FATHERS AND SONS IN THE ARAB MIDDLE EAST

Also by the author

Yusuf Idris: Changing Visions

An Arabian Mosaic

A Matter of Fate

Arab Women Writers: An Anthology of Short Stories

Mothers and Daughters in Arab Women's Literature:
The Family Frontier

Fathers and Sons in the Arab Middle East

Dalya Cohen-Mor

Parts of Chapter 1 and Chapter 2 appeared in my previous work, *Mothers and Daughters in Arab Women's Literature: The Family Frontier.* Leiden: Brill, 2011. Copyright © 2011 by Koninklijke Brill NV, Leiden, The Netherlands. All rights reserved. Reprinted by permission of the publisher.

First published in 2013 by
PALGRAVE MACMILLAN®
in the United States—a division of St. Martin's Press LLC,
175 Fifth Avenue, New York, NY 10010.

Where this book is distributed in the UK, Europe and the rest of the world, this is by Palgrave Macmillan, a division of Macmillan Publishers Limited, registered in England, company number 785998, of Houndmills, Basingstoke, Hampshire RG21 6XS.

Palgrave Macmillan is the global academic imprint of the above companies and has companies and representatives throughout the world.

Palgrave® and Macmillan® are registered trademarks in the United States, the United Kingdom, Europe and other countries.

ISBN: 978–1–137–33519–7

Library of Congress Cataloging-in-Publication Data is available from the Library of Congress.

A catalogue record of the book is available from the British Library.

Design by Newgen Knowledge Works (P) Ltd., Chennai, India.

First edition: November 2013

10 9 8 7 6 5 4 3 2 1

For Ziv,

A loving heart is the beginning of all knowledge.
Thomas Carlyle

Contents

Acknowledgments

While working on this research project, I was fortunate to have received assistance from several sources. First and foremost, I thank Professor Paul Poppen, chair of the Department of Psychology at George Washington University, where I have been a research fellow since 2006, for welcoming me to his department and facilitating my efforts to bring this project to fruition. This work would not have been possible without his continuous interest and support.

This study was informed by my stay as a Peace Corps volunteer in Jordan. I lived with a large Bedouin family who treated me as a member of their household. This gave me a unique opportunity to observe from close quarters their family life and patterns of interaction. My host family was related to one of the biggest families in the village, and I was introduced to many of their relatives, friends, and neighbors. During this period, I taught English at the village girls' school and interacted with the teachers, all of whom were extremely open and eager to exchange information with me about family life, family values, and cultural norms in Jordan and America. My stay in the village, as well as my visits to the capital city of Amman, to Al al-Bayt University in Mafraq, to Mu'tah University in the province of Karak, and to the village of Taybeh that overlooks the magnificent rocks of Petra, has given me invaluable insights into contemporary Arab life as manifested in Jordan. I was especially amazed to see the effects of the rapid social change currently underway in the village and the city. The march to progress in Jordan, as in varying degrees throughout the Arab region, is incontestable. I hope that the aspirations of the many Arab men and women who have anonymously contributed to this work will be realized in the near future.

This study is my second exploration into Arab family life. As with the first volume, *Mothers and Daughters in Arab Women's Literature: The Family Frontier* (Leiden: Brill, 2011), I am greatly indebted to the work of others in Middle Eastern studies; without this extensive literature, I would have been lost in the field. I thank Brill Publishers for permission to reuse some material from the first two chapters of my book. Finally, I want to extend a special thanks to all the Arab authors who appear in this volume for allowing me the use of excerpts from their works of prose and poetry for the purpose of review or criticism and to illustrate or buttress a point. I also thank their translators, editors, and publishers for permission to reprint these excerpts, as detailed in the endnotes, bibliography, and permissions.

Chapter 1

Introduction: Why Fathers and Sons?

The Legacy of Abraham

One of the most dramatic stories in the Bible is the one about the sacrifice of Isaac. God commands Abraham to offer his only son, Isaac, as a burnt offering on his altar. Without wavering or arguing, Abraham proceeds to carry out God's command. Genesis 22 tells the story:

> After these things God tested Abraham. He said to him, "Abraham!" And he said, "Here I am." He said, "Take your son, your only son Isaac, whom you love, and go to the land of Moriah, and offer him there as a burnt offering on one of the mountains that I shall show you." So Abraham rose early in the morning, saddled his donkey, and took two of his young men with him, and his son Isaac; he cut the wood for the burnt offering, and set out and went to the place in the distance that God had shown him. On the third day Abraham looked up and saw the place far away. Then Abraham said to his young men, "Stay here with the donkey; the boy and I will go over there; we will worship, and then we will come back to you." Abraham took the wood of the burnt offering and laid it on his son Isaac, and he himself carried the fire and the knife. So the two of them walked on together. Isaac said to his father Abraham, "Father!" And he said, "Here I am, my son." He said, "The fire and the wood are here, but where is the lamb for a burnt offering?" Abraham said, "God himself will provide the lamb for a burnt offering, my son." So the two of them walked on together. When they came to the place that God had shown him, Abraham built an altar there and laid the wood in order. He bound his son Isaac, and laid him on the altar, on top of the wood. Then Abraham reached out his hand and took the knife to kill his son. But the angel of the Lord called to him from heaven, and said, "Abraham, Abraham!" And he said, "Here I am." He said, "Do not lay your hand on the boy or do anything to him; for now I know that you fear God, since you have not withheld

your son, your only son, from me." And Abraham looked up and saw a ram, caught in a thicket by its horns. Abraham went and took the ram and offered it up as a burnt offering instead of his son. (1–13)[1]

The focus of the narrative is on Abraham's faith: in submitting to God's authority and demonstrating his willingness to sacrifice his son at God's command, he passed the ultimate test and became the model of faith. As for Isaac, he fulfilled his filial duty by submitting to his father's authority and acquiescing to serve as the sacrifice. The pattern of submission to authority that emerges from the story is intimately connected with the concept of fatherhood and patriarchal power: the son must obey his father just as his father must obey God, the Father of Creation. Significantly, Abraham establishes his authority over his son not through love and benevolence but through fear and aggression—the threat of death. The son does not try to escape or struggle or argue; he understands that it is his duty to obey. The binding ordeal (*akedah*) is a test of his mettle: he must steel himself and show that he is not afraid, that he is tough and loyal and courageous. In essence, then, the binding serves as an initiation rite into masculinity. It is a rite of passage that marks Isaac's transition from the sphere of boyhood into the sphere of manhood.

The terse biblical narrative offers no details about the emotional state of father or son. What went through Abraham's mind as he prepared to sacrifice his beloved son? Did his heart bleed for his son's fate or did he consider Isaac his exclusive possession to do with him as he pleased? What went through Isaac's mind as he saw his beloved father raise the knife above his head to slay him? Did he feel betrayed and forsaken? Was he paralyzed with shock and horror? Isaac does not cry out for mercy nor does Abraham shed tears of anguish. The scene is eerily silent, yet charged with enormous tension arising from conflicting emotions: love versus aggression, protection versus mutilation, loyalty versus abandonment, courage versus fear, trust versus betrayal, rebellion versus resignation, and attachment versus alienation. The elements for the closest—and the most tragic—father-son relationship are all here. Importantly, the biblical narrative states that Isaac's devoted mother, Sarah, died shortly after the episode of Isaac's binding. Did she die of shock on learning what transpired between her husband and her son? On hearing the dreadful news about the near death of her only son at the hands of his own father? Isaac, then, was doubly traumatized: first by the harrowing experience of his binding, second by the loss of his mother. Yet Sarah *had to* die so that Isaac could leave the world of women and enter the world of men.

By becoming motherless, Isaac was "defeminized," and his initiation into masculinity was complete. Nevertheless, as a young boy he must have been brokenhearted over the loss of his mother. Did he blame it on his father? Did he ever forgive his father for either of these two traumatic childhood experiences? The book of Genesis has no recorded conversation between Abraham and Isaac after the binding episode. This silence may be a sign of distance, or conflict, perhaps even total estrangement between father and son.

The story of Abraham is regarded as "central to the nervous system" of Judaism, Christianity, and Islam,[2] the three monotheistic religions that have evolved from it, though in Islam it is believed that Ishmael, Abraham's son by his Egyptian slave girl Hagar, was the intended sacrifice rather than Isaac.[3] Imprinted on the hearts and minds of millions of people for centuries, the story's enduring legacy can be seen in many contemporary societies where child sacrifice takes the form of fathers sending off their sons to fight in "holy wars."[4]

Indeed, the thoroughly authoritarian model epitomized by this religious myth continues to shape the relations between fathers and sons in many patriarchal cultures around the world, among them Arab culture. As the Tunisian sociologist Abdelwahab Bouhdiba observes: "The authority relationship has deep roots in our traditional society. It binds not only man to woman and parents to children but also teacher to pupil, master to disciple, employer to employee, ruler to ruled, the dead to the living and God to man."[5] The pattern of submission to authority that Bouhdiba identifies as a characteristic feature of his society is closely bound up with the concept of fatherhood and patriarchal power in Arab culture. How does this firmly embedded pattern influence the son's sense of self and personality development? What effects does the subordinate position that the son occupies vis-à-vis his father have on the family dynamics in general and on his relations with the females in the family in particular? In what ways does what happens in the family impact the wider society?

This study explores the relationship between fathers and sons in Arab families. Drawing on insights from psychology, sociology, anthropology, religion, history, and literature, I try to unravel the mysteries of this complex bond. I use both early and contemporary writings of male authors from across the Arab world to illuminate the traditional and evolving nature of father-son relationships in Arab families, and how these family dynamics reflect and influence modern Arab life. Many aspects of the father-son relationship are analyzed in an effort to understand the forces that bring them together or drive them apart. The myriad patterns of this relationship are interpreted from various perspectives: psychological, patriarchal, cultural, historical, and socioeconomic. In the course of this exploration, many myths and stereotypes about Arab fathers and sons are shattered and new definitions of the relationship between them are demonstrated. The far-reaching implications of this male relationship, not only for men but also for women, the family, and the wider society, are carefully evaluated.

Why fathers and sons? There are several compelling reasons for focusing on this topic. First, the father-son relationship is central to and part of every man's life. Every man is a son; most sons also become fathers. The childhood experiences that the son acquires in his family home, including patterns of socialization and interaction, not only influence his psychological development and the establishment of future adult relationships, but also tend to be replicated in his own style of parenting and the kind of upbringing he gives his own children. Thus these experiences establish a legacy that is carried into future generations of family life.[6] As Peter Blos puts it: "Every father has first been a son; arriving at fatherhood and having a son weaves his own sonship existence into the new context of a generational continuum."[7] The desire to understand how the father-son relationship works, or fails to work, in Arab families, motivates this study. The first of its kind, this study offers a cross-cultural analysis of an intriguing topic of universal interest.

Despite the fact that the father-son relationship is pivotal to men's lives, it has until recently been shrouded in mystery. As the psychologists Robert J. Pellegrini and Theodore R. Sarbin point out: "The emotional life of men and boys has only quite recently come to the forefront of systematic attention from a number of professional perspectives. Clearly, the previous scarcity of such formal scrutiny reflects a traditional pattern of gender role definition observed in cultures throughout the world, whereby males are encouraged to minimize their public expression of sentimental acts and to maximize their expression of instrumental ones. Given this legacy, along with its homophobic component, it's not at all surprising that the issue of men's emotional relationships to one another has been widely ignored."[8] In the Arab world, to a greater extent than in the West, the father-son relationship has been shrouded in silence. The main reason for this situation is the concept of privacy and sanctity of family life. The Moroccan writer Leila Abouzeid explains: "A Muslim's private life is considered an 'awra (an intimate part of the body), and sitr (concealing it) is imperative. As the Qur'an says, Allah amara bissitr (God ordered the concealing of that which is shameful and embarrassing)."[9] Needless to say, the intense privacy surrounding personal and family matters is an impediment to research.

The anthropologist Suad Joseph attributes the paucity of information on Arab family life to the hypervalorization of the family. As she states: "In both scholarly research and popular culture, the centrality of family in the Arab world has been so axiomatic that there has been relatively little problematizing of the psychodynamics of family life."[10] Those who violate the sacrosanct space of the family run the risk of being accused of disloyalty and betrayal. Joseph notes that in view of this obstacle, the most profound insights into the forbidden grounds of Arab family life often come from autobiographical or semifictional accounts.[11] Crucially, the surge of interest in gender studies in the Middle East in recent years has focused primarily on women, with the aim of reversing the traditional neglect of women as a topic of inquiry. But as a result of this new emphasis on women, there are very few recent studies on men's relation to men within the Arabic-speaking world.[12] In addressing the relationship between fathers and sons, this work fills an important void in contemporary scholarship on Arab family life in general and the dynamics operating between male members of the family in particular.

There is another important reason for exploring this topic. The father-son relationship is a central site for the construction of the masculine self or masculine identity. Fathers model manhood for sons and exert significant influence on the formation of their basic personality. As scholars of family life have observed, although boys may spend more time with their mothers, sisters, and peers, they tend to be deeply involved emotionally with their fathers as role models. They identify strongly with them and look to them for cues on how to act out their male roles, including their future roles as fathers. Although gender roles are currently changing, fathers continue to be the primary transmitters of the basic rules of society to their sons. Due to this fact, they have a profound influence on how their sons live their lives.[13] Emphasizing the connection between a harmonious father-son relationship (which produces well-adjusted individuals) and a more harmonious society, the sociologist Lewis Yablonsky states: "A shift toward a more positive, intelligent enactment of the father role would affect the overall society. More effective fathering could virtually eliminate such social problems as crime, drug abuse and the violence that plagues our society."[14] These comments are especially applicable to the Arab world, where men have traditionally occupied the public sphere and where violence in various forms is rife.

The main goal of this study, then, is to illuminate a key family relationship that is crucial to the shaping of the masculine self, masculine personality, and male gender roles, and that has a profound influence on men's development and choices. In particular, the study seeks to elucidate the conflicts, both normal and pathological, in the father-son relationship, as these tend to have a negative impact on family life and the wider society. A better understanding of the father-son relationship would benefit not only men, who live these roles, but also women. As Yablonsky notes: "The subject is of equal importance to women, especially mothers, because they are central figures in the dramatic scenarios between fathers and sons, and the quality of their lives is crucially affected by the fathers and sons in their families."[15] Samuel Osherson expresses a similar view: "Women who want to raise emotionally intelligent boys want and need to understand what goes on between fathers and sons."[16] Ultimately, what goes on between father and son—and what is missing between them—proves to have lasting repercussions on a man's life, especially his relationships with his spouse, children, friends, boss, and colleagues.

My fascination with this topic derives from additional considerations. The Arab family is often described as "Arab society in miniature." This is because the same structure (hierarchical), values (patriarchal), and sets of relationships (vertical) that characterize the family prevail in the society at large. Given this analogy, a study of the father-son relationship opens a window into the most intimate aspects of Arab culture and society. Specifically, it reveals the inner workings of the patriarchal system—its ideology, institutions, moral code, gender and age domination, sexual division of labor, and mechanisms of reproduction. Since fatherhood is "a man's link with the future" in that his son carries his name and inherits his social, emotional, and financial legacy,[17] understanding the dynamics between father and son enables one to evaluate the potential that this powerful bond holds for democratizing the patriarchal family and, by extension, society as a whole.

Furthermore, through the lens of the father-son relationship it is possible to examine larger issues concerning Arab men, such as the code of masculinity, men's desire for freedom and equality, and men's attitudes toward women's emancipation. The process of modernization and, conversely, the wave of Islamism, which are concurrently spreading in various parts of the Arab world, specifically the changes they bring about in family values, roles, and relationships, are also mirrored in the father-son dyad. In many ways, the changing dynamics of interaction between fathers and sons reflect the changing rhythms

of life in Arab societies, the influences of socioeconomic transformations, the ongoing confrontations with opposing value systems,
and the struggle for freedom and independence. Most intriguingly,
the father-son relationship offers a rare glimpse into the "privileged"
world of men, highlighting the complexity of male bonding, the issue
of solidarity and brotherhood, and the challenge of social change in a
volatile region of vital significance in world affairs.

Conceptual Considerations and Underlying Assumptions

Like any personal relationship, the father-son dyad must be considered in the specific context—family, culture, society—in which it is
embedded. In this regard, the family form and composition, the patriarchal social order, the Islamic belief system, Arab values, and prevailing customs and traditions all play a role in shaping the father-son
relationship. Additional factors such as class, lifestyle (Bedouin, rural,
urban), occupation, age, generation, education, and basic personality
traits further affect the interaction between fathers and sons. Due to
all these variables, the father-son relationship manifests a wide variety
of patterns that reflect the intense yet ambivalent nature of this bond.
A perennial theme in contemporary Arabic literature and popular
culture, the father-son relationship is generally depicted as oscillat-
ing between two opposite poles: love and hatred, blame and guilt,
oppression and empowerment, admiration and resentment, closeness
and estrangement, friendship and animosity, harmony and conflict,
loyalty and betrayal, and so on. These dichotomous representations
reveal that the father-son relationship is tumultuous and exceed-
ingly complex. By exploring intimate portraits of father-son dyads in
autobiographies, fiction, poetry, and politics, I hope to unlock the
mysteries of this relationship, illuminate the dual, both positive and
negative, potential of this bond, and dispel the taboos, myths, and
stereotypes surrounding it.

Several conceptual considerations guide this study. First, it is
important to stress the dynamic nature of this relationship, which
evolves over the entire life cycle of men, from childhood through
adulthood to old age. Throughout these developmental stages, the
father-son relationship is renegotiated and redefined as both father
and son adjust to changes in their needs and abilities. Second, it is
necessary to rectify the imbalance in emphasis on the father as the
active member in this dyad and the son as the passive one. Both father
and son play a vital part in this relationship, alternately being active

and passive, depending on the stages and circumstances of their lives. Although it is ordinarily the father who serves as a role model for the son, it is not uncommon for the son, once he has become an accomplished adult, to introduce his father to new ideas and values. The mutual dependence and reciprocity that characterize this relationship are readily observed in the son's caring for his elderly parents. Third, ideas about good or bad father-son relationships vary within the culture over time and over the course of an individual's life. It is useful to identify such changes and understand how they relate to specific developments in men's lives and the society at large.

While the father-son relationship has preoccupied contemporary Arab male writers, most of the literary works, whether autobiographies, memoirs, novels, novellas, short stories, poems, or plays, have focused on the son's story. As a result, the son's narrative predominates in the literature and occupies center stage. Privileging the son's story over the father's implies that instead of hearing two voices, readers are often left with one voice that claims to tell the whole story. This study aims to present the narratives of both father and son, thus giving due consideration to each party in the relationship, examining each perspective, and interpreting each side.

Most importantly, the Western reader must begin by discarding any preconceived notions about the father-son relationship. For example, it is a widespread sentiment in Western cultures that a son's ties to his parents weaken with marriage as he turns his loyalty and devotion toward his wife, whereas a daughter remains closely attached to her parents even after her marriage. "My son is my son till he gets him a wife, but my daughter's my daughter all the days of her life" runs a popular English saying. This sentiment is not characteristic of Arab culture, where custom dictates that a daughter's allegiance will be to her husband's family when she marries,[18] and where the mother-son relationship is recognized as particularly close and strong. Several factors enhance the strength of the mother-son bond in Arab culture. First, owing to the extended and patrilocal nature of the traditional Arab family, a newly wed couple takes up residence in the home of the husband's family. Thus, only the son continues to live with his parents, whereas the daughter leaves the parental home upon marriage (except if married to her paternal cousin, or *ibn 'amm*) and joins the household of her husband's family.[19] Furthermore, because the Arab family is patrilineal (descent is traced through the male line), the daughter is a member of her father's family, but unlike the son, she cannot pass this membership on to her children, who take their father's surname. This situation explains the meaning of the colloquial Arabic saying, *ibnak ilak wa-bintak la*, "Your son belongs to you but your daughter does not," which is quite the opposite of what the aforementioned English saying encapsulates. Hence cultural sensitivity is crucial in interpreting the father-son relationship in Arab families. Nothing can be taken for granted; while some patterns of interaction may turn out to be similar to those observed in Western families, others may prove to be utterly different, if not contradictory.

Since the traditional Arab family is characterized as patriarchal, much of the discussion in this work deals with father-son relationships in the shadow of patriarchy. Patriarchal society is the prism through which fathers and sons are seen and through which their relationships are shaped. It is therefore helpful to explain what the term denotes here. In its narrow definition, "patriarchy is a system in which the male head of the household has absolute legal and economic power over his dependent female and male members."[20] In its wider definition, patriarchy means "the manifestation and institutionalization of male dominance over women and children in the family and the extension of male dominance over women in society in general."[21] Marcia Inhorn delineates the characteristics of patriarchy as it relates to the Middle East: "Patriarchy is characterized by relations of power and authority of males over females, which are (1) learned through gender socialization within the family, where males wield power through the socially defined institution of fatherhood; (2) manifested in both inter- and intragender interactions within the family and in other interpersonal milieus; (3) legitimized through deeply engrained, pervasive ideologies of inherent male superiority; and (4) institutionalized on many societal levels (legal, political, economic, educational, religious, and so on)."[22] Soraya Altorki points out the variations that are possible within patriarchy rather than its uniformity across historical time and place, stressing that patriarchy manifests itself differently at different historical periods and in different classes.[23]

Given that men in Arab societies are the beneficiaries of the existing power asymmetry between genders, the questions that arise are: How do fathers and sons fare? Do male privileges bring them security and stability or stress and anxiety? How do these privileges affect the construction of masculinity and the male psyche? Do they enhance or undermine the son's personality development and functioning as a well-adjusted individual in society? This study argues that men too suffer under patriarchy, and that they too are trapped by its core values and expectations. Paradoxically, men are both the beneficiaries and victims of the prevailing patriarchal system.

Furthermore, the study argues that the power asymmetry that characterizes the relations *between* genders in Arab societies also has profound implications for the relations *within* genders. In the men's world, the male child is at the bottom of the hierarchy of power. He must learn to compete and fend for himself. He must obey his father's commands, serve him, and be subservient to him. Any infringement of rules by the son is met with harsh punitive actions by the authoritarian father. While the son derives comfort and reassurance from the warm and loving relationship that he has with his mother, he is well aware of her subordinate position and shares her fear that the all-powerful father might repudiate her or take another wife. He knows that one day he will take over his father's place within the household, but in the meantime he must accept his absolute will and put up with his own marginalization. Hence the questions: Is the men's world, in which the son is socialized, a site of male empowerment or oppression? Is the reality of this world conducive to male solidarity and unity, or conversely, to strife and animosity? A cursory look at the Arab region reveals a sorry state of affairs: despotic regimes oppress the masses; sectarian fighting destroys neighborhoods, suicide bombers kill innocent civilians; radical Islamists slay liberal intellectuals. As David Pryce-Jones observes: "In all relationships, domestic, private and public, internal and external, violence is not only customary but also systematic and utterly impervious to piecemeal reform or amelioration."[24] This study attributes male violence in Arab societies in part to the stresses and frustrations engendered by paternal authoritarianism and hegemonic (i.e., socially dominant) masculinity.

The main concern of this study, then, is to find out what brings Arab fathers and sons together and what drives them apart. Since the father-son dyad is not an island but part of the fabric of family life, it is necessary to examine the interrelationships among all family members. Specifically, how members interact with each other, and what the rules of relating are, is essential for understanding the father-son nexus. Three major relationships operate within the family: the marital relationship, the parent-child relationship, and the sibling relationship. Each of these relationships has a different set of mutual rights and obligations, as well as distinct patterns of communication and interaction, the totality of which weaves the fabric of family life. Family dynamics both shape the father-son relationship and are affected by it. The weak marital bond observed in traditional Arab families, for example, is compensated by a strong mother-son relationship, a situation that often generates resentment in the daughter and even alienation from the mother. The strong mother-son relationship frequently causes animosity between the son's mother and his wife, a situation that disrupts the emotional climate in the family and infuses it with tensions. It soon becomes apparent that an analysis of the father-son relationship necessitates an examination of the many significant others who influence the interaction between them: mother, brothers, sisters, grandparents, uncles, cousins, and even surrogates beyond the family circle, such as nannies, teachers, friends, and neighbors. These people comprise, as Yablonsky puts it, "the supporting cast of characters in the father-son life drama."[25] They communicate and interpret data about fathers to their sons and vice versa. Yablonsky notes that of all the intervening people who filter and reflect the images, sentiments, and attitudes between father and son, the mother is the most important figure of all. The way she mediates the relationship between father and son, and the way she depicts the father and feels about him, can have a great impact, positive or negative, on this dyad. These mediating characters become even more important to the father-son relationship when the father is remote and aloof, or when he is distanced from his son by long separations, divorce, or death.[26]

Still, what goes on inside the family is not merely the sum of its interrelationships. Many external factors have a reverberating impact on the functioning of the family and individuals within the family. Cultural norms, for example, play a pivotal role in determining how a family operates—what tasks it must fulfill and what strategies are appropriate for achieving them. Issues such as gender role expectations, the sexual code, rites of passage into manhood and womanhood, the custom of arranged marriage, the concepts of fatherhood and motherhood, the practices of honor crimes and blood feud are all grounded in the patriarchal values of Arab culture. Understanding these values is therefore crucial for understanding the forces that shape the father-son relationship.

Finally, the family is the site where the sense of self of sons and fathers is shaped. It is highly pertinent to examine how the experience of selfhood, especially the need to establish one's identity, express one's individuality, and gain autonomy, affects the relationship between them. An analysis of the family organization, hierarchies, and boundaries can shed light on adaptive or maladaptive thoughts, feelings, and actions of individual family members attempting to construct their own sense of self.[27]

Defining Basic Terms

Numerous scholars, both Arab and Western, have struggled with the question: Who is an Arab? The prevailing view considers the Arabic language the primary component of Arab national identity. The distinguished historian Albert Hourani, for example, states that Arabs are "more conscious of their language than any people in the world," and that "most Arabs, if asked to define what they meant by 'the Arab nation,' would begin by saying that it included all those who spoke the Arabic language."[28] He emphasizes that a full definition would require additional information, especially a reference to a certain process in history in which the Arabs played a leading part.[29] The sociologist Halim Barakat suggests a broader definition in which the sense of Arab identity of the great majority of citizens of Arab countries is based on "what they have in common—namely, language, culture, sociopolitical experiences, economic interests, and a collective memory of their place and role in history."[30] He also takes into account the divisiveness and diversity of affiliations that characterize Arab identity.[31] In view of all these criteria, it is proper to conclude that an Arab is a person who identifies as such on ethnic, linguistic, and cultural grounds. The plural form, *Arabs*, denotes the ethnocultural group at large.

The term *Arab world* refers to the Arabic-speaking countries of North Africa, the Arabian Peninsula, and the Fertile Crescent. The Arab world covers an area of 5.25 million square miles, comprises 22 states, and has a population of 350 million people. Needless to say, the diversity that marks such a large region with numerous communities and subcultures makes it difficult to generalize about its inhabitants.

The Arab world constitutes the core area within the Middle East. Hence, in this study, the terms *Arab Middle East* and *Arab world* are used interchangeably. Geographically, the Arab world is divided into two major parts: the Mashreq (Arab East), which lies in Southwest Asia, and the Maghreb (Arab West or North Africa). Historically and culturally, these parts of the Arab world have developed differently. Domination by European colonial powers in the nineteenth and twentieth centuries contributed to this division. The countries of the Mashreq were mostly under British colonial rule (e.g., Egypt, Palestine, Iraq), while those of the Maghreb (e.g., Algeria, Tunisia, Morocco) were largely occupied by the French. French colonial rule explains the problem of biculturalism prevalent in the Arab countries of North Africa. While in the Mashreq the predominant language of the inhabitants is Arabic and the majority of literary works are written in Arabic, those coming form North Africa are mostly written in French, which is accepted as the language of the educated classes.

Arabs differ in terms of nationality, religion, way of life (Bedouin, rural, urban), and local custom. Although Islam is often associated with the Arab world, not all Arabs are Muslims, and fewer than 15 percent of all Muslims are Arabs. The Arabs consider themselves the core of the Muslim nations because they were the originators of Islam and those who spread it in the world. While the overwhelming majority of Arabs are Muslims, there are sizable numbers of Christians who live primarily in Egypt, Syria, Lebanon, Iraq, Jordan, Palestine, and Sudan. Islam is the established state religion in many but not all Arab countries. Islamic law is dominant in the legal system in some countries, especially those of the Arabian Peninsula, while others have secular codes. However, personal status laws, or family laws, remain under the jurisdiction of Islam (for Arab Muslims) and Christianity (for Arab Christians) throughout the region. Sectarian affiliations abound in the Arab world: while the majority of Arab nations adhere to Sunni Islam, Iraq has a Shi'a majority, and Lebanon, Yemen, Kuwait, and Bahrain have large Shi'a minorities. Other prominent sects are the Alawites of Syria and the Druze of Israel and Syria, who are considered Arabs but not Muslims. Ethnic groups within the Arab world include the Berbers of North Africa, the Kurds of the northern parts of Iraq and Syria, Circassians, Assyrians, and Armenians. Formerly there were significant numbers of Jews who lived in many Arab countries, until their mass emigration/expulsion following the establishment of the State of Israel in 1948. Two of the largest Muslim nations in the Middle East, Turkey and Iran, are non-Arab.

Politically, various forms of government are represented in the Arab world, most of them authoritarian. Some of the countries are monarchies, others republics. Saudi Arabia and Sudan are Islamic states. Following the popular uprisings in the Arab region in 2011, the old, despotic regimes in Tunisia and Egypt were replaced through free elections with Islamist governments. In Libya, a new, secular government was democratically elected at the end of a hard-won civil war. At the time of writing this book, Syria is still in the throes of a long and brutal civil war, and Egypt has experienced a military coup that deposed its Islamist president, Mohamed Morsi, after one year in office. Economically, there are rich, petroleum exporting countries (OPEC) like the four Persian Gulf states of Saudi Arabia, United Arab Emirates, Kuwait, and Qatar, and poor countries like Egypt, Yemen, and Jordan. The economic disparities between oil-poor and oil-rich

Arab countries lead to extensive labor migration from the former into the latter.

On the whole, the Arab world exhibits a great deal of plurality and heterogeneity. As Barakat sums it up: "The Arab world in its present circumstances does not constitute a single coherent system or civil society as much as a multiplicity of societies."[32] These societies differ not only from one Arab country to another but also internally, from city to village to tribe. Generally speaking, patriarchal modes of domination tend to be weaker in modernizing milieus (e.g., urban areas) and stronger in traditional milieus (e.g., the countryside). Everywhere, class and educational differences affect people's attitudes and practices.

Defining the Arab family is not a simple task. The difficulty lies in the immense variation in family forms and organization in Arab societies. The social scientists William C. Young and Seteney Shami acknowledge that "anthropologists no longer try to arrive at a universal definition of the family; decades of research in a wide variety of societies have demonstrated that no matter how we formulate a definition of 'the family,' there will always be exceptional cases which do not conform to it strictly."[33] In their view, the most useful approach to the study of the Arab family is to go beyond description, whether statistical or ethnographic, and focus on understanding the processes or mechanisms that produce certain characteristics and forms of families in certain circumstances.[34]

This study delineates the basic characteristics of Arab families while highlighting the changes in traditional patterns of family life that have occurred in recent decades. The diversity encountered among Arab families results from a constellation of factors, including lifestyle (Bedouin, rural, or urban), class, level of education, as well as religious and sectarian affiliation. In describing aspects of Arab family life, I have relied on ethnographic and sociological studies available on the topic.[35] I have also drawn on the myriad depictions provided in the literary works of Arab writers included in this study. In synthesizing all these sources, I have taken care not to portray the family as a monolithic institution but rather to emphasize the dramatic adaptations that it has undergone since the colonial period.

Sources, Methods, and Approaches

This study draws on a wide variety of sources to explore the relationship between fathers and sons in Arab families. These sources include psychology, sociology, anthropology, history, religion, and literature.[36] I synthesize ideas from these various fields and bring together strands of thought and debate that are frequently kept apart because of disciplinary boundaries.[37] In doing so, I broaden the picture of father-son relationships and offer several vantage points on the manner in which they are constructed, negotiated, and defined. Such an integrative approach is more productive in illuminating the many interlocking facets of the relationship, although it presents a more formidable task.

The works of literature discussed in this study include autobiographies, memoirs, biographies, novels, novellas, short stories, essays, and poems written over the past half century by male authors from across the Arab world. These works paint penetrating portraits of Arab family life and offer fascinating insights into the psychodynamic forces that shape intimate family relationships. A large number of these works are analyzed in depth to find out how the father-son relationship is represented and experienced by men, what kinds of patterns it manifests, and in what ways it influences the course of male development. As these works are written by and about men and narrated from the perspectives of both fathers and sons, they offer a wealth of information on the topic of this inquiry.

The literary works were selected on the basis of several criteria. To begin with, they had to be written by and about men so as to depict the male experience from the male perspective. Naturally, the father-son theme had to figure prominently in these texts, or at least to be a vital part of the narrative. In addition, the voices of both fathers and sons had to be represented in the selection in order to paint a balanced picture. I also strove to introduce male writers from different generations and from different parts of the Arab world, though Egypt, which is the most populous Arab country and the center of Arab cultural life, is more largely represented. The literary merit or artistic quality of the text was also an important consideration. I made a great effort to include a variety of genres and styles of writing, early publications as well as more recent ones, and works by both established and emerging authors. While these objective criteria guided the selection of texts for discussion, the ultimate decision was also influenced by personal taste—an unavoidable factor in such a process.[38]

In this study, works of literature are treated as a source of knowledge and information about social, historical, and political phenomena.[39] This approach was necessitated by the intense privacy surrounding family life in Arab societies, a situation which results in lack of direct methods of investigation and in a paucity of publications on the topic.[40] As mentioned earlier, the domain of family life is regarded as sacrosanct, and those who open it to public scrutiny are branded as traitors and are ostracized. The vehicles of fiction and poetry offer writers a veil of nonaccountability: they can express intimate and critical reflections about their lives or their societies and at the same time shield themselves from potential persecution or accusations of betrayal. That this strategy is not infallible is borne out by the well-publicized trials of many Arab writers who did not escape the watchful eye of the censor.[41] Still, resorting to fiction and poetry does enable writers to engage freely in self-analysis, a process that facilitates self-liberation. Further, the blurry line separating the factual from the fictional in creative literature highlights the immense power of this medium to bridge the gap between the self and reality, to transcend reality by recreating it, and to give an individual reality a more universal meaning.[42]

There are additional merits to using literature as a source of knowledge and information. Literary texts paint intimate portraits of a given society, depicting all aspects of life and components of reality. In portraying the concerns and interests that motivate the characters, whether real or imaginary, the writer chronicles the times and circumstances of their lives, including the ruling political system, prevailing customs and traditions, religious beliefs, social norms, and popular attitudes. The literary scholar Trevor Le Gassick calls contemporary imaginative literature "the most revealing window into the closest workings of a society's values and orientations."[43] The novelist and sociologist Halim Barakat regards literature as "a way of exploring human behavior like science and philosophy."[44] He argues that literary texts are not only works of art but also social documents: "Poems, stories, novels, plays, paintings, graphics, and songs constitute historical sources of knowledge about society as well as aesthetic objects to be appreciated in their own right."[45] In his view, the novels of Naguib Mahfouz "portray Egyptian life and society more comprehensively and accurately than the works of all the social scientists put together."[46] The British novelist John Fowles echoes this view when he says that Mahfouz's *Miramar* "allows us the rare privilege of entering a national psychology, in a way that a thousand journalistic articles or television documentaries could not achieve."[47] Given the "view from within" that literary works offer, and the fact that most Arab societies are not readily accessible through other means of investigation, these works can be an invaluable aid in cross-cultural research, of which this study is a part.

Of equal importance is the reciprocal relationship that exists between literature, culture, and society. While literature is influenced by the conditions of the society in which it is generated, it also exerts its own influence on society. As Barakat points out: "A work of art both reflects and shapes reality at the same time."[48] Deeply anchored in the world that produces it, the literary text helps to reproduce ideologies, popular images, and values. "Literature is both a central cultural production and a participant in the creation of culture," observes Magda al-Nowaihi.[49] Highlighting the connection between literary texts and the existential actualities of human life, Edward Said argues that "the realities of power and authority—as well as the resistances offered by men, women, and social movements to institutions, authorities, and orthodoxies—are the realities that make texts possible, that deliver them to their readers, that solicit the attention of critics."[50] He criticizes the tendency among Western social scientists to exclude literature from studies of the Middle East, affirming that "a literary text speaks more or less directly of a living reality."[51] Since the relationship between fathers and sons is a cultural construction that eventually finds expression and representation in literary texts, one can draw on these texts as a valid, even vital, source of information for understanding the relationship.

Of all the critical approaches to literature, this study relies primarily on the psychological one. This choice was guided by the nature of the parent-child relationship, for "fathering" has increasingly come to connote what "mothering" does, namely, "a psychologically based role," which consists in "psychological and personal experience of self in relationship to child or children."[52] Scholars of family life have drawn extensively, though not exclusively, on psychoanalytic theory for the study of child rearing.[53] Significantly, the key terms used to describe the interactional dynamics of the parent-child relationship come from the realm of psychology: bonding, symbiosis, separation, individuation, autonomy. Given that the psychological approach to literature is concerned with understanding the psychical life of the individual—the deep mental, emotional, and motivational forces that shape personality and influence behavior—it is uniquely suited for this study. Moreover, the psychological approach is the ideal tool with which to interpret dreams, symbols, archetypes, and other forms of subliminal communication that we find in literature.

It is self-evident that no interpretative technique can fully fathom that which lies at the heart of a literary work. Any approach to literary criticism will result in oversimplification, and each approach has its limitations. The insights gained through the psychological frame of reference are therefore supplemented with biographical details, and the literary worlds are examined against their cultural, social, and historical backgrounds. Each text is analyzed systematically, first for its explicit message, and second for its symbolic, deeper meaning.

No analysis, however meticulous, can exhaust the rich interpretative possibilities of a literary work, particularly when the text contains symbols, the complex and ambiguous nature of which allows for more than one interpretation. Nevertheless, I had to come to some conclusions. Although at times I state my conclusions emphatically, I do not mean to rule out other points of view. My comments and observations are intended as plausible explanations, and I encourage the reader to delve independently into the literary texts in search of other answers.

Organization

This volume comprises six chapters, each of which examines the father-son relationship from a different perspective and draws on a different set of texts and insights to illuminate the power and meaning of this relationship for men, the family, and society.

Chapter 1 or the Introduction explains the objective of this study, the rationale for undertaking it, the methodology that guides it, and the corpus of literature that informs it.

Chapter 2 provides essential background information on male development in relation to psychological processes, social contexts, and historical perspectives. Traditional patterns of Arab family life and child socialization are contrasted with modern trends in family organization and parenting styles resulting from the rapid social change currently in progress throughout the Arab region. The influence of the mother and other family members on family dynamics and the interaction between fathers and sons is considered. The chapter concludes with a close look at the traditional code of Arab masculinity, highlighting the norms that put men in an untenable position and lead not only to male gender role strain but also to conflicted interpersonal relationships, especially between fathers and sons.

Chapter 3 presents intimate portraits of father-son relationships in ten autobiographical works by male authors from across the Arab world, five of them are Muslims and five are Christians. The texts are analyzed in depth and the authors' experiences of family life, of growing up male, and of the relationship with their fathers are compared. Dominant patterns of interactional dynamics between fathers and sons are identified and discussed. The underlying causes of the success or failure of each case of father-son relationship are explored and the influence of this relationship on the self-development and career choices of the author is assessed.

Chapter 4 deals with intimate portraits of father-son relationships in Arabic fiction. A variety of male-authored novels and short stories dramatizing different issues and problems that arise at different stages in the father-son relationship are analyzed. The analysis focuses on traditional and nontraditional forms of Arab masculinity, the culture-specific obstacles that Arab sons face in their struggles for authentic and autonomous selfhood, and the unique rebellions and visions of the future that they adopt.

Chapter 5 looks at representations of father-son relationships in poetry, the Arabs' literary medium par excellence. Many male-authored poems that depict the vicissitudes of the father-son bond are presented and interpreted. Several prominent themes, central among them the quest for freedom from paternal authority, are explored. Given that Arabic poetry has traditionally been closely connected with public life, especially the political sphere, the final section of this chapter examines Arab politics. Drawing on recent events in the Middle East, as well as on the biographies of several Arab rulers, the section discusses the authoritarian nature of Arab regimes, the image of the ruler as father, the phenomenon of "hereditary presidency" where leadership of an Arab republic is passed from father to son, and the popular uprisings by young men and women that spread throughout the Arab region in 2011 and came to be known as the Arab Revolutions or Arab Spring.

Chapter 6 offers the main conclusions of this study. It sums up the salient motifs that run through the myriad portraits of father-son relationships assembled in this work and examines their implications for men, the family, and the wider society. The dramatic events of the Arab Spring are revisited inasmuch as they reflect, as well as influence, the evolving dynamics between fathers and sons. In assessing future trends of development, special attention is given to the formidable challenges facing fathers and sons at a time when life is changing rapidly throughout the Arab region and the roles of the family, as well as their own roles within the family, are changing too.

Every study has its limitations, and this one is no exception. To begin with, it is impossible to exhaust all the readings on this fascinating topic. One can find many other literary texts to illustrate various points in the discussion and expand the volume of this work. The field of Arabic literature continues to grow, and new writings become available all the time. In addition, this study is concerned with the male perspective—all the texts analyzed are written by and about men—for the obvious reason that the relationship under scrutiny exists between men. It may be worthwhile to examine literary texts that present the female perspective on this topic. I hope that this work will stimulate other scholars to undertake a comparative study that explores the differences and similarities between the male and female perspectives. Finally, to achieve definitive conclusions on father-son relationships in Arab families would require some empirical data from field studies. Notwithstanding the absence of such data, given the paucity of research on the psychodynamics of family life in Arab societies, the present study may prove to be a useful source of reference.

Chapter 2

The Voyage to Manhood:
The Elusive Quest

Insights into the Making of Men

In recounting the path of his formal education, the famed nineteenth-century English essayist and critic Thomas De Quincey describes the peculiar predicament he found himself confronted with after completing public school: "England...sends her young men to college not until they have ceased to be boys—not earlier, therefore, than eighteen." Forced to wait a couple of years before being considered eligible for matriculating at Oxford or Cambridge, the author asks in bewilderment: "But when, by what test, by what indication, does manhood commence? Physically by one criterion, legally by another, morally by a third, intellectually by a fourth—and all indefinite." De Quincey's efforts to define manhood highlight the elusive and complex nature of this concept: between the two spheres of boyhood and manhood there is no clear line of demarcation. The change is a long process occurring over a variable period of time: "It is hard to say, even for an assigned case, by any tolerable approximation, at what precise era it would be reasonable to describe the individual as having ceased to be a boy, and as having attained his inauguration as a man." Moreover, the four traditional standards of maturity—the physical, legal, moral, and intellectual—rarely happen concurrently in any individual. Considering that the markers to manhood are so vague, how can a person know when, if ever, he has reached this aspired state of being? Baffled, De Quincey repeats his question: "How, under so variable a standard, both natural and conventional, of everything almost that can be received for a test or a presumption of manhood, shall we seize upon any characteristic feature, sufficiently universal to serve a *practical* use, as a criterion of the transition from the childish mind to the dignity (relative dignity, at least) of that mind which belongs to conscious maturity?" After a lot of searching, De Quincey finds only one reliable criterion: "It lies in the reverential feeling, sometimes suddenly developed, towards woman, and the idea of woman. From that moment when women cease to be regarded with carelessness, and when the ideal of womanhood, in its total pomp of loveliness and purity, dawns like some vast aurora upon the mind, boyhood has ended; childish thoughts and inclinations have passed away for ever; and the gravity of manhood, with the self-respecting views of manhood, have commenced."[1] Thus De Quincey acknowledges the pivotal role that women play in male development.

The key issues of what it means to be, and how one becomes, a man have stimulated a great deal of inquiry in the social sciences. From psychology to sociology to anthropology, scholars have grappled with the concept of masculinity, seeking to construct models and theories that unravel the "manhood puzzle" or "masculine mystique." The standard psychoanalytic view of male development is based on Freud's interpretation of the myth of Oedipus, whose journey and fate came to represent the archetypal male struggle for identity. As William S. Pollack sums it up: "For Freud and generations of psychoanalysts and child researchers who followed, the myth of Oedipus was the central paradigm for illustrating unconscious forces at work in self and gender identity formation in childhood, especially for little boys. The story came to represent, in particular, a boy's unconscious sexual wishes for his mother, fears of retributive castration by his father, and finally, the renunciation of this wish—leading to a more stable sense of self through the boy's identification with his father's masculine role."[2] Orthodox Freudian theory, then, links core sexual and gender identity to the crucible of the Oedipus complex and its resolution.

The Freudian psychoanalytic model of male development was criticized for being a reductionist argument, for having a defensive character, and for providing a negative image of masculinity. As Stephen J. Bergman observes: "Identification with father comes through competition, fear, and renunciation, not through a wish to connect. It sets the stage for hierarchy—that is, patriarchy—for dominance, entitlement, ownership of women, and men's fear of men."[3] Barry Richards makes a similar remark: "In this model the identification with the father is defensive, and arises out of the need to defend against castration anxiety. The identification is made in fear; it is what Anna Freud ... was to term 'identification with the aggressor.'"[4] The strongest challenge to orthodox Freudian theory came from feminist scholars, who argued that it is a theory of "libidinal determinism" and that it does not provide an adequate account of either male or female development in Western society, much less in other cultures.[5]

Post-Freudian ego psychologists, as well as feminist theorists, have proposed alternative models of male psychosexual development that accommodate social and relational factors.[6] They trace the development of gender identities to earlier patterns of attachment and separation in the so-called pre-Oedipal period. Within this psychodynamic perspective it is assumed that all infants, male and female, establish a primary identity, as well as a social bond, with the nurturing parent, the mother. Not only do they experience themselves as part of the mother, but they also experience the world through her touch, voice, and smell, and develop a core sense of self that is basically feminine. As infants grow, they reach the critical threshold of separation/individuation, what Margaret Mahler calls "'hatching' out of a matrix of embeddedness by which a person becomes more internally organized, 'field-independent,' emotionally controlled, with clear boundaries and an unfolding individuality."[7] At this juncture the boy faces the special problem of overcoming the previous sense of unity with the mother in order to achieve an independent identity defined by his culture as masculine. This task entails separating from the mother both psychically and interpersonally. The girl does not experience this problem as severely because her femininity is reinforced by her original symbiotic unity with the mother and an ongoing relational attachment to her.

Nancy Chodorow argues that by retaining their identification with their mothers, girls separate in a less definitive way than boys, and mature with a greater capacity for empathy and bonding: "From the retention of pre-Oedipal attachments to their mothers, growing girls come to define and experience themselves as continuous with others; their experience of self contains more flexible or permeable ego boundaries. Boys come to define themselves as more separate and distinct, with a greater sense of rigid ego boundaries and differentiation. The basic feminine sense of self is connected to the world, the basic masculine sense of self is separate."[8] This distinction entails different relational abilities and needs: "Masculine personality, then, comes to be defined more in terms of denial of relation and connection (and denial of femininity), whereas feminine personality comes to include a fundamental definition of self in relationship."[9] While women tend to look for intimate involvement with others in their adult relationships, men tend to exhibit ambivalence toward women and intimacy, both needing emotional nurturance but avoiding closeness because of the threat that it poses for the masculine sense of separateness.

Chodorow's primary concern is the reproduction of familial and gender relations. She observes that the archetypal family unit in Western industrialized society is characterized by the father's relative absence and the woman's exclusive mothering. This arrangement, or gendered division of labor in child care, has a crucial influence on the development of infants, predisposing them to inherit gender personalities that mirror the inequalities between men and women. In this way men's dominance and women's tendency to nurture and mother are reproduced across generations. In her view, only a shift in child care from exclusive female mothering to shared parenting by both sexes can break the cycle's repetition.[10] Her work, using and revising psychoanalytic object-relations theory from a feminist perspective, offers fresh and intriguing insights into "core gender identity—that is, socially induced psychological constructions of femininity and masculinity."[11] However, her model of gendered personality development was criticized for failing to account for differences among men or women, for glossing over the effects of class and race on the formation of masculine or feminine sensibilities, and for obscuring cultural variations in the caretaking of children.[12]

Feminist scholarship has contributed greatly to the study of men and masculinity in demonstrating the centrality of gender as an organizing principle of social life. Feminist-inspired critique of the hegemonic definition of masculinity, held as the norm against which both genders were measured, has promoted new approaches focusing on the diversity of gender patterns among men. Rather than a single version of masculinity—white, middle age, middle class, heterosexual—the term has been expanded to include multiple forms of masculinities, among them working-class men, men of color, gay men, as well as younger and older men. That masculinity is socially and historically constructed and hence subject to change is now a widely accepted view, known as social constructionism.[13] Within this perspective, the meaning of masculinity varies from culture to culture, within any one culture over time, and over the course of an individual's life.[14] As Michael Kimmel and Michael Messner state: "Men are not born, growing from infants through boyhood to manhood, to follow a predetermined biological imperative, encoded in their physical organization. To be a man is to participate in social life as a man, as a gendered being. Men are not born; they are made. And men make themselves, actively constructing their masculinities within a social and historical context."[15] Current Western studies of men and masculinity consider the ways in which men differ in their gender role expectations by factors such as race, ethnicity, class, age, religion, sexual orientation, region, and nationality. Attention to non-Western societies and traditions has increased, and a growing number of researchers are exploring how the voyage to manhood is experienced across cultural boundaries, what social ends codes of masculinity serve, and how they affect the lives of men, women, and children.

Studies on gender in the Arab world have tended to focus almost exclusively on women. By necessity, male ideology, institutions, and practices were discussed insomuch as they impact women's status and lifestyles, gender relations, and gender inequality. However, issues of male identity and sexuality in a region regarded as one of the seats of patriarchy have rarely been the topic of critical inquiry. Recent publications have begun to address this imbalance, emphasizing cultural sensitivity in examining processes of self-development and gender identity in Arab societies.[16] The social scientist Mervat Hatem, for example, shows that two of the core assumptions of Western psychology, the nuclear family as the central site for the construction of self, gender, and identity, and individualism as a universal cultural ideal, are not borne out in Egyptian society, where the extended family is prevalent and communal values are stressed. Hatem uses the feminist synthesis of Marxist and Freudian paradigms to gain an understanding of the psychodynamics of mothering and gender in Egyptian families. She finds that despite important cultural and socioeconomic differences between Egyptian and American/Western societies, the psychodynamics of mothering and gender are similar. For example, the Egyptian male personality, like its American counterpart, is based on the repudiation of the female aspects of personality, notably nurturance and connectedness; it also enjoys relatively more autonomy and firmer ego boundaries. In contrast, the Egyptian female personality is based on stressing nurturance at the expense of autonomy. A girl develops a self that is put into the service of others and rarely used for her own purposes. This extroverted self and its fluid boundaries distinguish the personalities of women from those of men in Egyptian families.[17]

Addressing the issue of heterosexual relations in Egyptian society, Hatem writes that the gender asymmetry that the child experiences during the Oedipal phase is so deeply internalized that it does not disappear as a result of education and work. Rather, it is manifested in adult identity problems and heterosexual tensions. Women's employment outside the home, often a necessity dictated by poverty, and women's education have weakened the patriarchal concept of masculinity but resulted in heterosexual animosity. Because Muslim ideology regards heterosexual intimacy and romantic love as a threat to patriarchal control, the emotional relations between men and women are undermined by male anxiety. In this situation, the only outlets for emotional satisfaction are the special relationship between mother and son and friendships between members of the same sex. Hatem observes that these outlets are fraught with danger: "The incestuous and homosexual potential of these relations make them very problematic to the stern Muslim culture."[18] Delineating the rivalry over the husband's affection between the wife and her mother-in-law as "the classic triad in Egyptian family life," she critically remarks: "The vulnerability of Egyptian masculinity is seen in its inability to resolve the tensions between mother and wife who lay conflicting claims to it." In her view, heterosexual tensions and ambiguities are likely to persist in Egyptian society, unless gender roles undergo fundamental redefinitions.[19]

The most intriguing insights into Arab men and masculinity come from the work of the Moroccan sociologist Abdessamad Dialmy, who examined the concept of sexuality in contemporary Arab society.[20] Dialmy argues that the traditional Arab organization of sexuality revolves around two poles: "One pole, which is superior, active, and dominating, is made up of men, and the other pole, which is inferior and passive, is made up of wives, children, slaves, homosexuals, and prostitutes."[21] A key characteristic of this asymmetrical polarity is the construction of all sexual passives in the image of the woman, for "they share with her the reception of the phallus and subjection to its domination—phallocracy."[22] The dichotomy of active/passive is reflected in the construction of two sexual genders: man, and not man. The Arabic language itself points in this direction by providing two distinct expressions: *maleness* (*dhukura*), denoting the biological given, and *manliness* (*rujula*), denoting the construction of man as social domination. By contrast, the term *femininity* (*unutha*) refers both to the female (the biological) and to the woman (the subordinate social gender). The distinction between man and not man, as well as between maleness and manliness, is achieved through a basic rite of passage—circumcision—which rids the boy of the membrane of femininity, the foreskin, and marks his transition from the world of women to the world of men.

Dialmy states that the active/passive dichotomy is central to the traditional Arab organization of sexuality. It is predicated on a masculinist definition of the sexual act as penetration: "Man is not only male; he penetrates and is not penetrated."[23] This definition essentially equates manhood with virility. Virility encompasses sexual prowess, multiple sexual partners, and fertility. The multiplicity of sexual partners entails the fragmentation of active man's desire so that he does not become dependent on any sexual passive, especially a woman. The act of defloration, which is one of the most important rites of passage for both genders, testifies to the virginity of the bride and the virility of the groom. Virginity is the basis of family honor, especially the honor of its men, for "masculinity is seen as the capacity to act, and the capacity to act is not only the ability to sexually penetrate but also the ability to prevent sexual penetration."[24]

Dialmy observes that within a perspective that reduces sexual activity to penetration, "this act becomes a fundamental condition for the construction and empowerment of the Arab male ego and for securing his mental health." Furthermore, "this pattern in the integration of sexuality into the personality of the Arab man makes sexuality the basic determinant of the masculine personality and, moreover, turns sexuality into a pivotal meaning of life for the Arab man."[25] By contrast, the significance of childbirth for the Arab woman's sense of femininity outweighs that of sexual activity. In fact, patriarchal ideology distinguishes between the respectable woman—the wife—and loose women (prostitutes, songstresses, lovers), who are the object and true site of lust. The respectable wife is not expected to seek sexual pleasure. Her sexuality is confined to satisfying her husband's desire and producing a large number of children, preferably male. The Arab man's fear of female sexuality and his desire to control it are expressed in the practice of female circumcision, which functions as a defense mechanism, preventing a girl from premarital sex and a wife from marital infidelity.

Dialmy acknowledges that his analysis is "merely a provisional approximation because Arab sexuality, like all social phenomena, unfolds in specific historical and social conjunctures and is always contingent and contestable, that is, historical."[26] He mentions the development of new sexual trends in the Arab region, including new forms of marriage (visitation marriage and de facto marriage), as well as the increase in prostitution and premarital sex. He also addresses the issues of honor crimes, impotence problems, HIV/AIDS, and sex education. His final conclusion is that despite socioeconomic changes, "Arab sexuality continues to be predicated on domination and hierarchy between men and women, between the older and the younger, between the normal and the 'queer,' and between the clients and the sex workers."[27] Lamenting the paucity of studies on Arab sexuality, Dialmy describes the formidable obstacles facing research into the topic in the Arab world: "The Arab researcher in this field still suffers from lack of recognition, regardless of the exhaustive effort and trouble taken in collecting and interpreting the data. The researcher also feels isolated and is often subjected to rejection, threats, and persecution, for when the researcher lays bare the sexual reality, this disturbs all sorts of social activists, be they technocrats, politicians, or feminists alike. Sexuality in and of itself continues to be semi-banned in teaching. It is an intellectual taboo for the various Arab peoples and a political taboo for the ruling Arab regimes and, moreover, for the Arab feminist movements themselves."[28] In Dialmy's view, the ruling regimes avoid the study of sexuality out of fear that their political rivals, especially fundamentalists, will gain scientific evidence that Islamic morality is not respected and current sexual conducts and practices are incompatible with Muslim Law. Even the Arab feminist movements are guilty of silence on the topic: "Sexual rights still constitute one of the taboos of Arab feminist movements. These movements hide their political and intellectual coyness in this area behind the logic of priorities—the priorities of education, employment, and health for women."[29] Dialmy believes that the strategic goal of the Arab feminist movements to share in political power is the main reason for their avoidance of the sexual rights and needs of women as a demand and as a topic of research. He advocates the establishment of "an Arab sexual democracy that moves sexuality from a religious order to a civil order," carefully explaining that the secularization of sexuality does not necessarily mean the rejection of Islam and religious values, but rather their retention at an individual level, as a free choice among a variety of possibilities. This will enable Arab researchers to study sexuality freely and to reintroduce it into the Arab discourse.[30]

The foregoing discussion dealt with prevailing theories of male development in Western and Arab societies, focusing on the work of leading scholars who have attempted to place masculinity in relation to psychological processes, social contexts, and historical perspectives. The following section looks at Arab family life and patterns of child socialization in order to find out how these factors influence the construction of masculine identity and gender roles.

Growing Up Male in Arab Families

In his account of the Middle East's cultural psychology, Gary S. Gregg highlights the difficulty of describing a "typical" path of development through the life span in the Arab region: "Not only does socialization vary from milieu to milieu but twists of fate often make it impossible for families to follow cultural models of child-rearing and for young adults to take up the roles and identities their culture prescribes. Differences in temperament, birth order, intelligence, and family organization exert such profound effects that the cultural patterns that create shared experiences simultaneously provoke diverging reactions to them."[31] Nonetheless, Gregg affirms that the Arab region constitutes a "culture area" with distinctive patterns of development from infancy to old age. He believes that it is useful to describe these patterns in general as long as one continually emphasizes the diversity within the region. In what follows, traditional patterns of Arab family life and child socialization are contrasted with modern trends in family organization and parenting styles resulting from the rapid social change currently in progress throughout the Arab world.

At the outset of this account, two qualifications need to be made. First, there is no monolithic family. As mentioned earlier, constructions of family vary considerably across the classes, and there are always exceptions to rules within class.[32] Second, nowadays, as in the past, the lives of men and women are difficult to place in a strictly traditional or modern category. Therefore, in this account I use the terms *traditional* and *tradition* versus *modern* and *modernity* as useful simplifications. These terms are porous and not static; they are always changing. Not only does the traditional pattern show many variations but there was never a period of "true" tradition in Arab history, just as currently there is no truly modern society in the Arab region.[33]

Traditional Patterns

The traditional Arab family has been described as extended, patriarchal, patrilineal, patrilocal, endogamous, and occasionally polygamous.[34] In the typical patriarchal family, the father has absolute authority over all members of his household. His authority derives from being the provider and the owner of the family's property. The father's supreme position as *rabb al-usra* (i.e., "lord of the family" or paterfamilias) contrasts with the subordinate status of his wife and children, who are socially and economically dependent on him. They are expected to submit to his rule, obey his wishes, and treat him with deference. Relationships within the patriarchal family are organized hierarchically by age and gender: the young are subordinate to the old and females to males. With the power and authority vested solely in the father, the internal boundaries of the family are clear, and everyone knows his or her place in relation to other family members. Although recent advances in women's education and employment, as well as the effects of modernization, have undermined the authority of the father, the patriarchal tradition still persists, and patriarchal attitudes and practices remain strong, especially in the countryside.[35]

All studies of socialization patterns in the Arab world report early differentiation in the handling and care of boys and girls. Since Arab culture places a much higher value on boys than on girls, the overwhelming desire of all parents is to have sons, and most frequently sons are favored at the expense of daughters. Furthermore, there are two sets of gender role expectations, one for boys and one for girls. While female socialization emphasizes domestic tasks and the home domain, male socialization emphasizes external work and the public domain. Boys have most of the rights and few restrictions, whereas girls have most of the duties and multiple prohibitions.[36]

The process of socialization takes place primarily within the home, where children are under the exclusive care of their mother and other female relatives during the first seven to nine years of their lives.[37] The virtual monopoly that the mother has over her young children is the result of the traditional division of labor, which assigns the wife to the home domain and the husband to the public domain. The wife is responsible for running the household and raising the children, whereas the husband is responsible for the livelihood of the family and its standing in the community. As the authority figure, the father is feared and obeyed by all the family members, and his relationship with them tends to be distant and formal. By contrast, the mother is loving, affectionate, and nurturing. Constantly present and involved in her children's daily activities, she also serves as a buffer or mediator between them and the father, often preventing or mitigating a harsh command or punishment. As a result, children, especially sons, develop a stronger emotional attachment to the mother, who enjoys more demonstrations of affection and deference than the father.

The socialization of boys and girls takes different paths around the age of seven to nine. The boy leaves the women's world, in which he was protected, pampered, and admired, and enters the men's world, represented by the father, in which he is viewed critically. The girl continues to be socialized by her mother and other female relatives living in the extended household.[38] Generally, more boys than girls are sent to school, where they learn to read and write. Mervat Hatem, describing the socialization of boys in Egyptian families, writes that "whether in school, in the fields, or in some skilled craft, a boy's maleness becomes identified with distinct non-female occupations and the beginning of exclusive interaction with members of the same sex."[39] In the men's world, the boy is at the bottom of the hierarchy of power and must learn to compete and fend for himself. But men's company also has its benefits: he can attend their gatherings and participate in their activities, such as going to the men's *hammam* (public bath)—formerly one of the traditional institutions for the construction of male identity—or the barber's shop, or the neighborhood café.

Early on, boys and girls are taught to submit to the authority of the father who, as the head of the family, lays down the law. The father's methods of socialization are harsh and involve the use of punitive, forceful disciplinary actions. The father places greater demands on the son than the mother does, and expects higher standards from him. As Abdelwahab Bouhdiba writes: "There is a terrible image of the father: *Ab*. This all-powerful, all-serious colossus cannot but represent an impenetrable wall between the child and his father."[40] Consequently, boys tend to develop an idealized image of the mother, who "appears even more as a font of affection, all the more precious in that it is a restful oasis in the arid social desert."[41] With time, the son learns that he is superior to his sister but inferior to his father: he must satisfy his wishes, obey his orders, and be subservient to him. He also learns that he can treat females, younger or older, and boys younger than him as his inferiors, but his father and other older men are his superiors. The girl learns that she is subordinate to, and must serve, the men in her family—father, brothers, and in due course husband and sons. In this sharply hierarchical context, both the boy and the girl internalize their specific position in relation to other family members and acquire ways of behavior that are appropriate to their age and gender.[42]

Ritual events in the lives of boys and girls contribute decisively to their differential identity and personality development. Central among the initiation rites through which masculinity is formally constructed is circumcision. Mervat Hatem highlights the importance of this event in Egyptian families: "The Egyptian definition of masculinity, like that of the West, requires the repudiation of the mother and any aspects of the personality associated with women. The Egyptian repudiation of the mother takes place in two stages. The early circumcision of male children and their integration into male work arrangements serve to assert the authority of the father and the repression of the attachment to the mother."[43] Considered obligatory for all Muslims, the circumcision of boys usually takes place between the ages of three and seven, although in some parts of the Arab world the operation is performed at adolescence.[44] A public, joyous, and festive occasion, circumcision marks the boy's acceptance of male identity and the transition from babyhood to boyhood. According to the patriarchal perspective, circumcision rids the boy of the membrane of femininity—the foreskin, and it is therefore a break between the boy and femininity. This break is further signified by symbolic acts of defeminization that accompany the ceremony, such as wrapping a girl's headcloth around a boy's neck and then casting it off in favor of a man's garment.[45] While the ritual is subject to variations by region, setting (Bedouin, rural, or urban), and social class, it is always a solemn celebration exceeded in scope only by wedding festivities.

Hamed Ammar observes that the operation, especially when done without anesthetic, is associated with castration anxiety in the dreams of young boys.[46] The boy suffers the pain of mutilation and the awful expectation of the ordeal by being dressed up and paraded around in advance. Some fathers induce a state of anxiety in their sons by threatening to recircumcise them even if they are already circumcised.[47] Abdelwahab Bouhdiba notes that because circumcision is performed at an age when the boy is already aware of "the exorbitant privileges that go with being a male," he is gripped by fear that his penis will be cut off if it is not circumcised, or that what remains will be cut off after circumcision. As he elaborates: "Such a fear is part and parcel of the paradox and contradiction of childhood experience. There is a symbolic valorization of the phallus and an obsessional fear of losing it. This situation is likely to last for a long time, especially in an authoritarian society and one in which the terrifying father holds all kinds of goods, pleasures, wealth—and women—in 'trust' for him."[48] The boy's castration anxiety becomes more acute in a family environment where the father's authority is exercised by means of corporal punishment.

While male circumcision is a joyous, festive, and public event, female circumcision is a private affair, often performed secretly and in strict female company. Male circumcision is regarded as a test of courage that infuses the boy with a feeling of self-importance and achievement. By contrast, female circumcision is largely an act of degradation that serves to intimidate the girl's sexuality and accentuate her inferiority in relation to boys. Considered an indispensable prerequisite for marriage, female circumcision signifies the girl's assumption of her female identity. It is not a universal practice and has no religious sanction. The age at which it is performed is not fixed and varies between six and twelve. A mainly Nilotic custom that is no longer practiced among the upper classes, the ritual is still widespread among the lower classes in several Arab countries, notably Egypt and Sudan.[49]

Bouhdiba sees an intimate connection between the ceremonies of circumcision and marriage, which, in traditional circumstances, follows soon after puberty: "It is as if circumcision were only a mimicry of marriage and the sacrifice of the foreskin an anticipation of that of the hymen.... It is as if circumcision were a preparation for deflowering."[50] He notes that both circumcision and defloration are characterized by sexual mutilation. The bride is deflowered on her wedding night, with family members anxiously awaiting outside the bedroom the display of the bloodstained sheet as proof of her virginity—and of the family honor. The sacrifice of the hymen, much like that of the foreskin, is accompanied by festivities, violence, blood, pain, and exhibitionism.

Despite progressive efforts in recent decades to make primary education universal, the majority of Arab children, particularly in Bedouin and rural areas, get little formal schooling. More boys than girls are sent to school at all levels, despite the fact that women have gained the right to education. Statistically, the Arab region has one of the highest rates of female illiteracy—as much as one half, compared to only one third among males.[51] In large villages, there may be several traditional Koran schools, or *kuttabs*, where children memorize the Koran and learn to read and write. The religious socialization of boys is further enhanced by attending the mosque.[52]

As boys and girls approach adolescence, they prepare to assume adult roles. Until recently, adolescence, as perceived in Western modern thought, scarcely existed: "One moved from babyhood through childhood to puberty and adulthood."[53] Morroe Berger observes that "it is only in the educated urban class that adolescence has become the kind of 'problem' period between childhood and adulthood that it is in the West. In the desert, in the villages and among the uneducated urban masses adolescence is hardly long enough to be considered a special interval. In these communities, when the girl approaches twelve or thirteen and the boy fourteen or fifteen they must begin to carry a full adult share of the family's burdens and to think about their own marriage as well."[54] Marilyn Booth describes the uneven emergence of adolescence as a recognized stage of life primarily in metropolitan areas.[55] Considered a period fraught with sexual temptation, in milieus where adolescence is recognized as a developmental stage, as among the educated urban class, the differential treatment of boys and girls is intensified.[56] For a boy, this is a time of growing freedom, but for a girl, adolescence entails more limitations on her freedom of movement, the way she dresses, and the company she may keep, in an effort to control her sexuality.

Although both Arab men and women have to abide by a strict sexual code, it is women who bear the brunt of sexual repression. Traditional Arab culture places a prime value on a girl's virginity, which is the basis of family honor, especially the honor of its men, whose masculinity is reflected in its control of female sexuality. While honor in its nonsexual connotation is termed *sharaf,* a woman's sexual honor is called *'ird.* The *sharaf* of the man depends almost entirely on the *'ird* of the women in his family. Under all circumstances, a girl must preserve her virginity intact until her marriage. To lose her virginity to anyone but her husband is the gravest sin she can commit. Correspondingly, the greatest dishonor that can befall a man results from the sexual misconduct of his daughter, sister, or cousin.[57] In a situation where a girl brings dishonor on her family by losing her virginity, it is incumbent on her paternal relatives—her father, brother, or uncle—to avenge the family honor by severely punishing her. In conservative circles, this means putting her to death. Capital punishment is considered the only way to cleanse the stain inflicted on the family honor. Public opinion in many Arab countries permits crimes of honor, and the courts treat them leniently.[58] Consequently, from early childhood a girl grows up in constant fear of losing her virginity. This fear is shared by her male guardians, who find themselves burdened with the heavy responsibility of having to safeguard the girl's chastity—and the family honor.

Marriage, the only legitimate framework within which the individual's needs for sex and procreation are met in Arab societies, is the ultimate test of a son's or a daughter's loyalty to the family. Traditionally, marriage has been seen as a union between two families rather than as an individual choice. The practice of endogamy favors marriages contracted within a relatively narrow circle: the same lineage, sect, or community. Marriage outside one's own group is frowned upon and discouraged, sometimes forbidden or even punished. The rising cost of the bridewealth (*mahr*) is a target of constant criticism. Arranged marriage is the predominant pattern in traditional milieus, but in the more urbanized, educated, and economically privileged social sectors, young adults have more opportunities for dating, romance, and choosing their marriage partners based on personal attraction and affection.[59]

In conclusion, child socialization in Arab families, as elsewhere, is a process of teaching the young to function as adult members of society. However, certain features of this process are specific to Arab culture. The attitude to childhood is a much-discussed point. Morroe Berger oberves that "children in the Near East are made to get over their childhood as early as possible."[60] Hamed Ammar notes that "in adult eyes, the period of childhood is a nuisance, and childhood activities, especially play, are a waste of time."[61] Abdelwahab Bouhdiba is highly critical of this attitude: "Precisely because of its excessive masculinity the social world is inevitably perceived by the child as castrating.

Paternal authoritarianism cannot fail to devalue childhood in the same way that it devalues femininity."[62] Marriage, which in traditional circumstances takes place soon after puberty, marks the end of childhood and the assumption of adult responsibility for the creation of another family unit, with its own children to socialize.[63]

The heavy emphasis on family loyalty is another culture-specific feature of socialization in Arab families. The growing child has to learn that the interests of the family come first and to govern every action with the family viewpoint in mind. In fact, the primacy of the family in the loyalty scale is regarded as a sacrosanct value whose violation carries the risk of social, economic, and emotional penalties.[64] As a result, notes Halim Barakat, "the interests of both the individual and society are denied for the sake of the family."[65] The frustrations of young men and women who must give up their personal desires regarding education, employment, career, or marriage because of family needs can run very high. Hence rebellion against the family is not an uncommon event in the life cycle of sons and daughters.

Underlying the parent-child relationship is a paradigm of submission to authority, which is yet another characteristic of socialization in Arab families. The child is expected to obey parental orders under all circumstances. Disobedience to parents is considered the gravest sin after polytheism, and divine retribution in the form of consignment to hell awaits the son or daughter who commits this transgression. Besides unconditional obedience, the child must honor and respect the parents at all times, and always strive to please them and win their satisfaction (*rida*), as opposed to provoking their anger (*ghadab*).[66]

Bouhdiba observes that the authority relationship is deeply rooted in traditional Arab society: "It binds not only man to woman and parents to children but also teacher to pupil, master to disciple, employer to employee, ruler to ruled, the dead to the living and God to man."[67] Other Middle Eastern scholars have drawn an analogy between the Arab family and Arab society, noting that similar sets of values and relationships prevail within both the family and the wider society. They thus see the family as a small-scale mirror image of society. Hisham Sharabi, for example, considers the patriarchal family to be the model of both traditional and partly modernized or neopatriarchal Arab society.[68] He emphasizes the repressive nature of both the family system and the larger social system:

In its basic features the family is the society in microcosm. The values that govern it—authority, hierarchy, dependency, repression—are those that govern social relations in general; the conflict and antagonism, the sociability and incoherence, which characterize relations among the members of the family, also characterize those among the members of the society. The hierarchical and authoritarian structure of the family finds its reflection in the structure of society (irrespective of its "social system"), and the individual is equally oppressed in both. As a system, the family simultaneously embodies and sustains the larger social system.[69]

Sharabi highlights the parallel in the dominance of the father and of the ruler, the axis around which the family and the nation are organized: "Between ruler and ruled, between father and child, there exist only vertical relations: in both settings the paternal will is the absolute will, mediated in both the society and the family by a forced consensus based on ritual and coercion."[70]

Halim Barakat shares this view, extending the analogy between the family and the society to all other traditional institutions:

> The Arab family has served as a society in miniature. As suggested earlier, similar sets of relationships prevail within both the family and the society as a whole, as well as in the economic, religious, political, and educational institutions. Stratified and patriarchal relations are common to all. For instance, each political leader, employer, and teacher behaves and is conceived of as a father. The ruler refers to the citizens as "my children" and may even name the country after his family. The employer-employee relationship is another form of parent-child or father-son relationship. The educational system (even at the college level) is also patriarchal; students are constantly referred to as "my children" or treated in a paternalistic manner. Vertical relationships continue to prevail and are regulated and reinforced by a general, overall repressive ideology based on *at-tahrib* (scaring) and/or *at-targhib* (enticement) rather than on discussion aimed at persuasion. Arab society, then, is the family generalized or enlarged, and the family is society in miniature.[71]

These scholars are concerned that the Arab family has become an obstacle to social change and progress. In view of the close similarities between the family and the society, it is not surprising that a literary work narrating "a successful challenge of repressive family rules reflects a collective dream of a freer and more equal society."[72]

Clearly, many aspects of the traditional socialization process can cause tension between fathers and sons and bring them into conflict with each other. But how representative is this portrait of growing up male in Arab families? As Gary Gregg writes, it is only fair to say that while the cultural prototype is borne out by ethnographic accounts, exceptions abound:

> In this prototypic world, children in the 7-to-12 age range develop with a complementarity of threatening paternal authority and protective maternal nurturance. But how do real families match up to the prototype? From my own fieldwork it is clear that some match almost perfectly. One young man who described his family in precisely these terms even offered a sociological view: In most families, he said, the child stays distant from same-sexed parent, who acts as disciplinarian, and seeks out closeness with the other one, who more freely expresses "fondness." "His father grabs him and beats him but his mother gives him compassion/kindness—that's the reason." But many families do not match the prototype. Just as not all fathers play the fearsome authority, so not all mothers are able or willing to play the nurturing protector.[73]

The many autobiographies and memoirs discussed in Chapter 3 illustrate these points. The mothers of Tawfiq al-Hakim and Yusuf Idris, for example, did not match the cultural prototype of "protective maternal nurturance," and the fathers of Mikhail Naimy and Jabra Ibrahim Jabra did not match the cultural prototype of "threatening paternal authority," but in the case of Edward Said, both his father and mother matched their respective cultural prototypes. Significantly, all the literary texts that are presented in this study document the patriarchal nature of the family. A prime example is Naguib Mahfouz's Cairo Trilogy, described by the Egyptian literary critic Sabry Hafez as "the patriarchal novel par excellence."[74] In the first volume of the Trilogy, the patriarch, al-Sayyid Ahmad, rules over his household with a heavy hand, imposing a strict set of rules on his wife and three sons. His arbitrary, often unfair, rulings affect even the most trivial aspects of their lives. Any form of disobedience is severely punished by him. Powerless, the wife and sons submit to his authoritarian regime, but when given the opportunity each of them rebels in an attempt to escape his control and gain a degree of personal freedom and autonomy.

Arabic proverbial lore possesses a wealth of advice on fathering sons. "When your son grows a beard, shave yours off," runs a popular saying,[75] implying that when the son becomes an adult, his father should relinquish his responsibilities to him (the beard used to be a symbol of manhood and prestige in the past). Another famous proverb counsels: "Bring up your son as a child and befriend him as a man."[76] And yet another proverb cautions: "The eye of the father is on his son; the eye of the son is on the stone" (i.e., on the gravestone, thus awaiting his father's death in order to inherit).[77] The prophet Muhammad is quoted as having said: "God's pleasure is in a father's pleasure,"[78] and "A father's wrath is the wrath of God."[79] And the Koran says: "Wealth and sons are the adornment of the present world" (18:46).[80]

Modern Trends

As the myriad narratives and testimonies assembled in this study show, the Arab family is the focus of rapid social change currently in progress throughout the Arab region. The process of modernization has brought about new conceptions of the family and gender roles, as well as changes in family relationships, parenting styles, child-rearing practices, and expectations for puberty and dating. "Traditional family life becomes increasingly burdensome to the Arab son or daughter brought up in a changing society that emphasizes education, nationalism and industrial development," writes Morroe Berger.[81] Many young adults resent the claims and constraints of the family, seeking autonomy and freedom to shape their own identities and futures. Rejecting the idea of arranged marriage, they seek romantic love and spouses of their own choosing. The rising status of women, particularly their access to education and employment, provides greater opportunities for direct contact between the sexes and the experience of dating. While the family remains the framework of everyday life and the primary source of support and security, its centrality as a basic socioeconomic unit has been undermined by the state and other competing institutions. State-sponsored education, employment, and welfare services have replaced some of the traditional responsibilities of the Arab family, thus reducing its function and power. In addition, there has been a shift away from the extended family to a modified version or a nuclear family, especially in the cities. Traditional patterns of marriage and divorce are also changing, partly because of legal reforms in the areas of polygamy, repudiation, and age of marriage. Different sets of relationships are developing within the family as fathers, no longer the sole breadwinners, are forced to relinquish their control of family life and share authority and responsibility with other family members. Since modernization is more advanced in the cities than in the villages, more changes can be observed in urban centers than in rural areas.[82]

Many factors have transformed the Arab family. Industrialization, urbanization, war and revolution, legal reforms, and foreign influences all have necessitated the development of new coping strategies for survival. New realities have caused family forms to proliferate. For example, international labor migration and greater geographic mobility have produced a rise in women-headed households where, in the absence of the husbands, the wives take charge of the family and manage its tasks.[83] Even where the extended family persists, it often assumes new functions, such as childcare for working mothers. Other important trends include smaller families and later marriages. Not only has the average age of marriage for both men and women increased, but also the age gap between the spouses has narrowed.[84]

The new or relatively new family forms develop different patterns of interactional dynamics. The husband-wife and father-child relationships are becoming more egalitarian, and the external boundaries of the family are becoming more open. Although the power asymmetry between men and women in the home has not disappeared, roles have become less separate and more fused as the spouses have begun to share activities and cooperate in making decisions, particularly regarding the family budget and their children's upbringing. While the importance of gender in child rearing remains crucial, the value of daughters relative to that of sons has increased as girls have become more educated and many work outside the home and contribute to the family income.[85]

Public education and new information technologies have been key factors in empowering young men and women and changing traditional attitudes toward gender roles and male-female relations. Educated youth of both sexes tend to adopt more liberal views of marriage, seeking a relationship based on love and equality rather than on parental approval and male domination. Cell phones, the Internet, cyber cafés, and shopping malls facilitate contact between young adults, giving them more opportunities for friendship, dating, and romance. However, these people tend to be from the more economically privileged, and more urbanized, strata.[86] Large social sectors in the Arab region still remain closer to tradition than to modernity. Regardless of modernizing forces, the family still enjoys a great solidarity, and young men and women show less alienation from the family than from any other social institution.[87]

In no area is social change more dramatic than in the emancipation of women. Legal reforms, public education, and access to the labor market have improved women's position in the family and in the wider society. The range of options available to women has expanded with respect to family formation, duration, and size. Trends include later marriages, smaller families, more schooling, more formal-sector employment, and greater decision making among women.[88] The most conservative reaction to the emancipation of women has come in the form of Islamic fundamentalism. Fatima Mernissi explains the fundamentalist backlash as a "defense mechanism against profound changes in both sex roles and the touchy subject of sexual identity."[89] At present, many Arab families are caught between conflicting value systems—old and new, traditional and modern, Islamic and Western. The emergence of competing agencies of socialization, including public schools, religious institutions, the mass media, and political parties or movements, adds to the dilemma facing many parents. Despite this state of flux, the Arab family continues to be the most important agency of socialization of young children throughout the Arab world.[90]

Pulled between tradition and modernity, the Arab family is in a transitional state. Given that the Arab family is society in miniature and that Arab society is the family generalized or enlarged, the transitional nature of the Arab family is mirrored in Arab society.[91] Some scholars maintain that the absence of both genuine traditionalism and authentic modernity in contemporary Arab society makes it neither traditional nor modern but rather neopatriarchal.[92] Other intellectuals see the family both as the means to, and the object of, social reform. While the public debate about the nature and future of the family goes on, this long-standing institution continues to give structure to the lives of millions of people throughout the many regions and countries comprising the Arab world.

Family Dynamics: Mothers and Others

In her study of family life in contemporary Egypt, the anthropologist Andrea Rugh writes that "if the two principles of same-sex closeness and greater closeness with mother are carried to their logical conclusion, one might then postulate that the inherent conflict in family life involves the father-son relationship."[93] Rugh explains that though the father-son relationship is strengthened by same-sex closeness, it is strained by the son's stronger attachment to the mother and the greater demands placed on him by the father. In addition, there is an element of competitiveness between father and son over the mother's affections, over their personal achievements, and over the need to assert hierarchical positions in the household. The son knows that eventually "he will take over the position of dominance within the household, but he is expected to suppress his desire to control until the right time comes," that is, until the father dies.[94] According to

Rugh, "if crimes can be considered a marker of where some of the tensions in the family lie, then one finds that between sons and their parents, the violent crimes almost always involve crimes between fathers (or father surrogates) and sons and usually are perpetrated by the sons on the fathers."[95] The primary cause of the initial dispute is money or property. By contrast, crimes that involve parent and daughter generally concern the girl's morality and are usually committed by the father or brother against the young woman (i.e., honor crimes).[96] Abdelwahab Bouhdiba attributes the violence in the father-son relationship to labor exploitation: "In terms of socioeconomic status it can be said that children have quite simply been exploited by the patriarchal socioeconomic structures to a relatively advanced age. In agriculture, in the crafts, in commerce, the child joins the family firm in which he works without being able to claim a wage.... Hence that stereotype of the son who waits endlessly for his father's death in order to inherit, that is to say, in order to reach economic autonomy—which he then establishes on the exploitation of his own children."[97] As evidence, Bouhdiba mentions the predominance of the theme of inheritance on radio plays, whether Radio Tunis, Radio Algiers, or Radio Cairo.

The Mother-Son Relationship

While the father-son relationship is frequently conflicted, the mother-son relationship is generally close and strong. Many scholars of Arab family life have observed that a husband's primary attachment is with his mother, rather than his wife, whereas a wife's primary attachment is with her son. The wife's behavior is attributed to the threats of polygamy and repudiation, which render the ties between the spouses weak and unstable. A mother always expects that her son will take care of her future, regarding him as her best insurance in sickness, old age, or divorce. Andrea Rugh writes that in Egyptian families a mother experiences her son as "her own personal ego extension" and competes with the father for his love and affection. She notes that "there is an underlying urgency to the mother's need to co-opt her son's affections": should her husband divorce her, she would need her son to support her.[98] Suad Joseph has examined the mother-son relationship in Arab Christian families in a village in Lebanon and found that the close bond between them conforms to the cultural norm of Arab Muslim families. She argues that a close mother-son relationship is not only functional but a plausible outcome of this patriarchal, patrilineal, and endogamous community.[99]

Other scholars view the closeness of the mother-son relationship as problematic and even dysfunctional. Halim Barakat, for example, describes the deep attachment that characterizes the mother-son relationship as verging on morbidity.[100] Hamed Ammar calls attention to the erotic element underlying the mother-son relationship.[101] Abdelwahab Bouhdiba criticizes what he calls the "prolonged uterine relationship" between a mother and her son, arguing that it has harmful effects on the development of the child's personality and later adult behavior.[102]

In her seminal study *Beyond the Veil*, the Moroccan sociologist Fatima Mernissi provides intriguing insights into the husband-wife and mother-son relationships in Arab families. She writes that conjugal intimacy is discouraged by Muslim ideology because it is perceived as a direct threat to man's allegiance to Allah, which requires the unconditional investment of all his energies, thoughts, and feelings in his God. In her view, the Muslim system is not so much opposed to women as to the heterosexual unit: "What is feared is the growth of the involvement between a man and a woman into an all-encompassing love satisfying the sexual, emotional and intellectual needs of both partners."[103] This is why the sexual act is considered polluting and is surrounded by ceremonies and incantations whose goal is to create emotional distance between the spouses and reduce intercourse to a strictly reproductive act. Erotic love is regarded as even more dangerous because it has the potential to grow into a profoundly fulfilling emotional bond that might compete with man's love for God. To eliminate the peril that the conjugal unit poses to man's total devotion to God, it is weakened by two legal devices, polygamy and repudiation, both of which are exclusively male privileges. Owing to these devices, the spouses are less inclined to invest emotionally in each other and the marital bond is weak.[104]

How, then, are the emotional needs of the spouses met if they are prevented from developing intimacy? Mernissi points out that in societies that establish a weak marital bond, the mother-son relationship is accorded a particularly important place. In Muslim societies, the mother-son relationship is the only context within which a man is allowed to love a woman—his mother, and a woman is allowed to experience warmth and affection from a man—her son.[105] Marriage promotes the Oedipal split between love and sex in a man's life: "He is encouraged to love a woman with whom he cannot engage in sexual intercourse, his mother; he is discouraged from lavishing his affection on the woman with whom he does engage in sexual intercourse, his wife."[106] Inevitably, this situation creates intense competition, jealousy, and antagonism between the mother and her daughter-in-law. The mother, who has control over the household as well as over her daughter-in-law, often interferes in her son's marital life. The wife is powerless vis-à-vis her mother-in-law until she gives birth to a son, who improves her status in the family and gives her prestige. The arrival of a male child sets a vicious circle in motion: since the son is the wife's exclusive possession, he becomes the object of her emotional investment—and the substitute for her unfulfilled heterosexual relations; therefore, she is bound to foster the same kind of relationship with him as the one existing between her husband and his own mother. In this way, the mother-son-wife triangle is perpetuated from generation to generation.[107] Mernissi states that this triangle is "the trump card in the Muslim pack of legal, ideological, and physical barriers that subordinate the wife to the husband and condemn the heterosexual relation to mistrust, violence and deceit."[108] Moreover, the structural instability inherent in the traditional Muslim family and its conflicted interpersonal relations have disastrous effects on child development.[109] In her view, while the pressures of modernization disrupt the patriarchal structure of the family and traditional patterns of male-female interaction, they increase the family instability by causing anomie—confusion of roles, ambiguity, and tension. This is due to the fact that existing norms have been shaken, but new ones have not yet come into place.[110]

Abdelwahab Bouhdiba examines the privileged relationship of mother and son in Arab families, affirming that it dominates all other types of interpersonal relationships within the group.[111] He calls attention to a striking paradox. On the one hand, there is systematic marginalization of the woman and the child, who are accorded no weight or autonomy in Arab Muslim society, because the only serious world is that of the adult male. On the other hand, in this male-dominated social system, the child is abandoned completely to the mother and is under her exclusive tutelage until the age of seven or nine.[112] The marginalization of the boy is temporary, because upon entering the *kuttab* (Koran school) he joins the adult male world and receives the necessary "apprenticeship of life." By contrast, the girl remains marginalized permanently, for her exclusion from the *kuttab* is just the first stage of "a state destined to continue, from womb to tomb, unchangingly." Bouhdiba defines the girl's socialization as "an apprenticeship in the superiority of the male," and a woman's life as "a conditioning to accept this situation—happily, which is to say by becoming alienated."[113] He notes that both the mother and the child are in a position of exclusion from the society at large, representing,

respectively, female and juvenile subcultures that do not converge with
the culture of the greater male-dominated society. Consequently, the
process of socialization is "polysegmented": the various social and
cultural experiences do not converge but rather diverge, creating tensions, conflicts, and contradictions that are unhealthy for the individual and the group.[114]

Bouhdiba introduces the concept of the "Judar complex" as a form
of the Oedipus complex peculiar to Arab Muslim culture. The name
originates from one of the stories in the collection of *The Thousand
and One Nights*. The hero, Judar the fisherman, guided by a Moorish
magician, sets out in search of a treasure buried in the depths of
the earth. To find the treasure, he must open seven doors, the last
of which is guarded by his mother. He must order her to undress
completely before him, and once she is totally naked she will vanish.
Then the spell will be broken, the door will open, and Judar will be
able to seize the treasure. During the first confrontation with his
mother, Judar hesitates to tell her to take all her clothes off, and so he
is defeated. The second time he does not flinch and orders his mother
to undress completely. As soon as her underwear drops about her
feet she vanishes, and Judar is able to seize the treasure.[115] Bouhdiba
interprets this tale in psychoanalytic terms: to attain psychological
maturity, "one must kill in oneself the image of the mother, profane
it, demythify it." The tale's message is that "it is only the image of
the mother that holds us back. In order to release consciousness...we
must free ourselves from the abusive presence of the false image, the
fantasy of the mother."[116] Moreover, the repudiation of the mother
is in her own interest as much as in her son's, for the tale goes on to
say that after seizing the treasure, Judar saves his real mother from
a life of poverty and humiliation. This act of filial duty is made possible only after the son's emancipation from his mother's dominant
influence. Thus, Bouhdiba concludes, "one could not have a better
demonstration of how the uterine relationship may be a source of
repression and how psychological maturity depends on the liquida-
tion of the survival of maternal desire."[117]

Bouhdiba argues that this myth comprises "all the elements, psychological and social, individual and unconscious, pathological and
normal, rational and oneiric that enable us to speak of a 'Judar complex' in the sense that one speaks of an Oedipus complex."[118] But
whereas Oedipus is guilty (he has committed patricide and incest),
Judar (who deals only with false appearances, and whose act is an
authentic liberation of himself and of his own mother), defines a type
of behavior free from all guilt, that is, an exculpated Oedipus. In

Bouhdiba's view, Judar is the archetypal image of the Arab Muslim male, and his mother is the faithful prototype of the Arab Muslim mother. He believes that in Arab Muslim society, a Judar complex underlies male personality and gender identity. This complex is manifested especially in the institution of marriage, whose instability reveals the man's inability to detach himself entirely from his mother and to perceive his wife—the woman—as a sexual partner and an equal.[119]

Instead of a polysegmented socialization, Bouhdiba advocates an integrated upbringing that allows the inclusion of the woman and the child in society, a situation that, if actualized, can lead to the convergence of the various interpersonal relationships. The child-mother relationship would then move in the same direction as that of the child-father and child-society, thus promoting the optimal functioning of both the individual and the society. Bouhdiba admits that this harmonious ideal is rarely achieved. At present, the process of modernization has accentuated the polysegmentation of socialization. While the mother and child have not yet really stopped being marginal, the father himself has become partially devalued, his authority being undermined by public education and improved employment opportunities for women and young adults. In other words, while the hierarchical relationship has lost its traditional economic basis, the egalitarian relationship has not yet come into being. Consequently, all interpersonal relationships are threatened by disintegration and divergence. This situation is disruptive both to the psychic equilibrium of the individual personality and to the social equilibrium of the group.[120]

The Sibling Relationship

Scholars of Arab family life have noted that the large size of the traditional family coupled with the siblings' closeness in age cause a high level of competitiveness among them. Not infrequently, sibling jealousy involves the parents as favoring one child over the others, particularly a boy over a girl. Polygamy, when practiced, produces great rivalry among children of different mothers but the same father. In many instances, parents deliberately provoke sibling rivalry in order to prod a child toward improvement and greater responsibility. They also use the motive of competitiveness as a means to toughen up a child, especially a boy, so that he may stand up to his rivals when he becomes an adult. Underlying this parental attitude is the assumption that exposure to competitive stress within the family is the best way to prepare children for life. Hamed Ammar views the sense of rivalry that is instilled by Arab parents in their children as one of the main sources for the Arab conflict proneness.[121] Morroe Berger sees rivalry as the flip side of intimacy, suggesting that "among Arabs intimacy and rivalry nourish each other."[122]

As with the husband-wife and father-child relationships, the sibling relationship is not egalitarian but governed by age and gender hierarchy (the young are subordinate to the old, and females to males). Traditionally, the eldest son enjoys a higher status among his siblings. He acts as his father's representative and disciplines his younger brothers and sisters, who tacitly acknowledge his authority and obey his orders.[123]

The brother-sister relationship is viewed as "running a close second" to the powerful mother-son relationship.[124] Characterized by unconditional love and mutual devotion, it is often described as "the only safe cross-gender relationship in otherwise relatively gender-segregated societies."[125] The brother is expected to protect his sister and take good care of her if she is needy, while the sister is expected to serve and obey her brother. The brother is also the jealous guardian of his sister's honor, and it is his duty—as it is his father's and uncle's—to avenge the family honor by killing a sister who has lost her chastity. Some scholars point out the incestuous tendencies underlying the brother-sister relationship.[126] The folklorist Hassan El-Shamy, for example, speaks of a "brother-sister syndrome" that is unrecognized and untreated in the Arab psychiatric literature, attributing this syndrome to the social and cultural conditions that characterize the traditional Arab family.[127] Other scholars focus on the romantic (love) and patriarchal (power) aspects of the brother-sister relationship, as well as on its function as a vehicle of gender role socialization in the service of patriarchy.[128]

The Kin Group

As stated earlier, the traditional Arab family is extended and tightly connected to a larger kin group. However, even when the family is not extended in the strict sense, it remains enmeshed in a web of intimate relationships that leaves limited room for the expression of personal autonomy. Little privacy is permitted, and the business of the individual is the business of the family. If a child is subjected to an undue disciplinary action by a parent, a close relative or a senior member of the group may intervene to mitigate the punishment. All members of the group help each other in times of need or crisis. They exchange gifts, celebrate festive occasions together, and visit each other regularly. The intense interaction with the kin group contributes to the socialization of the child, who is exposed to various role models, and imparts a strong sense of security and belonging to the individual member, who enjoys multiple sources of emotional and instrumental support. Specifically, a son whose father is absent owing to death, divorce, or the requirements of a job can seek compensation in surrogate relationships with other male members of the group. A grandfather, for example, can serve as a surrogate father figure for the grandson. Moreover, when both the father and grandfather are present, the grandson can observe aspects of the interactional dynamics operating between them. For women, the connection with the kin group is a vital means of reducing their isolation and developing supportive networks of relatives and friends. Social visits offer them opportunities to hear the latest news, meet new people, form new friendships, and select marriage partners for family members and acquaintances. Men find in the kin group peer company and an arena for the enactment of various forms of masculinity, both traditional and nontraditional. In many ways, the kin group contributes to the well-being of the individual. However, the flip side of this intricate web of relationships is obligation, control, and sometimes domination and exploitation. The duty to satisfy the demands and expectations of the kin group is burdensome to the individual, who is already bound by many commitments to his nuclear family.

Contradictions in Arab Masculinity

In his groundbreaking work *The Myth of Masculinity*, Joseph Pleck examines traditionally held beliefs about male gender roles in American culture. Deconstructing the model of male gender role identity, he proposes instead a new paradigm, the male gender role strain, thereby highlighting the conflicts and stresses that gender stereotyping and cultural expectations have created for men. Pleck identifies three varieties of male gender role strain, which he terms "discrepancy strain," "trauma strain," and "dysfunction strain." Discrepancy strain denotes the idea that a significant number of men exhibit long-term failure to fulfill male role expectations, a situation that has negative effects on their psychological well-being, particularly self-esteem, owing to negative social feedback. Trauma strain implies that even if male role expectations are successfully fulfilled, the socialization process leading to this fulfillment, or the fulfillment itself, is traumatic, with long-term side effects. Dysfunction strain suggests that the successful fulfillment of male role expectations can have negative consequences because many of the characteristics viewed as desirable or acceptable in men have inherent side effects, either for men themselves or for others. Pleck argues that the deeper the acceptance of the male gender role identity paradigm in the culture, the more widespread the experience of strain.[129]

The insights provided by Pleck's concept of male gender role strain, now widely accepted and assimilated into the cultural perspective on men and masculinity, are useful for the analysis of the male predicament in Arab societies. Specifically, they help to understand the ways in which Arab men manifest gender role strain, the sources of the strains that they experience, and the coping mechanisms that they adopt in their everyday lives.

At the outset of this analysis, it would be useful to describe the basic components of the code of masculinity in traditional Arab culture. Raphael Patai points out the pre-Islamic origins of this code: "In addition to bravery in battle, the old Arab ideal of *muruwwa* comprised such traits as patience in misfortune, persistence in seeking revenge, protection of the weak, and defiance of the strong. Complementary traits of *muruwwa* were loyalty, fidelity, and generosity. All these features together added up to a man's honor, which he was supposed to defend no matter what sacrifice it required."[130] He emphasizes that the virtues that were extolled in the odes of the pre-Islamic Arab poets: bravery (*hamasa*), manliness (*muruwwa*), honor (*sharaf*), and hospitality (*diyafa*), continue to occupy a central position in Arab ethics and are regarded as the most highly prized personal qualities.[131] David Pryce-Jones refers to shame-honor considerations as a defining frame for Arab masculinity: "Shame and honor closely define the roles of men and women and all transactions between them, validating and dramatizing them unforgettably and at all times. Honor for the male lies in fulfilling traditional masculine virtues, from being a 'warrior' to fathering children, sons above all. Honor for the female consists in modesty and faithfulness, the bearing of children, sons once again above all."[132] Julie Peteet sums up the main attributes of Arab masculinity in operational terms: "Arab masculinity (*rujula*) is acquired, verified and played out in the brave deed, in risk-taking, and in expressions of fearlessness and assertiveness. It is attained by constant vigilance and willingness to defend honour (*sharaf*), face (*wajh*), kin and community from external aggression and to uphold and protect cultural definitions of gender-specific propriety."[133]

Many "dark side" behaviors in Arab men can be characterized as a by-product of the imperative of preserving or restoring one's honor.[134] Prominent among these are various forms of violence, particularly honor killings and the blood feud, the former representing aggression against women, the latter against other men. As noted earlier, the honor of the man (*sharaf*) depends on the sexual honor (*'ird*) of the women in his family. Any sexual misconduct on the part of a wife, daughter, sister, or cousin is regarded as the greatest affront to a man's honor. This affront must be avenged, or else his honor is permanently stained. Pryce-Jones elaborates: "Immodesty or unfaithfulness forfeits [a woman's] honor and shames the men in the family in whose keeping this honor is vested. Men must put the lapse right at all costs, if need be killing the dishonored woman. Such tragic occurrences are commonplace, reported in the daily newspapers."[135] The task of killing the dishonored woman falls on the shoulders of her paternal relatives—her father, brother, or uncle. In such a situation, the psychological pressure to conform to the norms of masculinity often overrides all other considerations: "A man who kills his wife or daughter for her unfaithfulness, real or supposed, goes to prison glad to have preserved his family's honor. If he did not really wish to punish her, his only alternatives are to be dishonored himself or to leave the community altogether. The community thinks well of him as he pays whatever the penalty may be, valuing his action and disregarding the flagrant breach of the law."[136] According to psychologists, gender role strain in general leads to overconformity rather than to rejection of the cultural norms prescribed by hegemonic masculinity. This reaction is attributed to the overwhelming anxiety induced by the fear of the consequences of *not* conforming to the cultural expectations, for violations of gender roles incur sanctions ranging from public humiliation to social condemnation to ostracism. As the anxiety associated with such sanctions increases, individuals tend to regress to stereotyped forms of behavior.[137] The French social scientist Pierre Bourdieu, who examined the sentiment of honor in Kabyle society in Algeria, writes: "The fear of collective reprobation and shame...the negative aspect of the point of honour, is such that it compels a man most lacking in self-esteem to conform, with constraint and of necessity, to the dictates of honour."[138]

Closely related to shame-honor considerations is the concept of *wajh*, or "face," which is the outward appearance of honor, its "front" or façade. Under all circumstances, a man must be cautious lest his face should be "blackened"; he must always strive to "whiten" his face, and the face of his kin group. This "tyranny of the face"—the relentless pressure to save one's face at all costs—is the primary concern in weighing one's actions and words. It often results in a division between the public and private life of a man, who projects two different images, or two kinds of personality, one to the outside world and one to his family.[139] This duality is vividly depicted in Naguib Mahfouz's Cairo Trilogy in the figure of the patriarch, al-Sayyid Ahmad, who fasts and prays as fervently as he drinks alcohol and commits adultery. While a man will relax somewhat in the company of his kin, his true personality remains hidden even from them. Given that what motivates a man to obey the rules is not guilt but shame, instilled in him by shaming techniques throughout his socialization process, he often has no scruples about lying or cheating to protect his honor and avoid shame.[140] Thus his behavior may take the form of merely outward conformity with ethical demands whose substance is largely neglected. Pryce-Jones argues that "shame-honor ranking effectively prohibits the development of wider, more socialized types of human relationship," fostering hypocrisy, deception, and corruption.[141] As for the father-son relationship, he states: "Shame-honor considerations render it impossible for a son to grow up and assert his own individuality without upsetting, insulting, or otherwise calling into question his father's honor as head of the household and probably his mother's as well."[142]

The blood feud is another form of violence prescribed by traditional masculine norms in Arab culture. This ancient Bedouin custom calls for blood revenge (*dam butlub dam*, "blood demands blood") in the case of homicide, premeditated or accidental. Avenging a death becomes the duty of all the male members of the victim's kin group, who must fulfill it or else forfeit their honor. If the avengers cannot find the murderer, any member of the murderer's kin group is a legitimate target for blood revenge. Before long, the inexorable *lex talionis* or law of retaliation triggers a chain reaction that involves an increasing number of men and groups. The blood feud comes to an end only when the honor of the victim's family is restored, that is, when its members exact their revenge or a reconciliation (*sulha*) is arranged and appropriate damages paid.[143]

The duty of the blood revenge, which passed almost unchanged from Bedouin society into village life, is held as noble manhood. As with honor killings, a man finds himself in an impossible bind. He faces a tough choice: either to safeguard his honor and lose his humanity, or to safeguard his humanity and lose his honor. Some men choose to flee from their tribe or village to the city, where they hope to escape the pressure exerted on them by their male relatives to slay an innocent person for the sake of blood revenge.[144] Some scholars see a connection between the custom of blood feud and the Arab conflict proneness.[145]

Virility and fertility are key components of Arab masculinity. As previously stated, the rite of defloration testifies to the virginity of the bride and the virility of the groom. The consequences for either party who fails the test are catastrophic. The Algerian author Rachid Boudjedra condemns this practice: "Brutally and swiftly deflowering his bride, the husband is responding to a social criterion of virility, which is still very widespread. Deflowering is not a means leading to the consummation of the sexual act, but a proof of power to engender, to be given to friends grouped about the bedroom. Above all, here is a matter of male pride whose consequences may well be disastrous for the couple's future harmony."[146] This practice is only one of various obstacles on the road to marital life. The multiplicity of sexual partners allowed to the husband (wives, concubines, prostitutes, mistresses), in sharp contrast to the strict monogamy required of the wife, is another obstacle. But this male privilege is double-edged, for while having multiple sexual relations attests to a man's virility, it also entails the fragmentation of his desire and energy, so that he cannot develop close ties or an intimate relationship with any woman.[147] In this respect, both polygamy and repudiation, which privilege Arab Muslim men, destabilize the institution of marriage and prevent the spouses from investing emotionally in each other.[148]

Given the supreme value of virility in the code of Arab masculinity, it is not surprising that fertility should occupy a prominent place. Fertility serves as the ultimate proof of a man's virility. While a man acquires respect by having many children, it is especially sons who increase his honor. The prestige and social recognition that come from having sons is such that in traditional milieus a man who has only daughters is derided as *abu banat*, "the father of daughters."[149] Conversely, when blessed with male offspring, a man assumes the honorific title of "father of" followed by the name of his first born son. A man will go to great extremes to fulfill his desire for a son, including divorcing the wife who fails to bear him one or taking an additional wife.[150] Fertility entails heavy responsibilities for the father, who must provide for his children, and many sacrifices for the mother, who has to bear and rear them.[151] Despite the heavy burden for the family and society, most parents aspire to live up to the prophet Muhammad's dictum, "Get married, reproduce and let your number increase."[152] Needless to say, this attitude interferes with family-planning programs in a largely developing region where poverty and overpopulation combine to set a vicious cycle in motion.

The emphasis on virility and fertility can have debilitating effects on the male psyche. Marcia Inhorn describes the stigma attached to male infertility in Egypt.[153] The Lebanese psychiatrist John Racy reports that impotence and related problems in men are among the commonest reasons for seeking psychiatric help in the Arab East.[154] Abdessamad Dialmy calls attention to the phenomenon of the "Viagra freak," namely, healthy males who consume Viagra although they do not suffer from sexual dysfunction at all.[155] He notes that this phenomenon reveals the Arab man's constant fear of impotence and his "desire for a continuous guarantee of virility—that elementary dimension of the Arab definition of masculinity."[156] In his view, the promotional image of Viagra answers special needs in the emotional makeup of today's Arab man: "The economically vanquished Arab male—who is unable to justify his patriarchal control and privileges by rights of what he spends on his wife—requires something through which he can compensate for his economic incapacity. Intensified sexual activity becomes a means of compensation as well as a way to strengthen control."[157] Men's sexual activity, however, is compounded by the so-called madonna-whore complex, that is, the ideological separation between the respectable woman—the wife— and the loose woman—the songstress, the prostitute, the lover. The respectable wife is confined to satisfying her husband's desire and producing a large number of male children, whereas the loose woman is linked to sexual pleasure. In addition, the hegemonic definition of male sexuality in Arab culture stigmatizes and marginalizes certain categories of men, specifically homosexuals and transsexuals.[158] Subordinate masculinities are not determined by sexual orientation only; they include the factors of age, generation, class, ethnicity, and religious affiliation. Thus, sons are subordinate to their fathers, the younger generation to the older generation, the working class to the upper class, Berbers to Arabs, Copts to Muslims, etc.

The foregoing account shows that many of the norms of masculinity in traditional Arab culture are difficult to live up to. Specifically, the three fundamental male gender roles or the three *Ps—procreator, protector, and provider*—are fraught with inconsistencies and contradictions. The Arab male finds himself torn between autonomy and conformity, personal aspirations and family obligations, patriarchal ideology and objective reality. At times masculine role norms require a response that conflicts with his own judgment and humanity. Should he protect his honor at all costs or the life of his daughter? Should he allow his wife to work outside the home or stoically carry the heavy burden of being the sole breadwinner in the family? Should he bring numerous children into the world when he can barely afford to feed them? Such ambiguities and stresses, conflicting demands and expectations, can generate feelings of inadequacy, frustration, rage, and alienation in Arab men, resulting in dark side behaviors.

In conclusion, as in other patriarchal societies, the defining characteristics of Arab masculinity are inseparable from the totality of gender relations. As the Moroccan anthropologist Abdellah Hammoudi sums it up: "Manhood is defined by, among other criteria, the authority exercised over a woman, the maintenance of her inferior status, and the procreation of sons."[159] The feminist scholar Deniz Kandiyoti argues that the subjection of Muslim women through seclusion and polygamy ultimately mutilates and distorts the male psyche. While the little son shares with his mother a profound sense of fear of the father and understands the sources of her misery at an early age, he has an inordinate amount of power over her, because she depends on him to move through the streets and bazaars. Skeptical about the deeper motivations of Middle Eastern male reformers who have supported the cause of women, Kandiyoti wonders whether they were not in fact rebelling against their own lack of emancipation from paternal control. Her examination of personalized accounts of boyhood by male writers such as Abdelwahab Bouhdiba and other male narratives such as biographies and novels brings her to the conclusion that "quite often, male reformers were not speaking from the position of the dominating patriarch, but from the perspective of the young son of the repudiated or repudiable mother, powerless in the face of an aloof, unpredictable and seemingly all-powerful father."[160] In her view, this perspective explains why in some instances male reformers speak in a tone that is not just rational and didactic but strident and full of rage and disgust. Rhetorically, she asks: "Was I hearing the rage of an earlier, subordinated masculinity masquerading as pro-feminism?"[161]

Historical changes in the labor force and the organization of the family have made it even more difficult for Arab men to develop a secure sense of masculinity. Women have become more assertive following improvements in their status, particularly with respect to education and employment. The process of modernization and the influences of the mass media, satellite television, and the Internet have undermined patriarchal authority. Sons rebel against their fathers, seeking independence and freedom from family control. Often better educated than their fathers and capable of supporting themselves economically, young men are no longer willing to accept their subordinate status in a family system that makes many demands but offers few advantages.

As a result, the generation gap becomes more pronounced, and the father-son relationship more conflicted.

Some scholars see a connection between the rising popularity of Islamist movements and the crisis in Arab masculinity.[162] While it is true that different people join an Islamist movement for different reasons, the desire of many men to regain control over their families—wives, sons, and daughters—and reassert patriarchal authority cannot be discounted. Two much-quoted sayings of the prophet Muhammad run: "God's pleasure is in a father's pleasure" and "A father's wrath is the wrath of God." In this sense, then, the return to the literal teachings of the Koran, as well as the rallying to fight in the cause of Allah (i.e., jihad) can be seen as coping mechanisms for men whose masculinity is insecure or in crisis.

Chapter 3

Fathers and Sons in Personal Histories

Cross-Generational Echoes: Grandfathers, Fathers, Sons

The father-son relationship, like any relationship, is not self-contained. Each father and son brings to the relationship influences, elements, and traces of myriad other relationships, primarily with family members. Not infrequently, the father's style of parenting mirrors that of his own father before him and is also replicated by his son. In general, the interactional strategies, role models, values, obligations, and set of expectations that operate within a specific family form trends or orientations that persist from generation to generation. While the family legacy is a major factor in shaping the nature of the father-son relationship, it does not necessarily follow that all sons conform to the patterns established in the family. Some sons reject their fathers' models of behavior rather than emulate them, and seek alternative styles of interaction with their children. Attempting to avoid their fathers' shortcomings, they strive to be lenient, supportive, and affectionate with their own sons if, for example, they have experienced their fathers as strict, distant, and cold. In such instances, rejection becomes a mechanism of change and progress. The cross-generational movement, then, is not entirely predictable. At times the father-son relationship shows similarities across generations; at other times, it reveals dramatic changes. This variability results from differences in the personalities of the players involved (i.e., father and son), and from differences in the historical context in which the family is embedded, specifically the dynamic interplay among various social, cultural, religious, economic, and political forces at work.

The cross-generational echoes of the father-son relationship are rarely explored in modern Arabic autobiography. The Arab autobiographer tends to focus on a single father-son relationship—his own, often privileging his narrative over that of his father. Only seldom does the autobiographer chronicle the father-son relationship across several generations that include the grandfather, the father, the son, and the grandson, thus depicting not only the here and now (i.e., the present), but also the there and then (i.e., the past). Such a broad perspective is useful because it highlights the evolutionary nature of fatherhood and sonhood and shows how they change over time. Moreover, by portraying past father-son relationships, the autobiographer arrives at a better understanding of his own relationship with his father and the effects that it had on his life.

Jurji Zaydan's *Autobiography*

Jurji Zaydan (1861–1914), a Syrian Egyptian journalist, novelist, and historian, was one of the major contributors to the Arab Awakening (*nahda*) of the late nineteenth and early twentieth centuries. Zaydan founded one of the earliest magazines, *Al-Hilal,* in Cairo in 1892, which is still popular today, and a publishing house, Dar al-Hilal (1891), which has become one of the largest in the Arab world. Zaydan's literary output was large: he wrote 22 historical novels and romances, more than a dozen scholarly works on Arab history, Arabic language, and Arabic literature, and countless articles. He is credited with introducing a new genre into Arabic literature, the historical novel, and a new literary style, the direct or semijournalistic style. Despite his many accomplishments, the work for which Zaydan is frequently cited is his autobiography, an incomplete text published posthumously.[1] It is considered the first true autobiography in modern Arabic literature because it focuses on the development of the author's personality, both psychologically and intellectually, rather than on the mere facts of his public life.[2]

Zaydan's autobiography covers only the first period of his life, from 1861 until 1883, when he left Beirut for Cairo. Written in 1908 when he was approaching 50, it was stimulated by the departure of his son, Emile, for Beirut, where, like his father, he was to study at the American University of Beirut (formerly called the Syrian Protestant College). In recording his childhood memories, Zaydan was fulfilling a promise he made to his son.[3]

The central theme of Zaydan's narrative is that of the self-made man. Born in Beirut into a working-class Greek Orthodox family, he received only basic education because his father, who owned a small restaurant, took him out of school at the age of 11 to help him with his heavy work. Despite this setback, Zaydan continued to study on his own and, at the age of 19, passed the entrance examination of the Syrian Protestant College, enrolling in its medical school. This was a turning point in his life. After completing the first year, he relocated to Cairo, where he took up journalism and gradually established himself as a respected scholar and publisher. His success was remarkable: from the humble background of a poor Arab Christian and Syrian émigré, he rose to play an important role in the cultural life of Egypt's predominantly Muslim society.

The path of Zaydan's career was paved with many obstacles, economic, educational, social, and religious. How did he overcome all these hurdles? When one looks closely at his struggle for self-fulfillment, it becomes clear that the source of his strength was the stable family environment in which he grew up and the positive values and role models that he internalized at home. Both his father and mother were hard workers who denied themselves for the sake of the family. Zaydan says of them: "I grew up seeing my father leaving his restaurant in the morning and returning only about midnight, and observing my mother never standing still from morning to dusk. She herself ignored visits, festivities, social and even religious gatherings. Only rarely did she go to church to pray. She was more interested in conducting her household and educating her children. Thus I grew up and became accustomed to this way of life. It ingrained itself on my mind that man was created to work and that sitting around without work was a great disgrace" (p. 22). Hard work, then, became a motto in Zaydan's life and the key to his success. The narrative abounds with references to "perseverance in work" (p. 36), "activeness" (p. 22), "punctuality" (p. 22), and "steadfastness and effort" (p. 45). The young Zaydan worked as a waiter, cook, and accountant in his father's restaurant by day and studied independently at night. He was the only student among his classmates at the Syrian Protestant College who had to support himself by taking up various jobs. Despite carrying a double load, Zaydan finished the first year at medical school with distinction. Characteristically, he downplayed his scholastic aptitude and attributed his extraordinary achievement to hard work: "At the root of my success were my consciousness of time and perseverance" (p. 49).

Zaydan's family was of meager means and humble origins. His father came to Beirut as a child and was not yet ten when his own father had died and he became the head of the family, having to support his mother and three siblings. A poor boy who never had a chance to go to school, Zaydan senior "did not have any skills and his will to work was his only capital" (p. 17). From a bread seller to a baker to a restaurateur, he managed to make a living and take care of his family. Given this history, it is not surprising that the father expected that Jurji, his eldest son, should share with him the burden of earning a living if necessity arose. The father's view of education was narrow and practical: he wanted his son to learn enough reading and writing so that he could take over the bookkeeping in his restaurant, a task he himself was unable to do because he was illiterate. With this goal in mind, he sent Jurji to school at the age of 4, which was rather unusual in those days. The same economic consideration made him interrupt his son's schooling at the age of 11. A waiter who also served as a bookkeeper for him suddenly left, and he needed someone to replace him. He initially told his son that he would be absent from school temporarily, saying, "Come assist me for seven or eight days until I find someone to replace you" (p. 22). Duty-bound, Jurji obeyed, only to watch in dismay as these seven days stretched into seven or eight years. Despite being trapped in the restaurant during most of his youth, and arguably being exploited as child labor, Jurji never questioned his obligations to his family and accepted his father's demand for self-denial and self-sacrifice on his part.

The mother was a staunch supporter of her son's educational aspirations. She hated the filth and long hours associated with the trade of restaurants and considered associating with the customers, most of whom belonged to the lowest classes in Beirut, a danger to decency and propriety. For her, education was a means to secure her son's future and liberate him from a life of drudgery, deprivation, and low station. She constantly pleaded with her husband to allow Jurji to return to school, encouraged her son to continue studying on his own, and gave him all her savings when he announced his decision to apply to the Syrian Protestant College. No wonder that Zaydan was closer to his mother, in whom he found an ally, than to his father, whom he obeyed and respected, but also resented. The narrative contains a warm tribute to his mother's generosity and many acts of kindness, and indirect criticism of the father's stinginess and narrow-mindedness.

Altogether, in assessing the factors that contributed to Zaydan's success, his childhood comes first and foremost. The first 11 years of his life, which are also the formative years, were nurturing enough to give him a firm moral foundation and strength of character so that he could cope with subsequent hardships and challenges effectively. The narrative reveals that the family was close-knit and cohesive. His mother instilled in him ambition and motivation, whereas his father instilled in him willpower, discipline, and responsibility. Even the many years that he spent working at his father's restaurant were not a complete waste: he developed outstanding social skills, having to deal with different types of customers, skills that later helped him in his professional career. During this period he also met people like Iskandar al-Barudi, the teacher he credits with preparing him for the entrance examination of the Syrian Protestant College: "It was he who placed me at the gates of knowledge and prepared me for the world of culture" (p. 43). Besides this teacher, who provided him with a new role model, Zaydan writes that he derived enormous inspiration from a self-help book titled *The Secret of Success* by Samuel Smile. Reading about the lives of ordinary men—among them barbers, shoemakers, servants, and artisans—who reached the top "through their diligence and efforts and self-reliance" stirred him so much that he was unable to sleep or finish reading the book (pp. 44–45). All these factors combined to facilitate Zaydan's voyage of self-discovery and self-attainment. Since the narrative ends with his departure from Beirut to Cairo, it does not contain information on the second chapter of his life—the years he lived in Egypt. However, it is known that his relocation to Cairo—the cultural center of the Arab world then as well as now—opened many doors to him and gave him opportunities that he would otherwise not have had, partly because of his Greek Orthodox background.

Undoubtedly, the greatest obstacle that Zaydan had to overcome to fulfill his dreams was his father's reliance on his help. As he writes: "My father believed that my leaving would lead to closing the avenue to a livelihood for my family" (p. 43). Ever the dutiful son, he aspired to become a physician rather than a teacher because "from this profession I as well as my family can make a living" (p. 44). He saw a way out of his obligations to his father when the latter went into partnership with a friend and no longer depended so heavily on his services. Although at this point the father did not object to his son's plans to resume his formal education, neither did he offer to financially support him. However, after Zaydan got into medical school and completed the first year at the top of his class, he took pride in his son's achievements. And after Zaydan went to Cairo, where he abandoned the pursuit of medical education in favor of journalistic activities, the father expressed his disappointment, demanding that his son return to Beirut to enter into a "decent" profession such as becoming a lawyer or a physician.[4] Thus the father had come a full circle, from obstructing his son's formal education to insisting that he should complete it.

Zaydan's only act of open rebellion against his father concerned the choice of a spouse. In 1891, with the founding of his publishing house and the publication of his first historical novel, Zaydan's career was established, and he decided to marry Maryam Matar, a simple teacher. His decision met with bitter opposition from his parents, who disapproved of the woman's humble origins. According to Thomas Philipp, "a drawn out and unfriendly correspondence between Zaidan in Cairo and his father in Beirut began. Friends interceded on both sides, and finally consent for the marriage was obtained."[5] A few years later, the devoted son had his parents, brothers, and sisters follow him to Cairo. Two of his brothers worked with him in his publishing house, Dar al-Hilal.

On the basis of Zaydan's correspondence with his son Emile between 1908 and 1912, when the latter was studying at the American University in Beirut, and the reminiscences of Zaydan's four children, Philipp concludes that Zaydan had close ties with his sons.[6] The sample of five letters to Emile included with Zaydan's autobiography reflects love, care, and devotion. Zaydan confides in his son about a humiliating experience in his professional life, when a position offered him in 1910 at the newly founded Egyptian University (today Cairo University) to teach a course on Islamic history was cancelled unceremoniously because of religious prejudice: he was a Christian Arab. Further, Zaydan expresses great interest in the subjects that his son is studying, advises him on various issues, responds promptly to all his needs and requests, sends him generous amounts of money, and keeps him informed about every family member and family affair. As a father, then, Zaydan was keen on giving his son what he himself lacked in his youth: formal education, material comfort, and emotional support. In this instance, the cross-generational echoes of the father-son relationship reveal a dramatic transformation from ignorance to literacy, from poverty to prosperity, and from distance to intimacy.

Ahmad Amin's *My Life*

Ahmad Amin (1886–1954) appeared on the Egyptian cultural scene a generation after Jurji Zaydan. Born into a conservative middle-class Sunni Muslim family in Cairo, he was educated at al-Azhar and the Shari'a Judicial School with the goal of becoming a Shari'a judge. After his graduation in 1911 he served as a jurisprudence teacher and then as a judge, subsequently abandoning these activities in favor of a career as a professor of Arabic studies at Cairo University. Regarded as one of Egypt's distinguished scholars in the second quarter of the twentieth century, he wrote more than 20 books on Islamic civilization and edited several works of classical Arabic literature and Islamic philosophy. He is best known for his series on Islamic intellectual history, titled *Fajr al-Islam* (The Dawn of Islam), *Duha al-Islam* (The Forenoon of Islam), and *Zuhr al-Islam* (The Noon of Islam). His autobiography, *My Life*,[7] published toward the end of his life, is noted for its simplicity and sincerity, as well as for its penetrating portrait of Egyptian society in transition from tradition to modernity.

Arranged chronologically, the purpose of Amin's autobiography is self-analysis: describing people and events that shaped his character and influenced his career and thought. Amin declares right at the outset that he is the product of nature and nurture:

> If any man inherited what I did and lived in an environment like mine, he would have been me or very nearly so. My formation has been influenced to a great extent by what I inherited from my forefathers, the economic life that prevailed at our home, the religion that dominated us, the language that we spoke, the folk literature that was related to us, and the kind of upbringing that was in my parents' mind though they could not express it or draw its outlines, and so on. I did not make myself: God made me by way of the laws He prescribed for heredity and environment. (p. 10)

In depicting his upbringing, Amin's relationship with his father takes center stage. He paints a critical portrait of his father, at whose hands he experienced a joyless childhood and youth. An extremely religious man who worked as a teacher at al-Azhar and an imam (prayer leader) at a mosque, the father ruled over his household with a heavy hand. He was a harsh disciplinarian who beat up his children and wife (pp. 18, 25, 38, 47), led a semisecluded life on the upper floor of his house (p. 16), never smoked, joked, amused himself, or sat in a café (p. 18), never chatted kindly with his children and rarely met with them except to give them lessons or supervise their studies (pp. 16, 139). Strict, stern, and ill-tempered, he was the embodiment of threatening paternal authority. Amin admits: "That was why we felt at ease and a little joyful when he was away from home, and were afraid and held our breath when he returned" (p. 139). In contrast to the aloofness, formality, and harshness of the father, the mother represented protective maternal nurturance. "Our conversations, jokes, and play were with our mother" (p. 16); "When our father was mad at us, we took shelter in her tenderness and sought comfort in her affection" (p. 194). An uneducated, simple, and kind woman, the mother suffered a lot in her life. Three of her six children died in their youth, leaving her brokenhearted and depressed, and she lacked intimacy and companionship with her husband. As her only surviving son, Amin did his best to make her happy when he grew up. Recalling her difficult marital life, he acknowledges that he felt pity for her: "My father treated her severely and robbed her of her power; he repressed her personality, deprived her of her sphere of influence, and let his personality dominate hers" (p. 194).

Amin recounts that as a result of the father's somber personality, his home was serious and reserved and had little laughter or mirth. He calls it a "negatively happy home," by which he means a home not lacking in food, clothing, and shelter—the basic necessities of life. As for "positive happiness," which entails joy, fun, and laughter, it was almost nonexistent at his home because of his father's humorless disposition (p. 81). The effects of this upbringing on the young Amin were detrimental. The revealing words that he wrote on the back of a picture taken shortly after his marriage at the age of 30 sum it up: "With a heart full of sorrow, I say that I did not take advantage of the period of boyhood and youth as I should have. Neither mirth, activity, and entertainment however innocent, nor love found a way to my heart. I acted as an old man since youth, and this undoubtedly was a result of my home upbringing which was based on fear and intimidation, for my home had no semblance of fun or joy at all" (p. 123).

Central to Amin's complaint that he was oppressed as a child is the rigorous, mostly traditional, program of learning that his father made him follow from an early age. The *kuttab* (Koran school) was his first encounter with formal education. Amin hated this school and its master, whose ineffective method of instruction and reliance on corporal punishment produced "dead souls and broken spirits" (p. 34). He was not free to play at the end of the school day or on holidays, for his father gave him additional lessons: "In my father's room at home, I had another *kuttab* on Fridays and in times of leisure. My father was 'our master' and I memorized there something new and heard something old" (p. 35). Amin followed this program for about five years during which time he memorized the Koran and learned reading and writing. Then his father took him out of "those detestable *kuttabs*" (p. 36) and enrolled him in a government elementary school.

Amin writes that he loved this school, which offered him modern secular education. However, as the father was undecided regarding his son's future, whether to direct him toward the religious side and prepare him for al-Azhar or toward the secular side and educate him in public schools, he filled his son's free time with supplementary religious studies. The double load was exhausting, and the boy

Amin barely coped with the pressure. Occasionally he rebelled and neglected his extracurricular religious lessons, for which his father punished him with a severe beating. When his mother tried to intervene on his behalf, she was beaten too.

At the age of 14, Amin experienced a severe psychological crisis when his father took him out of the secular school and enrolled him in al-Azhar. Suddenly, the adolescent Amin had to wear a robe, a cloak, a turban, and red leather shoes instead of a suit, a tarboush, and ordinary shoes. He looked odd and felt awkward and ashamed. His friends made fun of him and abandoned him, and he became lonely and depressed. "I was like a branch cut off a tree," he writes, "or a sheep isolated from a flock or a stranger in a country other than his own. I begged my father to return me to my school but he turned a deaf ear to me" (p. 41). The traditional methods of instruction at al-Azhar aroused in him bitter memories of his days at the *kuttab*. Although he survived the crisis and completed his four-year studies at al-Azhar successfully, he remained highly critical of its teaching methods, curriculum, and goals.

Despite his many grievances against his father, when Amin looks back on his life, he acknowledges the immense debt that he owes him: if it were not for his father, he would not have finished his studies at al-Azhar and would not have been admitted to the Shari'a Judicial School. It was his father's preoccupation with his education that secured his future and helped him find his place in the world. Thanks to his father, he learned patience and perseverance in studying, and clarity and simplicity in writing—qualities that served him well in his subsequent activities as a jurisprudence teacher (1911–21), a judge (1921–26), and a scholar and professor of Arabic studies (1926–46). Amin expanded his religious education through independent readings in Western science and literature and by visiting several European countries, among them England, France, and the Netherlands.

On the whole, Amin's feelings toward his father were ambivalent. On the one, hand he hated him for being a tyrannical figure and an ill-humored recluse. On the other hand, he admired him for being an excellent teacher, a good provider, and a pious man. He also appreciated his father's sense of duty toward his children's education, both boys and girls, and the fact that he sent his daughters to school at a time when most people regarded educating girls as an "unforgivable crime" (p. 140). Amin acknowledges that his relationship with his father improved after he grew up and "became free from his protection and severity," that is, he became an independent adult. At that point, "I began to be aware of his merit. My fear of him turned to love and respect" (p. 141). In addition, the tragic loss of his brothers brought son and father closer together: "After he was bereaved of two of his children, my affection for him increased and I made every effort to do what pleased him. On his part, he gave me love and tenderness in return for mine and left me free to dispose of his money and his affairs, while he occupied himself exclusively with his sorrow, his sickness, and his religion" (p. 141).

In an attempt to rationalize his father's tyrannical behavior, Amin writes that his father suffered greatly from hernia and chronic constipation. He believes that these ailments were the reasons for his father's "irritability and for spoiling his and our lives," for depriving their home of mirth and laughter, and for "leading a secluded life, in which my father was inclined to be alone with himself and his pains" (p. 138). Afflicted with hernia at the age of 40, the father, who did not believe in medicine, refused to undergo an operation until he was 80. He died shortly after having the operation, with Amin at his side. Amin finds another explanation for his father's behavior in his humble origins. Born into an Egyptian peasant family, the father fled from his village in his youth with his older brother, arriving in Cairo penniless. They encountered much misery and hardship in their early days, until the older brother became a well-earning craftsman. Rather than asking his younger brother to help him earn a living, he sent him to school and paid his expenses. Amin's father excelled in his studies and joined al-Azhar. Reluctant to burden his brother financially, he lived frugally and asked him only for the bare necessities. The studies at al-Azhar were long, difficult, and tedious, but Amin's father succeeded by virtue of his patience and perseverance. Amin believes that all of this took a heavy toll on his father: "His life was all seriousness, and that exhausted him and destroyed his health" (p. 13).

While Amin accepted his father for what he was, he sought satisfaction for his emotional and intellectual needs elsewhere. He found a surrogate father figure in Atif Bey Barakat, the principal of the Shari'a Judicial School where he was a student for four years and then a teacher for another ten years. Calling Atif Bey "my second and spiritual father" (p. 141), Amin says of him: "He received me from my father who had given me my first education, and he gave me my second education" (p. 141). Atif Bey had a great influence on Amin's career and thought. After Amin's graduation, he appointed him a teacher and attached him to his classes on ethics, thus becoming his mentor. A prominent professor with modern education and progressive views, he introduced Amin to English writings on ethics, which opened his mind to Western culture and values. He taught Amin, who was intensely religious, to

rely on rational argument and analytical thinking. As Amin acknowledges: "He influenced me immensely in making reason the judge over
religion, for until that time I used to make emotion the judge, not
reason" (p. 87). Atif Bey's ideas of reform in Egyptian culture and
society resonated with his young disciple, who believed in change and
progress. Amin's close friendship with Atif Bey lasted for 18 years,
from 1907 until his death in 1925. He recalls the deep sorrow he felt
at his passing: "I grieved for him as much as for my father" (p. 141).

For a person who, as a young boy, experienced paternal repression
and later, as a scholar, espoused modern ideas and wrote in a reformist
vein, how did Amin relate to his wife and children? Was he strict or
lenient, authoritarian or egalitarian? Paradoxically, Amin shows a conservative attitude toward marital life and the upbringing of children.
He had an arranged marriage and established a traditional pattern of
family life in which he earned the family's living and his wife ran the
household and raised the children. Amin admits that he was uninvolved with the daily care of his many children (he was blessed with
ten children, two of whom died in childhood), a situation that freed
him to pursue his intellectual activities: "The credit for that goes to
the mother who carried for me the burdens which she could, while I
contented myself with supervising the children's academic and moral
growth though I failed to sit and play with them enough and secluded
myself for long stretches of time at my desk" (p. 127). In this respect,
then, Amin had unknowingly internalized his father as his role model.
As for his children's upbringing, he candidly states: "I was strict with
my first children and severely supervised their studies and morals. I
used to punish them for the least deviation and allowed them no freedom except within limits in accordance with my mentality at the time.
But my severity could not be compared with that of my father. As my
age advanced and my thinking developed, I reduced my interference
and increased the amount of freedom they enjoyed" (p. 129). Both as
a husband and a father, then, Amin followed the traditional cultural
models. Moreover, when he compares his generation's upbringing with
his children's, he expresses nostalgia toward the former and criticism
toward the latter. In his view, the collapse of patriarchal control—the
father's authority—destroyed the harmony of family life: "The home
has become a small parliament which is neither well-organized nor
just" (p. 19). With no single authority to judge them or weigh one of
them against the other, family members have "clashed and conflicted
and contested with one another. Their victim was the home's happiness, peace, and tranquility" (p 19). While Amin acknowledges that
modernity has introduced improvements in child-rearing practices and

methods of pedagogy, along with "many other kinds of bliss," such as material comforts (e.g., electricity, telephone, radio), he is disenchanted with some of its aspects. If the *kuttab*, where he was educated, was too strict, then the kindergarten, where his children were educated, is too indulgent: "I am afraid that we were as excessively harsh in my days as we are excessively lenient in my children's days" (p. 35). In particular, Amin bemoans the diminished importance of the neighborhood, which played an important role in his own education. As he sums it up: "I realize the great difference between my generation's upbringing and theirs, the abundance of our experiences and the paucity of theirs, the diction of our language and theirs, our knowledge of the soul of our nation and their ignorance" (p. 32).

Overall, the father-son relationship in this narrative, which is set in a turbulent period of history when Egypt moved from British colonial rule to independence and witnessed two world wars, speaks of the generational conflict. Amin's dual perspective on the father-son relationship, first as a son and then as a father, reflects the changes in the rhythms of life in Egyptian society and the inevitable clash between opposing value systems: old and new, religious and secular, traditional and modern. Although Amin's attitude toward traditional Arab culture is mixed, being critical of some aspects and supportive of others, his narrative reflects a reformist spirit. For him, the solution for the generational conflict is a compromise between tradition and modernity: instead of rejecting one for the other (e.g., preferring the kindergarten over the *kuttab* or personal autonomy over paternal authority), one should take the middle road: "Life is not pure seriousness and misery, nor is it pure fun and bliss. The best kind of teaching is one that portrays all kinds of life" (p. 35). Amin believes that he succeeded in guiding his children properly: at the time of writing his autobiography, his two daughters were happily married, four of his sons had graduated in engineering, the fifth followed his advice to study law, and the sixth was eligible to study medicine but preferred to go into engineering. Judging by his sons' career choices, it is obvious that he let them follow their own inclinations even though it meant favoring the secular direction over the religious path.

Nurturing Fathers: Bonds of Love

Mikhail Naimy's *Seventy: A Life Story*

The Lebanese poet, fiction writer, and literary critic Mikhail Naimy (1889–1989) was a member of the Mahjar group—Arab writers who immigrated to America during the late nineteenth and early twentieth centuries. Naimy, together with Gibran Khalil Gibran and other Syro-Lebanese immigrants, founded in New York in 1920 the Pen Society (*al-rabita al-qalamiyya*)—the first modernizing school of Arabic literature. Naimy helped to introduce into the Arabic literary tradition new forms of writing: free verse, the novel, the short story, the essay, and the drama, and laid down the principles of literary criticism. During his exceptionally long and fruitful career, he produced more than 30 volumes of fiction, poetry, drama, literary criticism, and essays, as well as Gibran's biography and his own autobiography.

Naimy's autobiography, *Seventy: A Life Story*,[8] is a work of monumental scope that covers his life from early childhood to the age of 70. Arranged chronologically, it comprises three volumes, each of which deals with a well-defined period in his life. The first volume, with the subtitle "The First Stage," describes his childhood and youth in his native village Biskinta (Lebanon), Nazareth (Palestine), and Poltava (Ukraine). The second volume, titled "The Second Stage," chronicles his stay in America from 1911 to 1932. And the third volume, "The Third Stage," depicts his years in Lebanon, from his return to Biskinta in 1932 up to 1959. Altogether, Naimy's autobiography offers a comprehensive portrait of his psychological and intellectual development, with ample references to the vicissitudes of his family—his parents, sister, and brothers.

Naimy was born into a poor Greek Orthodox family in a small village situated on Sannin, one of the highest mountains in Lebanon. His father eked out a living by cultivating a small patch of land called Shakhroub, which belonged to his forefathers. When Mikhail was ten months old, the father immigrated to America in the hope of making a better life for his family. The first recollection in the autobiography depicts the little boy's longing for the absent father. It tells how his mother, illiterate like all the other adults in the family, taught him to repeat with her the Lord's prayer, adding at the end: "Son, say with me, O Lord, bless my father in America with success. May the soil he touches turn in his hands to gold. O Lord, bring him safe to us. Lord, preserve my brothers" (1:15). Thus the sorrows of separation and longing for the absent father featured in the boy's life from the very beginning.

The father returned home after six years, poor as he had been and grieving over the death of his beloved sister, who had left with him. Naimy, who was almost seven years old at the time, bonded with him immediately. "I remember that my father, with his European dress, his tall frame, ample moustache, handsome features and soft, bright

eyes, came up to my expectations of him."[9] Possessing no other skills
than ploughing and sowing, the father went back to his rocky strip of
land, toiling endlessly to provide for his family. Naimy's recollections
of his father are filled with affection and respect: "I can close my
eyes right now and see my father as he was then, simple and sincere,
modest and decent in thought and speech, driving his oxen ahead of
him with his right hand gripping the plough and his left the goad."[10]
He recalls that his father beat him only once, and that was when he
lied to him that he went to Mass when he had not: "As he hated lies,
so my father hated hypocrisy, flattery and putting off fulfillment of
a promise."[11] Although the father respected the church and devout
churchmen, he disdained exterior appearances: "Religion in his view
consisted in a moral outlook and good works rather than in obser-
vance of the conventional duties and rituals. For this reason he did
not always refrain from work on Sundays and holidays; a day's work
was in itself a day's worship."[12] Hard work and high morals, then,
were the core values that the father instilled in his son.

Naimy recounts that as he grew older he learned that it was his
mother's idea that his father should seek his fortune in America. An
ambitious and stubborn woman, the mother had higher aspirations
for her family: "She wanted her husband to be free of the drudgery of
plough and hoe, and her sons to be educated at the best schools so as
to become men of rank and consequence, objects of envy, not subject
to it."[13] After her hopes were dashed and the father returned from
America only to work again on his small strip of land, she did not
allow any of her sons to miss one day of school to help him. "I don't
want our children to inherit the trade you inherited from your father,
and to get as little out of life as you have—this she would tell father
in our hearing."[14] The mother raised a large family consisting of five
sons and one daughter. While the adult Naimy gives her credit for
striving to secure a better future for her children, his sympathy clearly
lies with his father. Moreover, when he compares the personalities of
his parents, the mother's image appears decidedly negative:

> Father was never hurt half so much by the sting of the briars or his
> struggle with the boulders as by the sting of my mother's tongue
> and his struggle with her character. She was stubborn where he was
> patient, ambitious where he was diffident. He was peaceable, she was
> not afraid of a quarrel; where he was the quiet and contemplative type,
> she tended to be argumentative, dictatorial and energetic. His emo-
> tions were stored too deep for his tongue to haul up, hers erupted from
> her eyes, her features and her tongue. The clashes between them are
> perhaps my most unpleasant and painful childhood memories.[15]

Nevertheless, Naimy acknowledges that his parents complemented each other: thanks to his mother's ambition, persistence, and budgeting, he and his siblings received decent schooling, and thanks to his father's patience and fortitude in the face of constant toil and hardship, the family had stuck together.

As a young boy, then, Naimy experienced his mother's ambitions as a source of conflict and disharmony in the family. In addition, he complains that she was a harsh disciplinarian: when he used an improper word, she pulled his ears until he screamed, and when his brother Haykal skipped school, she tied him to a pole and flogged him hard with a mulberry stick. By contrast, the father rarely punished his children physically. His gentle and kind disposition was, in the adult narrator's view, the reason for his failure to make it in America. "I marveled at how he—by nature honest, trustworthy and content with little—was able to survive for six years in a land where it was hard for the immigrant to attain any degree of success unless he were wily and ambitious and prepared to dispense with honesty and trustworthiness in the interest of making money."[16]

Despite his family's poverty, Naimy paints a positive image of his childhood, recalling that he roamed freely on the slopes of Mount Sannin amid cool rivulets, tall trees, bright flowers, and singing birds. His description of Shakhroub, where he spent his summers helping his father till the land, betrays his deep attachment to the landscape of his childhood.[17] The attachment to nature was intimately connected with his attachment to the father who tilled the land and lived in close proximity to it. Hence Naimy's recollections of his father are intertwined with the scenery of Shakhroub: "Father would take his oxen to Shakhroub early in spring, when the snow had melted and the ground was ready for the plough. He would stay there alone, like a hermit, until the rest of the family joined him at the end of the school year."[18] Naimy recounts that seeing his father at work had a spellbinding effect on him: "I experienced a kind of magic at the sight of my father taking a handful of seed, then casting it to right and left, his eyes on the ground inspecting how it was distributed, his legs moving rapidly, his face that of a worshipper performing the most sacred of his devotions."[19] The attachment to nature played a major role in shaping Naimy's literary sensibilities: as a Mahjar writer he was influential in spreading romantic attitudes among his contemporaries in Arab countries. Ultimately, the attachment to the landscape of his childhood was what brought the adult Naimy, after years of living in exile, back to his birthplace.

Naimy's formal education began at his village elementary school, which the Russians, who patronized the Greek Orthodox in the

Middle East, founded in Biskinta in 1889. From there he went on to the Russian Teachers' Institute in Nazareth (1902–6), and finally to the Theological Seminary in Poltava in the Ukraine (1906–11). Living in Russia, he became fluent in the Russian language and well-versed in Russian literature. The exposure to Russian culture and way of life opened new literary and intellectual horizons for him. According to Hussein Dabbagh, "by the end of his stay in Russia, he had acquired all the qualities of a rebel," questioning the church's teachings on the one hand, and the Arabs' concept of literature on the other hand.[20]

The second stage in Naimy's life, to which the second volume of his autobiography is devoted, describes exposure to yet another culture and way of life: American. In 1911 he joined his two older brothers who lived in Washington State, and a year later enrolled as a student of law and English literature at the University of Washington, Seattle, graduating in 1916 with a double degree. The English language afforded him a window into Western literature, and he read all its classics with the same zeal that he had read the classics of Russian literature. After one year of service in the US Army in France during World War I, he settled in New York, where he rose to the forefront among the circle of Arab immigrant writers. Imbued with modernist and antitraditional ideas, Naimy was committed to transforming Arabic literature in content and form. This was a period of prolific literary output for him: he published a book of literary criticism (*Al-Ghirbal*), a volume of poetry (*Hams al-jufun*), drama (*Al-Aba' wa-al-banun*), short stories (*Kana ma kana*), and essays (*Al-Marahil*).

After the death of his close friend Gibran Khalil Gibran in 1931, Naimy decided to return to Lebanon. In the following year he left New York for the haven of his childhood: Biskinta, Shakhroub, and Mount Sannin. Living in solitude in a little hut that he built for himself in Shakhroub, he came to be known in the Arab world as the "hermit of Shakhroub."[21] He spent the next 50 years in this little hermitage, where he devoted himself to his literary activities and wrote, among other things, Gibran's biography and his own autobiography.

Naimy's life was exceptional in many ways: as a writer who experienced three worlds, Arab, Russian, and American; as an immigrant who returned to his homeland; and as an individual who never married and chose to live in self-imposed isolation. Significantly, in renouncing Western civilization and returning to his native village, Naimy was following in his father's footsteps. Just as his father had been unable to reconcile himself to the American way of life and had given up the pursuit of the dollar in favor of a simple rural life lived among family and kin, so did Naimy. Disillusioned with the modern world of "machines and crises," he decided to leave New York, a city he referred to as the "frightful whirlpool."[22] His renunciation of Western civilization and materialism, then, was modeled on that of his father. It is no accident that he chose to dwell in Shakhroub, the land that was so dear to his father and where the father used to stay alone, "like a hermit," during the ploughing and sowing seasons. In New York, Naimy suffered from a sense of exile and alienation, but in Shakhroub he regained his sense of harmony and belonging based on family ties, attachment to the land, and connection to his native culture.

The father died in his son's arms in 1937, five years after Naimy's return to Biskinta. The event is movingly described in a chapter titled "Bu Dib Takes Leave of Shakhroub" in the third volume of the autobiography.[23] In this chapter, Naimy artistically interweaves his father's thoughts on life and death with his joy at the sight of water springing forth from the earth of his beloved Shakhroub.

Why had Naimy never married? Interestingly, in his autobiography the author mentions several love affairs, both with Russian and American women. Was he afraid that the presence of an ambitious wife in his life would be a source of conflict and disharmony, as it had been for his father? Did he regard marriage as a burden that would prevent him from pursuing his literary and intellectual interests? Naimy's own comments on the topic are difficult to understand. He acknowledges that it is not easy to repress sexual desire and claims that he managed to do so by turning his mind and heart toward something "more sublime." As he states: "I no longer look upon women the way the male looks upon the female. Mine is the outlook of a man who believes that his nature and that of the woman are complementary, not through the close union of their bodies, but through the union of their souls, and that the physical union hampers the union of their souls. This is the reason why I discarded the idea of marriage altogether."[24] Considering the yearning for immortality that Naimy expressed in his writings, as well as the loving ties that he shared with his father, it is quite enigmatic that he chose to live alone and not father a son of his own.

Jabra Ibrahim Jabra's *The First Well*

The figure of a poor but kind father who is devoted to his family is also encountered in the childhood memories of the Palestinian writer Jabra Ibrahim Jabra (1920–94). A versatile author whose works include novels, short stories, essays, prose poetry, as well as literary and art criticism, Jabra was educated at the Arab College in Jerusalem and at Cambridge University in England, where he studied English literature and earned his master's degree. Forced into exile in 1948, he moved to Iraq, where he lived and worked until his death.

In *The First Well: A Bethlehem Boyhood*, the first volume of his two-part autobiography,[25] Jabra describes the years of his boyhood in Bethlehem, his birthplace, and later in Jerusalem, where he moved at age 12 with his parents. The title of this volume, as he notes in his introduction, carries a dual meaning. Literally, it refers to the well of water that was a basic necessity in the courtyard of each house in which his family lived in those days. Metaphorically, it refers to the fountain of his earliest experiences—his childhood, which constitutes a vital source of nourishment for him, both emotionally and artistically. As he puts it: "The well of one's life is that same primary well, without which living would not be possible. Experiences gather in it as water does in a well—to be turned to in times of thirst. Our life is but a chain of wells. We dig a new well in each phase.... The first well is the well of childhood" (p. xxi).

Jabra was born into a poor family belonging to the Syriac Orthodox Church. The family, which consisted of the parents, a maternal grandmother, and five children, lived under harsh economic conditions: cramped housing, shortage of food and clothing, and chronic lack of money. The father, an unskilled laborer, scraped a living as a construction worker for some time and later as a hospital gardener, until bad health forced him to leave his job and stay permanently at home. Not surprisingly, most of the narrator's negative recollections revolve around persistent material want, be it school items such as a pencil and a notebook, or home furnishings such as a chair and a clock, or basic footwear such as a pair of shoes. Jabra recounts that to ease the problems of their daily survival, his parents insisted on observing all the days of fasting of the Orthodox Church: "Fasting for us solved problems in a way that pleased both God and man, for we abstained from eating meat, fish, eggs, greasy foods, and all kinds of dairy products. All these cost money, which we did not have. And so, we pleased God by fasting and made a virtue of necessity" (p. 58). The family's poverty was the reason they moved frequently from house to house, compelled to find a place with lower rent and bigger space to accommodate their growing number. All the "houses" that the family occupied consisted of a single room, without electricity or running water, which served all their needs and was occasionally shared with their domestic animals, such as chicken and sheep.

While the material world in which the boy Jabra lived was marked by deprivation, his emotional world was immensely rich and comforting. He was surrounded by a loving and close-knit family that provided him with a warm and stable home environment. The mother, Maryam, was the pivot around which the family life revolved. Frugal and resourceful, she managed to run the household on meager means and look after her husband and children. Jabra admiringly says of her: "My mother worked like a man, perhaps even harder. She started to move about at the crack of dawn and did not stop working until the day had passed and everyone had gone to sleep" (p. 122). He describes her as a proud and generous woman, but quick-tempered and strict. If he misbehaved, as when he skipped school and lied about it, she gave him a good spanking. An illiterate woman who believed in folk medicine, she valued education and sent Jabra to school at an early age. Although she never complained, she had known many sorrows: she was widowed at 17 when her first husband, along with her brother, died in tragic circumstances, leaving her with an infant son. Then she married Jabra's father and bore him eight children, four of whom did not survive.

While the mother was the disciplinarian in Jabra's life, the grandmother was a source of unconditional support and affection. Jabra recounts that she protected him when he got into trouble and covered up for him. She also indulged him by giving him money to buy "luxury" items such as a pencil and a notebook. "I had a special relationship with my grandmother behind my mother's back" (p. 10), he writes, affirming that he was deeply attached to her. His privileged relationship with his beloved grandmother was cut off when his older brother Yusuf moved to Jerusalem in search of a job and took her with him to look after his affairs. Until the family's reunion in Jerusalem two years later, Jabra saw them only occasionally when they came for short visits.

Yusuf, who was four years older than Jabra, served as a role model for his younger brother. Jabra writes that he admired him and strove to emulate him: "He and his friends appeared to me to belong to a world other than mine—the world of adults. Whenever he said anything, I was all ears, and I felt he was admitting me into his world" (p. 23). Yusuf was the person who introduced Jabra to the realm of books and literature and motivated him to go to school and learn. For a boy raised by illiterate parents, Jabra acknowledges that his brother was his gateway to knowledge: "My brother Yusuf was my teacher most of the time" (p. 28). When at the age of 12 Yusuf left the Syriac Orthodox School, claiming that he was not learning anything new in it, and entered the secular government school, Jabra soon followed in his footsteps. When Yusuf dropped out of school and took a job at a grocery store to help support the family, Jabra announced his intention to do the same. But Yusuf objected to this idea, yelling at his brother: "Is it necessary that my misfortune be also yours?" (p. 116). Thus, thanks to his brother's self-sacrifice and his parents' encouragement, Jabra was able to continue his formal education and secure a better future for himself.

Jabra identified strongly with his father. The narrative contains many tender recollections of the father that highlight the close ties they shared. Jabra recounts that as a child he slept next to his father, "being unable to sleep anywhere but near him" (p. 29). The father used to tell him stories after he came home from work; he played with him a game of solving riddles; he took him to church to pray together and celebrate the holidays; he never yelled at him and never hit him, even when he deserved a punishment. Deeply religious, the father taught his son Christian values and "glorified virtue, ascetic life, and poverty," convinced that it is "easier for a camel to pass through the eye of a needle than for a rich man to enter Paradise" (p. 99). Jabra paints a highly sympathetic portrait of his father as a decent and hardworking man, a loving husband, and a caring parent. He admired his father for his impeccable morals, kind nature, and devotion to his family, qualities that he never lost, despite his many hardships, both physical and economic.

Poor as he was, the father's greatest ambition was to educate his children. He forbade Jabra to drop out of school to help him earn the cost of living, as Yusuf did against his wishes, declaring that "if it were up to me, I would return him to school tomorrow—and let us die of hunger" (p. 117). To help Jabra prepare his lessons and study for his exams, he volunteered to wake him up at three o'clock every morning. This meant staying awake much of the night to listen to the bell of the Terra Sancta monastery strike the hour because the family did not own an alarm clock. When Jabra, at the end of the fifth grade, was expelled from school for unknowingly breaking one of its regulations, the father immediately came to his rescue. He went to the principal and pleaded with him, saying: "It is as if you have killed him, and me too, Mr. Principal.... Meanwhile, I am as you see" (p. 181). Moved by the father's devotion to his son's education, the principal forgave Jabra and allowed him to return to school, telling the father: "I am proud to see a man in as bad a condition as you are, who insists on educating his son" (p. 181). Thus, thanks to his father, Jabra was able to continue his education.

As a boy, Jabra found several avenues of escape from his wretched living conditions. "School to me, with its students and teachers, its books and atmosphere, was an escape and a refuge, like nature" (p. 154), he writes. The church, with its various festivals, ceremonies, and traditions, was another haven. The neighborhood that he belonged to offered him activities, excitement, and entertainment. Above all, Jabra had the wings of his imagination to carry him away from his harsh reality into the realm of magic and dreams. All these escape routes not only helped him cope with poverty but also played a major role in shaping his budding literary and artistic sensibilities.

The father's illness left indelible marks on Jabra's psyche. The father suffered from sciatica, which is caused by strenuous jobs and is common among construction workers. Manifesting as severe pain in his left leg and being unable to control its movement, the father's condition slowly worsened until he could no longer work. This scared Jabra, as it did the entire family, and created an acute sense of insecurity in him. He understood that his father might die, and that his death would cause enormous misery for his family. He also understood that he might have to drop out of school in order to support his family. He watched in fear mixed with hope as his father, driven by desperation, allowed quack doctors to perform dangerous procedures on him for exorbitant amounts of money. The sight of his father so weak and vulnerable saddened Jabra and accelerated his process of maturation. Aware of his obligations to his family, he became extremely motivated to succeed in his studies so he could get a good job. "All I wanted was to secure success so that I would not 'fail' and would not be expelled from school before I obtained a piece of paper enabling me to work as a teacher in some school in order to help my family with the salary I earned" (p. 161). The father's illness heightened Jabra's identification with him and reinforced his sense of duty toward him. There was a reversal of roles between father and son, where Jabra felt it was his turn to protect his father and look after him.

At 11, Jabra's thoughts about his father are full of compassion and admiration: "I knew that my father owned nothing in this world other than the clothes on his back. But he owned his songs and tales, and his love that flooded everything around him. He owned his bodily strength, which had begun to abandon him, and he owned his spiritual strength, which would never abandon him. I never heard him utter a word of abuse, and he wanted me to be like him in this regard" (pp. 136–37). One of the final episodes in the narrative reveals the close bond between father and son. Jabra, aged 12, wanted to help his father carry a heavy car tire. He carelessly rolled it, causing it to spin out of control and fall into a deep ravine. Although his father eventually managed to retrieve it, Jabra felt bad about his reckless action. As he recalls: "I rushed to him, and he saw the tears flowing from my eyes as I was shaking uncontrollably. He patted my head with his free hand and said, 'Don't, man! Isn't it a shame? I'm your father and you can always depend on me!'" (p. 152). The father's kind words aroused tremendous gratitude and appreciation in his son: "He appeared to me to be a towering and beautiful giant, like the azarole tree that I liked. He never raised his hand to hit me, whatever I did, and he never shouted at me in anger" (p. 152). This episode marks the last time that Jabra saw his father radiating strength and vigor. Thereafter his condition deteriorated rapidly, and he resigned to his fate. Jabra was keenly aware of his father's transformation: "Youth began to leave him quickly, though he was only in his late thirties. The vitality he exhibited when he sang lessened, and he no longer danced with his friends at weddings. He told fewer tales until he said one day, 'From now on, it is your turn. You will sing to us, you will tell us tales from the books you read, and you will be the ones to shake the earth with your friends when you dance'" (p. 153).

Jabra ends his narrative when he turns 13 and is about to embark on the next stage of his life—adolescence. He provides some highlights of what is yet to come: his sexual awakening, his studies at the Arab college in Jerusalem, and his scholarship to study abroad. He also mentions some devastating blows: the death of his young sister and the loss of his homeland. Although the events and experiences of his youth and adult life were greater and more complex than those of his childhood, he declares that Wordsworth's observation, "The Child is father of the Man," is particularly true for him (p. xvii). His childhood shaped his personality, nourished his spirit, and stimulated his mind. It was the fertile ground in which his literary and artistic interests took root and blossomed. And it never ceased to inspire his creativity and sustain his inner self: "Childhood remains the source of a magic, constant and beyond explanation, the fountainhead of a radiance which cannot be defined" (p. xviii).

Jabra's personal account demonstrates that poverty does not necessarily produce abusive and conflicted family relationships. Quite to the contrary, his family was able to develop close and loving ties that gave Jabra a sense of safety and security and protected him from feeling self-pity, failure, or alienation. In particular, his father's humanity stands out as the guiding force in his son's life. Jabra's identification with his father and his lifelong suffering is reflected in his writings, which show a strong empathy for the plight of the poor and dispossessed members of society. Also, as a Palestinian refugee, the issue of his lost homeland—the site of his cherished childhood—features prominently in his literary works, whether implicitly, as in *A Cry in a Long Night* (*Surakh fi layl tawil*, 1955), or explicitly, as in *The Ship* (*Al-Safina*, 1970). However, instead of imposing an ideological scheme on his novels and short stories, Jabra chose to depict the experience of life in exile, the feelings of siege and frustration, and the yearning for salvation, thus giving his works a deeper, universal meaning.

Authoritarian Fathers: Conflicted Ties

Edward Said's *Out of Place*

Unlike the character of the poor but kind father in the autobiographies of Mikhail Nainy and Jabra Ibrahim Jabra, the personal accounts of Edward Said and Tawfiq al-Hakim portray the character of a wealthy but tyrannical father who fails to bond with his son and constantly clashes with him. Edward Said's narrative in particular invites a comparison with that of Jabra Ibrahim Jabra because both authors came from Christian families in Palestine, pursued higher education in the West, and lived their adult lives in exile.

Edward Said (1935–2003) was professor of English and comparative literature at Columbia University in New York. A celebrated but controversial figure, he represented the influential school of literary and cultural criticism known as "postcolonial studies." His seminal book, *Orientalism* (1978), which examines how Western scholars write about the Orient in general and the Middle East in particular, is credited with helping to change traditional scholarship in this discipline. The anticolonial perspective that characterizes his work was not limited to the academic realm. Said became the most outspoken advocate of the Palestinian cause in the United States, tirelessly expounding his political views in books, television interviews, newspaper articles, and public lectures.[26]

In his memoir, *Out of Place*,[27] Said offers an intimate account of his childhood in the Middle East, where he was born and spent his formative years, and of his adulthood in the United States, where he received his college and university education. Written after he was diagnosed with cancer in 1991, the memoir aims to record not only the events of his life but also "an essentially lost or forgotten world" (p. ix), as many of the situations, places, and people he knew no longer exist.

Said was born in Jerusalem into an affluent Palestinian family whose primary place of residence was in Cairo. His father, Wadie, a Protestant Jerusalemite, immigrated to the United States in 1911, when he was 16, and volunteered for service in France during World War I, which earned him an American citizenship. Returning to Palestine in 1920, he became a successful businessman, called himself William to emphasize his adopted American identity, and in 1929 relocated to Cairo, where he established a prosperous company for office equipment and stationery. Three years later he made an arranged marriage with Said's mother, Hilda, the daughter of a Baptist minister from Nazareth. He was 37 and she was 18, fresh out of the American School for Girls in Beirut, where she had been a student for five years. Edward, the couple's only son and the eldest of five children, was named after the Prince of Wales. Said writes that he always lived with a divided identity. Even as a child, he realized that his first name was British, his last name was Arabic, and his nationality was American. Adding to his sense of confusion was the fact that his parents were "two Palestinians with dramatically different backgrounds and temperaments living in colonial Cairo as members of a Christian minority within a large pond of minorities" (p. 19). Linguistically, he was split between Arabic, his native language, and English, the language of his formal education. Geographically, he was caught between four locations: Palestine, the home of his extended family up to 1948; Lebanon, where he spent every summer for 27 years; Egypt, where he lived and attended school up to the age of 16, and the United States, where he settled down after graduating from Harvard University. As a result, he developed a feeling of "always being out of place" (p. 3). As he acknowledges: "I have retained this unsettled sense of many identities—mostly in conflict with each other—all of my life, together with an acute memory of the despairing feeling that I wish we could have been all-Arab, or all-European and American, or all-Orthodox Christian, or all-Muslim, or all-Egyptian, and so on" (p. 5).

Said grew up as a member of Cairo's westernized privileged class. He describes his early life as one of "inordinate and untoward luxury" (p. 197), which included a spacious apartment in Zamalek (a suburb inhabited by foreigners and wealthy locals), a staff of servants, expensive clubs, trips abroad, and private schools. Said attended exclusive British and American schools, including two years in Cairo's Victoria College—then the "Eton of the Middle East" (p. 180). After school he participated in a variety of extracurricular activities: piano lessons, tennis, horse riding, and other sports, arranged by his parents so he could learn discipline and finesse. Isolated from ordinary native

Egyptians and protected from everyday life and problems, Said states that "school, church, club, garden, house—a limited, carefully circumscribed segment of the great city—was my world until I was well into my teens" (p. 22).

Said writes that he experienced the cocooned existence that his parents created in Cairo as "claustrophobic" (p. 194) and "eerily out of touch" (p. 269). On the one hand, he was disconnected from the real world; on the other hand, he was constantly supervised at home and restricted by a rigid set of rules. As he recounts: "I never went out with girls; I wasn't ever allowed to visit, much less frequent, places of public entertainment or restaurants; and I was always warned by both my parents not to get close to people on the bus or tram, not to drink or eat anything from a shop or stand, and above all to regard our home and family as the only refuge in that vast sty of vices all around us" (p. 28). These instructions reflect a deliberate effort on the parents' part to make the family their son's primary orientation or, as Said puts it, to keep him and his siblings "psychologically enclosed within our own tight family circle" (p. 163). He disliked his family life, which he characterizes as "dour and explicitly formal" (p. 203), and felt repressed, sexually and otherwise. Looking back, he concludes that the "gigantic cocoon" (p. 12) in which he lived had detrimental effects on him.

Said portrays his father as an unsophisticated character but a tough and brilliant businessman who ruled over his employees "as absolute monarch, a sort of Dickensian father figure, despotic when angered, benevolent when not" (p. 93). He complains that his father subjected him to a grueling regimen of schedules, chores, and assignments and used violent methods to discipline him, from slapping to punching to whipping. Strict and extremely demanding, the father constantly pressured his bright but rebellious son, found fault with every detail of his physique, and instilled "a deep sense of generalized fear" (p. 66) in him, which he spent most of his life trying to overcome. Resentful, Said says: "My father came to represent a devastating combination of power and authority, rationalistic discipline, and repressed emotions...from my childhood through my twenties I was very much controlled by him" (p. 12). Time and again, he criticizes his father: "He managed to combine harshness, unreadable silence, and odd affection laced with surprising generosity which somehow never gave me enough to count on" (p. 28). Overall, he depicts his relationship with his father as hopelessly conflicted, "the familiar terrain of dominance and subterranean resistance" (p. 261). The only redeeming quality that he finds in his father is that he was an excellent provider: "None of us had a day's worry about anything material" (p. 78). In fact, despite his severity, the father was quite generous to his son: he always encouraged him "to travel, continue piano studies, live well, always willing to foot the bill" (p. 65). Eventually, he let his son go his own way, quietly selling the family business the year his son got his PhD in literature. He died in 1971 after a ten-year battle with malignant melanoma.

In assessing his career, Said attributes the driving spirit that brought him his various achievements to his father, admitting that "however unpleasant, his force and sheer presence had provided me with an internalized framework in a world of volatile change" (p. 261). Particularly during the difficult time of his own battle with leukemia, Said found a coping mechanism in the very regimen of tasks and schedules that his father had inculcated in him as a child. He recounts that 20 years after his father's death, in the course of a psychoanalytic session with his therapist, he experienced a kind of epiphany about his father: "Perhaps, for oedipal reasons, I had blocked him, and perhaps my mother with her skill at manipulating ambivalence had undermined him. But whether this was true or not, the gap between my father and me was sealed with a longstanding silence" (p. 262). Belatedly, he finds himself shedding tears of sorrow and regret "for the years of smoldering conflict in which his domineering truculence and inability to articulate any feeling at all combined with my self-pity and defensiveness kept us so far apart" (p. 262).

In contrast to the conflicted relationship that Said had with his father, he shared a strong bond with his mother. As he candidly writes: "My mother was certainly my closest and most intimate companion for the first twenty-five years of my life" (p. 12); "It was exclusively to my mother that I turned for intellectual and emotional companionship" (p. 13). Said portrays his mother as a warm and affectionate woman who instilled in him a love of music and literature. At the same time he criticizes her for being manipulative, neurotically difficult to please, and deeply ambivalent about the world—and her own son. In comparing the personalities of his parents, Said remarks: "My mother possessed a powerful, sensitive intelligence, which I was attracted to, but she tended to hide it to make herself seem like a helpless, much put upon adjunct to my father's strength" (p. 173). While his father's forceful personality intimidated him and made him feel inadequate, his mother's sympathy and affection empowered him and liberated his real self: "It was my mother's often melting warmth which offered me a rare opportunity to be the person I felt I truly was in contrast to the 'Edward' who failed at school and sports and could never match the manliness my father represented. And yet my relationship with her grew more ambivalent, and her disapproval of me became far more emotionally devastating to me than my father's virile bullying and reproaches" (p. 56). Despite his mother's moodiness, Said adored her and regarded her as his "point of reference" (p. 292). He always turned to her in times of crisis, as, for example, when he killed a motorcyclist in a car accident in Switzerland, and when his first marriage broke up and he divorced his wife.

Said admits that his attachment to his mother was so strong that as a boy he had no friends of his own age, and as a young adult it interfered with his relationships with his sisters and with other women (p. 221). Blaming his mother for her active role in erecting "prickly barriers" between him and his sisters, which persisted from their childhood into their adulthood (p. 294), he tries to rationalize her behavior by alluding to the blow she must have suffered when she was taken out of school in Beirut and given in marriage to a man 20 years her senior (p. 14), and by emphasizing her frustrations about her life in Cairo (p. 60). He writes that only as an adult he realized what his mother's deepest needs were and what he meant to her: "I was her only son, and shared her facility of communication, her passion for music and words, so I became her instrument for self-expression and self-elaboration as she struggled against my father's unbending, mostly silent iron will" (p. 222). Besides having similar traits and interests, mother and son also shared the same fate, for a year after she died of breast cancer he was diagnosed with leukemia.[28]

Said's departure to the United States in 1951 set him on the path of a distinguished academic career. He blossomed intellectually in Mount Hermon, a New England prep school, then went to college at Princeton University, then to graduate school at Harvard University, and in 1963 to a teaching post at Columbia, where he remained. Meanwhile, major political changes took place in the Middle East: Israel was established in 1948, the colonial Egypt of King Farouk disappeared by 1952 and the era of Nasser's regime began (1954–70), and Lebanon was transformed by 15 years of civil war (1975–90). Although Said made regular visits to the Middle East, mainly to Cairo and after 1962 to Beirut, where his parents relocated, he remained almost entirely disengaged from politics until his early thirties. What, then, suddenly motivated him to become involved in the Palestinian political struggle, so much so that he became the most prominent advocate of the Palestinian cause in the United States?

Said himself claims that it was the trauma of the Arab defeat in the Six-Day War (1967) that shocked him out of his earlier complacency, reconnecting him with his "authentic self" (p. 293). With so many dissonances in his life, cultural, linguistic, and geographic, perhaps it was only natural that he should embrace the Palestinian identity. After all, Palestine was where he was born and where his extended family had lived. At the same time, Said's strong identification with Palestine may have been the result of the "complexity of his background—privileged yet marginal, wealthy yet powerless."[29] This peculiar situation, manifested in his cocooned life in Cairo on the one hand, and in brutal encounters with colonial authorities at the city's British and American schools on the other hand, may have driven him to "empathize with dispossessed people, especially the victims of Zionism,"[30] which he equated with colonialism.

Most likely, Said's pro-Palestinian activism was a form of rebellion against his father.[31] The father loved America and wanted his son to become American and turn his back forever on the Middle East (pp. 10, 211, 294); he disliked his homeland, saying that Jerusalem "reminded him of death" (p. 6); he rarely talked about the loss of Palestine, imposing silence on the topic (pp. 115–17); and he hated and distrusted politics (p. 117). Participating in the political struggle for Palestine provided the son with a means of asserting himself vis-à-vis his authoritarian father. Thus, for Said, the "narrative of oppression" and the "process of liberation" became intimately connected on both the personal and national levels. Said makes an explicit reference to his quest for freedom when he mentions that he and his father were almost exactly the same age—16—when they came to the United States: "He to make his life, I to be directed by his script for me, until I broke away and started trying to live and write my own" (p. 8). Even as a young boy Said was motivated by the desire to prove to himself—and to his father—that "there was more to 'Edward' than the delinquent yet compliant son, submitting to his father's Victorian design" (p. 79). Hence his choice of intellectual pursuits can also be understood as a rebellion against the father who was a brilliant businessman but not much else.

Said's ultimate act of rebellion against his father appears to be the writing of his memoir, for Wadie upheld the concept of privacy and sanctity of the family. As Said emphatically states: "One of my father's ironclad rules was never to discuss the Said family at all; he often told me that a man's family is his honor" (p. 17). Be it consciously or unconsciously, Said's conflicted ties with his father motivated his actions and cast the longest emotional shadows over his life. Sadly, he says: "I called my father Daddy until his dying day, but I always sensed in the phrase how contingent it was, how potentially improper it was to think of myself as his son" (p. 18). Given these sentiments, it is fair to conclude that Said channeled some of his frustrations as a son and his resentment toward his father into his antiauthoritarian and anticolonial writings and political activities.

Tawfiq al-Hakim's *The Prison of Life*

Tawfiq al-Hakim (1898–1987) is regarded as the father of the modern Arab theater. He pioneered the dramatic form in Arabic writing and was the leading playwright of his time in Egypt. His literary career, which spans over half a century, from the 1920s to the 1970s, is characterized by an immense output that includes more than 70 plays of remarkable variety, as well as several novels, collections of short stories, and books of essays.

Al-Hakim's autobiography, *The Prison of Life*,[32] covers the first part of his life, that is, the years of his childhood and youth, until 1928, when he returned to Egypt from Paris as a "disappointment" to his family for failing to earn his doctorate in law. Al-Hakim's proclaimed goal in narrating his life history is to understand himself, especially the makeup of his nature, which he sees as the "motor" that determines his ability and controls his destiny (p. 3). For this reason, he does not keep to the chronological order of events. As he explains: "I have in most instances mingled times and occurrences in order to reach straight into the heart of the matter sought here—namely, the uncovering of something relevant to the formation of this nature of mine, behind the prison bars of which I have been thrashing all my life" (p. 208). Hence the title of his autobiography. Al-Hakim is aware that to achieve this goal, he must violate the concept of privacy and sanctity of the family by discussing his parents and family life. He therefore pleads with the reader: "Let us not shrink from overstepping a little our country's custom of placing one's parents and forefathers into rigid molds and fixed frames, befitting images of such perfection and piety and virtue as to defy any human analysis. We need a modicum of courage and candor in order to discover at least something of our nature's makeup—this nature which imprisons us throughout life" (pp. 3–4).

Al-Hakim was born into a middle-class Sunni Muslim family in Alexandria. His father belonged to a landowning family in the village of Saft al-Muluk, and his mother, whose hometown was Alexandria, descended of seamen with Turkish roots. Both parents had to struggle to get an education, the mother because it was considered shameful for young women of her generation to learn to read and write (p. 11), the father because his own father expected him to stay in the village and help him farm his land. Eventually, he made it to law school and after graduating joined the judiciary, where he worked his way up from public prosecutor to district magistrate. The couple had two sons, Tawfiq, the elder, and Zuhayr, the younger.

Like Edward Said, al-Hakim grew up in the shadow of an authoritarian father who wanted to mold his son in his own image. The antagonism between father and son, as the narrative's opening lines suggest, began the moment al-Hakim was born. First, the father was not present at his son's birth because he was working in a faraway village in the countryside. Second, the father did not like the names "Husayn Tawfiq" that the mother had chosen for his son. A comment written in his father's notebook, which al-Hakim found among his effects after his death, reads: "This name did not please me, and I determined to have it legally changed" (p. 5). The narrator construes these facts as evidence that his father rejected him, an interpretation that fuels his sense of resentment toward the father. However, when he thinks of his brother, Zuhayr, so named by the father after a pre-Islamic poet whose suspended ode he memorized, he feels fortunate that his father was absent at his birth: "No doubt if he had been present at my birth he would have given me the name of one of those poets, and I would today be known as Imru' al-Qays al-Hakim, or Tarafa, or Labid, or something of the kind—but God was merciful!" (p. 44). Interestingly, the father's notebook contained the text of a letter that he received from his brother-in-law with the news of his son's birth. In the letter, the brother-in-law says: "I saw him this morning, and found him to be like his father—except that he has no moustache!" (p. 4). This innocent remark foreshadows al-Hakim's artistic career. In Egypt of that time, a shaved upper lip was "the badge of the artist" (p. 169), for no one else dared to shave his moustache. Thus whoever shaved it off was "a rebel against the norm, mired in the company of artists" (p. 169). As it happened, when al-Hakim was a student at the College of Law in Cairo in the early 1920s, he shaved his moustache and spent the greater part of his time with artists, especially those connected with the theater.

Al-Hakim's childhood was not a pampered one: he never got toys from his parents and never had a birthday celebration. He portrays his parents' personalities as the total opposite of each other: the mother was lavish, strong-willed, gregarious, and ruled by her emotions, whereas the father was punctilious, ruled by a stern logical/intellectual tendency, and with a semiascetic approach to matters of pleasure or comfort, even to food (pp. 195–97). The family was not close-knit, and the parents did not cultivate intimate ties with their children. Most conspicuously, the traditional cultural model of a strong mother-son relationship is not encountered in this family. Instead of being the nurturing figure, the mother was constantly preoccupied with her material possessions and financial security, tending to the land that she bought and rented out in small plots to peasants. The father, who was the authority figure, was formal and remote. The family moved frequently from town to town because of the father's work as a district magistrate. The repeated transfers interfered with al-Hakim's education, for he could not stay in one school a whole year. Moreover, in most of these towns there was no primary school, only *kuttabs*. Only after the father was given a longer appointment as a judge in Cairo did the young al-Hakim enter a primary school. He was over ten years old then and placed in the first grade. "The decision was a blow to me" (p. 59), he writes, for he was eager to make up for the years wasted outside the system. When, in the middle of the second grade, he experienced difficulties with the schoolwork, he was afraid to tell his parents: his upbringing did not encourage such revelations. As he recounts: "Of course I did not dare confide in my parents, for they had never accustomed me to speaking frankly about my concerns. I knew in advance their reaction to any weakness in me: reproof and the threat of the cane. I was afraid to tell them that I could not follow the lessons lest I hear their usual shout: 'Because you are a dunce! Because you play!'" (p. 69).

Paradoxically, while in his capacity as a judge the father showed fairness and justice in his dealings with people, he was neither just nor fair toward his own son. The narrative abounds with incidents where the father maltreated his son: he routinely applied the cane and the bastinado to discipline his little boy (pp. 46, 68); he slapped him on the face, causing a nosebleed, when he could not explain a difficult word in a pre-Islamic ode (p. 72); he roughly cast him to the sea when he tried to teach him how to swim, traumatizing him for life (p. 73); and he locked him out of the house one night because he went to the cinema (p. 88). In addition to such harsh punishments, the father repressed his son's love for music, literature, and the theater. He forbade him to read novels or go to the cinema, deeming these activities detrimental to his education and future. The struggle between the authoritarian father and the budding young artist dominates the narrative and plays a central role in their troubled relationship. Al-Hakim writes that he used to hide under his bed in order to read his favorite stories and novels, as if he was committing a crime (p. 74). When he failed his first year in secondary school, his father and mother descended on the novels in his possession and tore them all to pieces (p. 87).

No wonder that the narrator regarded his father with fear and resentment rather than love and admiration. He criticizes him for failing to show understanding toward him as a child: "My father did not appreciate that there is different material to suit different ages. Like most fathers in those days, he treated me as if I was the same age as himself. He imposed on me what reading he liked and esteemed" (p. 73). But even as an adult, al-Hakim did not get the treatment befitting his age. He recalls that his father always addressed him as "You, boy—Tawfiq," even after he finished law school and was appointed a prosecutor (p. 37). His critique of the father also extends to his financial incompetence, the symbol of which was the family house in Alexandria. The father was a fool to buy the house in the first place, and later a bigger fool to undertake to renovate it. The problem was that he decided to be his own architect, contractor, and supervisor. Before long, the renovation project turned into a money pit. The "genial architect," as al-Hakim mockingly calls his father, had to mortgage the house heavily to pay for the costs of protracted construction and demolition operations. And after the house was finished, he failed to rent it to prospective tenants or holiday makers, and failed to sell it. Upon his death due to typhoid fever at the age of 65, all the money from his life insurance policies went into paying the debts on the house, or rather, "into stopping that gap, that drain that went under the name of a house" (p. 141). Resentfully, al-Hakim says that his father never consulted him on financial matters, even after he became a prosecutor (p. 92). Worse yet, his father gave him poor financial advice that caused him to lose the ten pounds that he had painstakingly saved out of his allowance throughout his school years (p. 37).

In the repressive home environment that al-Hakim experienced in his childhood, he had one ally—his maternal grandmother. A kind-hearted woman in her old age, the grandmother often interceded on her grandson's behalf, saved him from his father's cane, and spoke in his defense (pp. 68, 88–89). As a young boy he used to sit by her side and listen to her recounting her sorrows over her divorce and her two daughters, his mother being the younger one, who were bitter adversaries and constantly feuded with each other. Interestingly, just as al-Hakim's mother was not close to her sister, so also al-Hakim was not close to his brother. He attributes this fact to fundamental differences in their personalities: "Like my mother, the directions he took in life were strictly materialistic and practical. His hobbies were shooting, hunting, swimming, dancing, card-playing, and other things that I am incapable of describing or thinking about" (p. 44). As a result, there was little contact between them, even as adults: "Circumstances did not bring us together often. We did not correspond and did not visit each other even at times of serious illness" (pp. 174–75). These revelations clearly contradict another traditional cultural model: that of the strong bond between siblings in Arab families.

Like Edward Said, who blossomed intellectually after he left home for the United States and became free from family control, so also al-Hakim blossomed artistically after he left his parents' home in Alexandria and went to Cairo to complete his secondary education, moving in with relatives. Cairo, then as now the center of cultural activities in Egypt, gave him ample opportunities to pursue his interests in drama and the theater. Although the narrative's focus is on the author's development, his recollections about the Egyptian theater in the 1920s and 1930s are of great interest to the historian of Arabic literature. Free to come and go as he pleased, al-Hakim spent most of his time with artists, studying just enough to pass his school exams. After earning his baccalaureate, he enrolled in the College of Law. As it happened before, he failed the first year because of his extracurricular activities. Thereafter he worked steadily at the law until he earned his degree, though not with distinction, owing to his continuous involvement in theatrical troupes and the production of plays. In 1925, his father, hoping to improve his son's employment prospects and distract him from writing for the stage, sent him to Paris to earn a doctorate in law. Three years later al-Hakim returned to Egypt without the additional degree, but with cases full of books of literature. The narrative begins with the father's disappointment over his son's name and concludes with his disappointment over his son's failure to earn a doctorate.

The cultural encounter with the West broadened al-Hakim's horizons, fired his imagination, and unleashed his creative impulse. Although he had to work as a prosecutor to support himself, his quest for freedom, self-expression, and self-fulfillment was achieved through a literary career. Intriguingly, in exploring his artistic bent, al-Hakim believes that it is a seed he received from his father. Before his marriage, the father was known as the "artful poet-philosopher" (p. 26), a man with a liberated image and an inventive mind who loved to recite poetry and compose verses of his own. After his marriage, the father's duties and responsibilities as a judge and the head of a family stifled his poetic inclinations, so that he confined his energy solely within the framework of the bench and the family. In al-Hakim's view, "a father's frustrated wish is perhaps what he does pass on to his children" (p. 200). He sees himself as the product of psychological and biological determinism: "My father therefore cast upon my shoulders what his circumstances did not allow him to carry. I am the prisoner of the wish he did not fulfill, and indeed the prisoner of many things I have inherited from him, some good, some bad" (p. 200). Likewise, he inherited from his mother a combination of good and bad qualities. Altogether, this legacy constitutes the "prison" of his life, namely, his basic nature. He cannot escape from it. The realm where his freedom resides is his thought: "It is in this that I differ from my parents entirely. Here is the source of my real strength, with which I resist....Man is free in thought and a prisoner in his nature" (p. 201).

The narrative contains interesting cross-generational echoes. Some features of child socialization have clearly changed over time. For example, al-Hakim expresses his envy at the availability of children's literature for his little son, who can enjoy reading stories from Arab history and world literature in simplified language and with colorful illustrations (p. 74). His sense of envy is also aroused when he sees "young people reading novels, short stories, and plays without censorship or objection from their elders" (p. 74). In addition, al-Hakim depicts the psychological effects of growing up in the shadow of an important or well-known father. Once, when he was a ten-year-old boy standing in the morning assembly of a small town school, a man passed by whom the headmaster greeted with great respect and whom the entire assembly was asked to salute. That man was al-Hakim's father, so well respected because he was the town's judge. Al-Hakim recounts that he felt "a mixture of a little inner pride and a great deal of diffidence and embarrassment," and wished that he could "disappear into the belly of the earth" (p. 53). A similar incident happened to his own son when he was ten years old. A teacher had called him to the front of the class and stood next to him, delivering a long speech in praise of his father on the occasion of his being awarded a state literary prize. Al-Hakim writes that his son was too shy to tell him to his face what he had felt, but that he learned that he was extremely annoyed rather than "disturbed or embarrassed or scared as I had been" (p. 53). His son's reaction did not change when he grew older and he continued to be annoyed whenever attention was drawn to him because of his father.

As for the relationship between al-Hakim's father and grandfather, it is depicted as conforming to the traditional pattern of submission to authority. Despite the fact that the grandfather was a much-married man with numerous children, a situation that resulted in his losing most of his land, al-Hakim's father was dutiful toward him and extremely eager to please him. He honored him and defended him and his ways, including his multiple marriages. However, he himself refused to take another wife when al-Hakim's mother fell ill and became bedridden for a long time. He referred to his provincial father as an enlightened man who had studied at al-Azhar but who had to quit and return to his village to farm the land that he had inherited from his forefathers. Nevertheless, as a boy he had to plead with him to stay in school year after year until he completed his secondary education and was accepted to law school. Thereafter, the grandfather stopped insisting on agriculture as the necessary vocation for his male children and became eager "to see one of his sons in the ruling set!" (p. 19). Thus each of the men in al-Hakim's family—the grandfather, the father, and the son—set a new standard or role model for the next generation: the grandfather became an enlightened peasant who studied at al-Azhar, the father became a lawyer and a judge, and the son became a lawyer, an artist, and a writer. The autobiography shows the evolution of the father-son relationship and its influence on the son's development and choices over three generations of family life.

Abusive Fathers: The Scars of Neglect and Battering

The developmental trajectory of a young boy from childhood to manhood is greatly dependent on building a strong relationship with a father figure, ideally the boy's real father, who provides him with a role model. Nothing damages a young boy more severely than an abusive relationship with the father, on whom he is expected to pattern his male identity. Child abuse and neglect are attributed to a variety of factors, including a family history of parental abuse and neglect, the parent's characteristics and the "goodness of fit" with the child's characteristics, as well as contextual sources of stress such as marital conflict, poverty, unemployment, and alcohol or drug abuse. Studies show that children exposed to abuse and neglect are scarred for life psychologically and physically. They tend to suffer from poor self-esteem, emotional instability, depression, and negative attitudes toward work and life, and are also likely to exhibit maladaptive and antisocial behavior, even criminal. Moreover, they frequently establish a family legacy that impedes the functioning of successive generations. Notwithstanding the harmful effects of child abuse and neglect, there are always exceptional individuals who manage to overcome the deprivations they have suffered in their childhood and develop the skills necessary to become successful and well-adjusted adults.[33]

Hanna Mina's *Fragments of Memory*

The autobiographical trilogy of Hanna Mina, one of Syria's most prominent novelists, provides an intimate glimpse into the vicious cycle of poverty and child neglect. The first volume of the trilogy, *Fragments of Memory* (1975), like its sequels *Al-Mustanqaʿ* (The Swamp, 1977) and *Al-Qitaf* (The Picking, 1986), is described on the title page as a novel.[34] However, extratextual information, particularly interviews with the author in which he has affirmed that these texts depict personal experiences and real characters, lends support to an autobiographical reading of these works.[35] It is fair to assume that Mina's trilogy, like most forms of retrospective writing, combines fact and fiction about his childhood and youth.

Hanna Mina was born in 1924 into a poor family of Greek Orthodox Christian background in the coastal city of Latakia in Syria. He was the only boy after three girls, and remained so, as five more siblings who followed him all died of disease and malnutrition. When he was three years old, his father was hospitalized with a chest ailment and the doctors advised a period of convalescence in a rural area. The family migrated to the countryside and embarked on a journey of unimaginable suffering, including displacement, servitude, starvation, and oppression, which lasted for several years. At the age of eight, Mina returned with his family to the city of Iskenderun, where he started his schooling. After completing the elementary level, extreme poverty forced him to quit school and seek employment. He worked as a dock porter, sailor, barber, and journalist, and spent time in exile and prison due to his political views. A self-made, self-taught man, Mina survived his wretched childhood and rose above his humble origins to become a leading intellectual and writer in his country.

Fragments of Memory, set in the rural area of northern Syria at the time of the French Mandate, describes Mina's early years between the ages of three and eight, when his family was displaced in the countryside. *The Swamp*, set in the slum quarter of the city of Iskenderun, where his family settled, continues the narrative from the age of eight to fourteen or fifteen.[36] Told largely from a child's point of view, these volumes contain a wealth of information about growing up in Syria in the late 1920s and 1930s, focusing on the harsh living conditions of the peasants and the proletariat prior to and during the Great Depression (1928–35). Having experienced poverty and social injustice firsthand, Mina chronicles the exploitation of the peasants in the villages under a feudal system (vol. 1) and the exploitation of the proletariat in the city under a capitalist system (vol. 2). The devastating effects of colonialism are shown to impact both the village and the city: the first volume describes Mina's family raising silkworms in a village and how this entire industry came to an end with the introduction of cheap synthetic silk on the world market by the colonial powers; and the second volume ends with the departure of Mina's family from Iskenderun after France ceded the area to Turkey in 1939, despite the fact that most of the population there was ethnically Arab—an event that is nationally mourned in Syria to this day.

Mina paints intimate portraits of his parents' contrasting personalities and relentless struggles for survival in hopelessly adverse conditions. Both illiterate, the parents originated in the coastal village of al-Suwaydiya but became rootless through migration to the countryside and then to the city, driven by the need to find a means of livelihood. The father, Salim al-Misri, is depicted as a weak, unreliable, and failed man who never succeeded in any trade or job he took, except in getting drunk, wasting borrowed money, and cheating on his wife. Irresponsible, unfaithful, and addicted to alcohol, when the going got tough he simply abandoned his wife and children and disappeared for weeks on end, returning only after he sobered up and felt remorse. The cycle of failure—abandonment—drinking repeated itself every few months, much to the mother's—and her son's—fear and desperation. Contrary to the father's reckless and selfish behavior, the mother, Mariam, emerges as a saintly figure, utterly devoted to her children and the only source of security and nurturance in their lives. Gentle, loving, and protective, she held the family together and forgave her husband's transgressions time after time. Despite her ignorance and superstition, she insisted on sending her son to school, thus enduring additional hardships. At one point, with no one to turn to for help, as she was an orphan, and with no shelter, food, or work, she collapsed and suffered a nervous breakdown that lasted for several months. A resigned fatalist, she found comfort in the belief that everything in life is preordained and subject to God's will.[37]

Mina's childhood, then, was marked by traumatic experiences: his father's absence and neglect, his mother's nervous breakdown, his sisters' enslavement as domestic help in the houses of the rich, starvation, disease, homelessness, humiliation, and persecution by the corrupt authorities. These experiences left indelible marks on his mind. As he recounts: "We were a willow in the red desert dust, victims of the whirlwind and burning sun. A mother, two children, and a father who was a flop in a poor rural area. Poor to the degree that hunger, disease and superstition on one side of the scale were balanced by the

tyranny of a feudal system on the other" (1:104). While he acknowledges that countless other Syrian families lived in dismal conditions
in those days, he nevertheless condemns his father for compromising
the family's safety and bringing ruin on it: "I don't mean to imply
that it was our family's boat alone that experienced this buffeting in
the relentless sea of great poverty. But it, due to the irresponsibility of
its captain, was in a worse state of disarray in the struggle against the
tempest and more quickly lost in the tumult" (1:86). Mina's resentment toward his father is expressed with sarcasm when he says: "This
failure in his family and working life was a success in his love life"
(1:136); and "This wanderer, adventurer, drunkard, with no sense of
fear, this damned lecher was [my mother's] husband" (1:136). Above
all, he denounces the father for selling his young daughters one by one
into slavery in order to pay for his debts, his alcohol consumption, and
his senseless projects: "It was Father who concluded this contract and
handed over our sister to be crucified on the cross of service" (1:87).
This powerful image reveals the author's Christian background. The
only period when the father did not abandon his family as usual
was when he had an affair with a village woman named Zanuba and
became so attached to her that he stuck around. Although the situation was morally reprehensible, the son experienced his father's presence as a blessing: "Father did not leave, and fear and hunger did not
gang up against us. . . . Father was with us. How good it is for children
to have their father with them" (1:138).

As a child, then, Mina's world revolved around his mother: she was
his point of reference, his rock, his lifeline. He readily admits that she
meant everything to him: "She was my mother, something more precious than a mother. Not merely the mother who gave me existence,
but survival too. I did not understand how to separate my existence
from my survival" (1:120). When the mother had to leave him for a
few days to go and visit her sick little daughter who worked as a maid
in the city, he felt lost and forsaken: "That night, I experienced feelings of being an orphan, of lonesomeness and of being cut off from
everything dear and secure. I never worked as a servant child; I wasn't
plucked from my parents' side like my two sisters, destined to live far
away from them. That night I could appreciate in my imagination
what they endured in their alienated exile, and therefore I extol their
suffering and that of all children who have been deprived of their
childhood through death or poverty" (1:141).

Clearly, the adult narrator suffers from feelings of guilt on account
of his sisters' bitter fate. He is tormented by the fact that he was fed
and educated at their expense and through their exploitation. As he

writes: "My sisters' childhoods were sold for a year. Then Father borrowed against the coming year, and before it was finished he borrowed against the following one. I didn't realize that I was the one with the hungry mouth; that I was being nourished from my sisters' bodies, from their childhood, from their freedom; that I learned to read and write in the elementary grades from their ignorance. I assume they will never read these words, as they are illiterate and no one will ever volunteer to read them to them" (1:118). Mina tries to rationalize the preferential treatment that he received from his parents by claiming that as a boy he was useless and undesirable as a servant. But this is a lame excuse, for young boys are known to have worked as domestic help in the houses of the rich throughout the Arab region. (One example is the Moroccan writer Mohamed Choukri, as depicted in his autobiographical novel *For Bread Alone*.) Most probably, he was spared his sisters' lot because of his favored position as the only son in the family. The sad fate of his sisters, whose "childhood was being squeezed out like a lemon, burned up like a cigarette and turned into ashes" (1:118), explains to a large extent why the author turned to socialism as the solution to all social ills, from child labor to class differences to women's oppression.

Remarkably, despite his many grievances against the father, the adult son is willing to forgive him. This act may be attributable to the influence of Christian teachings that his mother instilled in him. It may also stem from the son's own need to come to terms with his father and attain a sense of inner peace. As he states: "I really forgive my father for much of the damage he caused us through his irresponsibility towards life. I do not reproach him for his pathological lust since he was not responsible for it, or for his intemperance, since he drowned his misery in intoxication. But as a child, I was unable to fathom that and my mother's remonstrances to him were mine too" (1:126). Critical of the father as he is, the son remembers fondly how he carried him on his back across a long thorny field on a hot summer day after they became exhausted from gleaning the grain (1:150). Importantly, the father was not physically abusive to his family and seldom hit his wife or children. The adult narrator chooses to exorcize the demons from his childhood by forgiving his father and accepting him for what he was: a victim of poverty, society, and his own nature.

Mohamed Choukri's *For Bread Alone*

In contrast to the conciliatory spirit of Hanna Mina, the Moroccan novelist Mohamed Choukri is unable to forgive his father, even after his death. In his two-part autobiography, *For Bread Alone* (1973) and *Streetwise* (1992),[38] he paints a gruesome picture of his father as a brutal and violent man. Choukri's account of his childhood and youth is a shocking narrative of physical, emotional, and verbal abuse at the hands of a monster father. His attack on the sacred image of the father in Arab society explains in part why he was unable to find an Arab publisher (the English version of *For Bread Alone* appeared a decade before the Arabic text) and why the Arabic edition was banned in most Arab countries, including Morocco.

Mohamed Choukri (1935–2003) is regarded as one of North Africa's most controversial and widely read authors. He was born into a poor Berber family in Beni Chiker, a small village in the Rif mountains, when northern Morocco was still part of the Spanish Protectorate. The Berbers, most of whom are Sunni Muslims, fought fiercely against Spanish and French occupation in the 1920s. Eventually submitting to the colonial powers, many of them served in the Spanish and French armies, where they were valued for their fighting skills.[39] Choukri's father, Haddou Allal Choukri, joined the Spanish army and took part in Franco's war, and then he deserted (1:64 and 2:124). Mohamed was seven years old when his family fled the great famine in the Rif and arrived in Tangier, then moved to Tetouan, where he grew up in conditions of extreme poverty. Eight of his brothers and sisters died of malnutrition or neglect, and another brother was killed by Choukri's father in a fit of violent rage. He ran away from home at the age of 16, embracing a life of homelessness and petty crime. At the age of 20, he decided to become literate, and in a period of 5 years passed from learning the letters of the Arabic alphabet to writing poems and stories. His vivid depictions of street life and sexual encounters in the bars and brothels of Moroccan cities broke all literary and religious taboos in the Arab world, earning him the title "l'enfant terrible" of modern Arabic literature. Largely self-taught, Choukri's exceptional life story culminated in becoming a professor of Arabic literature at Ibn Batutu College in Tangier, his beloved city and the setting of most of his stories. In addition to his autobiography, he penned two collections of short stories and published accounts of his encounters with the French writer Jean Genet, the American playwright Tennessee Williams, and the writer Paul Bowles, whom he befriended in the cosmopolitan circles of Tangier.

Choukri's life was a journey of discovery in an uncharted part of Maghrebi society—the backstreets of cities like Tetouan, Larache, and Tangier. His two-part autobiography chronicles both the misery and liberty of living on the fringes of Maghrebi society. The first volume,

For Bread Alone, covers the years between 1942 and 1955, from the age of 7 to the age of 20, when he made the decision to go to school and learn to read and write. *Streetwise*, the sequel, continues the narration from that particular point into the 1970s, focusing on the author's struggle, as a young adult, to educate himself and change the pattern of his life. Although the two volumes carry the subtitle "an autobiographical novel," no ambiguity exists with regard to the identity of the protagonist. In both texts he is explicitly identified with the author: his name and his parents' names are mentioned in full in several places (e.g., 1:50; 2:103). Given the taboos surrounding the subjects of sex and family life in Arab culture, it is fair to say that classifying his work as an "autobiographical novel" allowed Choukri to express himself more freely and at the same time assume a degree of nonaccountability. As previously noted, most autobiographies are a combination of fact and fiction, as well as of personal and social history. Interestingly, in an interview about his work, Choukri said that he considers *For Bread Alone* "a semidocumentary endeavor about an oppressed social group that included myself and my family."[40]

Choukri's abuse at the hands of his father began in his childhood and continued unabated into his early adulthood. The narrative abounds in incidents where the father beats up his son senseless for no apparent reason, intimidates him at the dinner table so that he doesn't dare to eat, throws him out of the house into the street, exploits him as child labor, tortures him by forcing him to eat a whole pot of tripe until he passes out and his stomach has to be pumped at the hospital, curses him, calls him derogatory names, humiliates him, and threatens to harm him. The very first page of *For Bread Alone* begins with the themes of starvation and battering. The father comes home and finds his two little sons crying for bread. He immediately explodes with anger and violence: he slaps and kicks Mohamed, yelling: "Shut up! If you're hungry, eat your mother's heart" (p. 7). Then he lifts him into the air and throws him forcefully onto the floor, kicking him until his leg gets tired. From cross-references (e.g., 2:36), it becomes clear that Mohamed is seven years old at the time. Mohamed's younger brother, Abdelqader, is not so lucky: when he doesn't stop crying for bread, the father twists his neck in a fit of rage, killing him instantly. The crime goes unreported, and the remorseless father is left free to carry on with his reign of terror: "Each afternoon my father comes home disappointed. Not a movement, not a word, save at his command, just as nothing can happen unless it is decreed by Allah" (1:9); "When he comes into the house, only he has the right to exist" (1:58). He hits the mother in front of her son, calling her "bitch" and "rotten whore" (1:9, 1:57). Unemployed, frustrated, and always in a bad temper, "he abuses everyone with his words, sometimes even Allah" (1:9).

Under constant threat for his survival, the son develops deep fear mingled with intense hatred toward his father. During the two years the father spends in jail as punishment for deserting from the Spanish army, he experiences a profound sense of relief living alone with his mother, despite their appalling conditions. He wishes the father were dead and fantasizes that he never returns home—but the father does return, and the hellish family life resumes. Embittered and vengeful on account of his jail time, the father reasserts his place in the family with greater tyranny and cruelty. He sends his wife to sell vegetables in the street, while he spends his days sitting in a café smoking, drinking, and chatting with fellow deserters from the Spanish army. He also forces the 12-year-old Mohamed to work for his living, saying: "Food costs money in this house. Unless you work, you've got no food or bed here. You understand?" (1:29). Then he proceeds to collect the money that his son earns with the sweat of his brow. The son is aware that the father is exploiting him and the mother, but is too weak to resist. Helpless, in his imagination he pictures killing him: "I was thinking: If there's anybody in the world I wish would die before his hour comes, it's my father. And if there were others, they would surely look like him. How many times have I killed him in my mind? All that's needed is for me really to kill him" (1:56). When he goes to the cinema, he fantasizes that his father is the villain in the film and that he pulls the trigger and shoots him to death (1:61). He admits that he is constantly filled with fear, even when the father is not around: "He is not at home, but he is here because I am afraid of him" (1:57); "His essence stays with us even when he is not there himself" (1:56). Inevitably, he seeks refuge in the street, but even there he is not safe from his father's clutches. As he recounts: "My father had a habit of stealing up behind me in the street and seizing my shirt collar. Then with one hand he would twist my arm behind my back, while with the other he would beat me until the blood ran. When that happened, I knew the thick military belt was waiting at home for me" (1:50).

The mother tries to protect her son from the father's brutality but is powerless in the face of his violent outbursts and usually ends up being battered herself. Fearing for his life, the teenaged son runs away from home and arrives in Tangier, where he lives in the gutter for four years. Finally resolving to change his way of life, he enrolls in a literacy school in Larache, where he succeeds in getting his elementary certificate and a grant to go to the teachers' training college in Tetouan. He returns to Tetouan in 1960 as a young adult in his mid-twenties, ready to begin his training as a primary schoolteacher. However, even after such a long absence the father's abusive behavior toward him still persists, and he treats him with the same hostility and aggression as before. Losing no opportunity to run his son down in front of neighbors and friends, the father says: "He's just an ignorant bastard like me. Don't tell me he's actually learnt anything! If you ask me, they must have made a mistake in the paperwork when they passed him" (2:102). Disillusioned, the son admits: "His resentment toward me was endless. If my mother ever protested, he'd beat her and curse her, just as he used to do with us. And the hatred seemed to pursue me even after his death" (2:102). Realizing that his father expects him to give him money out of his monthly grant, he spitefully remarks: "He was the kind of man who worshipped money more than he worshipped God, but he wouldn't lift a finger to earn it—he expected others to earn it for him. All my dormant hatred for him was rekindled. Relations between us had settled into a mutual loathing" (2:100). But this sorry state of affairs pains the son and ruins his peace of mind: "I didn't understand why he hated me so much. He never missed a chance of saying bad things about me, whether to my face or behind my back.... How much longer would I let him prey on my mind?" (2:100–101).

The father's inhumanity toward his son calls for some explanation. Importantly, Choukri himself does not try to understand the reasons for his father's abusive behavior toward him. Attempting to understand his father is one step toward forgiving him, and he is not prepared to forgive or forget. Therefore he makes no attempt to look into his father's background—his specific upbringing, family history, etc. Unlike Hanna Mina, he accepts no excuses for his stolen childhood and expresses no desire for reconciliation with his father. He declares this emphatically after he suffers a nervous breakdown and is discharged from a psychiatric hospital in Tetouan: "I spent two days with my family. There was still an icy silence between me and my father. Just to keep my mother happy, I kissed his head as usual, without a word passing between us. The pain that I'd had from him in my childhood, he was now getting back from me in his old age. There was no way that there could ever be a compromise between us" (2:202).

Attributing the father's inhumanity toward his son to poverty is not an adequate explanation. While it is true that poverty can lead to inhumanity, Choukri does not consider this to be a valid excuse.

On the contrary, he repeatedly states that he encountered true acts of kindness, compassion, and generosity among the poorest and lowest members of society—prostitutes, drug addicts, and thieves. It is most likely that the father's abusive behavior toward his son stemmed from a psychological impairment in his personality. Uneducated and jobless, he had anger-control problems, low frustration tolerance, poor self-esteem, and lack of empathy. He also suffered from paranoid delusions: he believed that Mohamed was not his own son and suspected that he was constantly scheming against him with the mother's help. In one of his confrontations with his son, he says to him: "I don't feel like your father. Who knows? Maybe somebody else was with your mother. You're nothing like me. More like her. She spoils you the whole time. You plot together against me. You defend each other. You never listen to what I tell you" (1:59). The rebellious son admits that he shared some characteristics with his father: "He and I were both as stubborn as each other. He disapproved of me as a son, and I disapproved of him as a father" (2:107). Another factor that negatively impacted the relations between father and son was the horrible death of Abdelqader, Choukri's younger brother. As a little boy, Choukri witnessed the killing, which was never reported to the police. Traumatized by this event, its memory haunted him throughout his life. He recalls his agitated state of mind at his brother's funeral: "I thought of how my father had twisted Abdelqader's neck. I wanted to cry out: He killed him! Yes. He killed him. I saw him kill him. . . . Then I was afraid he was going to kill me too" (1:10).

Altogether, the father's image in this narrative is monstrous. He personifies paternal abuse in its worst form. An utter failure in his roles as "man-the-procreator-protector-provider,"[41] he does not measure up to the norms of Arab masculinity. This may explain his high level of frustration and the need to fabricate stories about his bravery in the Spanish Civil War. As the son sarcastically remarks: "His friends in the Feddane, like himself, had been deserters in Franco's war. His stories were all lies. The only time my father was ever brave was in his war with us, and he began to lose that war once we started growing up" (2:125).

Choukri acknowledges that he grew up in a dysfunctional family. Calling his home "a house of daily conflicts between my parents" (2:104), and "the hut of disaster and ill omen" (2:108), he refers to himself as "a son of the gutter" (2:119). Perhaps because he ran away from home in his youth and settled in Tangier, he did not develop close ties with any of his surviving siblings, one brother and two sisters. The only close bond he had was with his mother. Affirming that he loved her, or as he puts it, "My love for her is bound up with my hatred for him" (1:57), Choukri states: "She always showed me more affection than she did to my brothers and sisters. Maybe this was because I was the eldest and had been saved from starvation by a miracle; maybe it was because I'd been born in the Rif and spoke with her in the language of her family; and maybe it was also because I was living away from home" (2:110–11).

When the father died of asthma in 1979, the family did not bother to inform Choukri, knowing the animosity that prevailed between them. However, when the mother died, Choukri's siblings sent someone to fetch him from Tangier. Grief-stricken, he arrived in Tetouan to attend her funeral, fully aware that "the umbilical cord had been cut and that the roots of my family tree had now rotted beyond the point of no return" (2:214).

Choukri's torturous relationship with his father scarred him for life. He became an alcoholic, a drug user, and a heavy smoker. He suffered from bouts of depression, repeated mental breakdowns, and he even attempted suicide. He never married, had no lasting relationships, and preferred the company of drunks and prostitutes in the bars and brothels of Tangier. In a public interview he declared that he decided not to have children for fear that he might repeat the pattern of violence that he experienced at home.[42] Choukri's talent for writing gave him a voice and saved him from poverty and marginalization, but not from the wounds of his battered childhood. Despite his remarkable success as an author, he lived alone, cared for by a servant. He died at the age of 68 of cancer of the throat, a disease that is closely associated with heavy drinking and smoking.

Absent Fathers: Efforts to Fill the Void

A father may be absent from his child's life either emotionally, when he is cold, aloof, and uninvolved in the daily activities of his family, or physically, when he works far away from home in another city or country. A more permanent paternal absence may be the result of sickness, divorce, or untimely death. In all these situations, the effects of growing up fatherless are profound for the child. Paternal deprivation is especially traumatic for the son, who usually acquires his masculine identity and role model from his father. How do fatherless boys in Arab families cope with such a critical void in their lives? What kind of compensatory strategies do they employ or have available to them that enable them to survive and even excel in a patriarchal society? In what follows, two examples will be discussed.

Halim Barakat's "Childhood Memories"

The childhood recollections of the novelist and sociologist Halim Barakat offer an interesting insight into the concept of orphanhood in traditional Arab culture. Born in 1933 into a Sunni Muslim family in Kafrun, a small village in Syria, and raised in Beirut, he received his doctorate in social psychology from the University of Michigan and later had a long career on the faculty of Georgetown University. He published scholarly works, novels, a collection of short stories, and a memoir.

In "Childhood Memories,"[43] Barakat describes his father's sudden death in his mid-thirties after a short battle with pneumonia. A poor villager with no material legacy to bequeath to his family, the father's death came as a shock to his wife and three little children. Barakat, who was ten years old at the time, remembers that his mother struggled unsuccessfully to make a living in the village and was finally forced to go to Beirut. After she had established herself there and found a place to live, she sent for her children. Barakat recounts that his mother never stopped grieving for his father and never remarried. What he finds even more striking is her interpretation of his father's death: "To this day, my mother insists that my father was the sacrifice for her life, that he died instead of her so that we would not be orphans. My mother used to say: 'The orphan who loses his father is no orphan.' She meant that the mother would not remarry after the death of her husband, but instead would devote her life completely to her children and then to her grandchildren. And my mother has done exactly that" (pp. 131–32). Clearly, by remaining available to meet her children's needs, emotionally and physically, the mother enhanced their ability to cope with the tragedy and develop normally. Moreover, her explanation of the father's death provided them with a "healing theory," a means of rationalizing the loss and finding some meaning and comfort in it. According to psychologists, a healing theory is especially important when trying to come to terms with a sudden and unexpected death: not only does it help the family to define the event in a way that does not deny the pain of the loss but it also enables them to establish once again a positive sense of control, fairness, and trust in the future.[44]

Interestingly, research shows that sons who experience absent fathers at a young age exhibit systematic deficiencies on many levels, emotional, cognitive, and interpersonal. However, sons whose fathers have died are exceptions to the rule: "In spite of the complete absence of their fathers they show fewer difficulties in adaptation than sons whose fathers are absent for other reasons. It seems that widows often have very positive memories of their husbands, and that they talk a lot about them; for their sons this helps create a positive symbolic image of the father that partially compensates for the fact that he is not present."[45] This observation is especially applicable to Arab culture, where widowed mothers tend to remain loyal to their husbands' memories and refrain from remarrying for the sake of their children.

The mother's unconditional commitment to the well-being of her child is acknowledged in Arabic proverbial lore. A famous Lebanese saying states: "The mother is the world" (*al-dunya umm*).[46] Another colloquial saying declares: "He who has his mother need have no worry." And yet another proverb highlights the contrast between the mother's devotion and the father's absence: "The mother builds a nest while the father runs away."[47] Hence the popular assertion, "A fatherless child is not an orphan," which encapsulates the idea that the mother is more important than the father as a source of love, care, and protection because of her lifelong devotion to her children. Especially in the case of boys, the strong mother-son relationship that is frequently encountered in Arab families is a critical factor in mediating the son's response to the loss of his father.

Yusuf Idris's "A Sketch of My Life as a Child"

The Egyptian author Yusuf Idris (1927–91), unlike his Syrian counterpart Halim Barakat, speaks of a childhood bereft of his father's presence because of the requirements of a job rather than death. A physician by training, Idris wrote innovative plays and novels, but was especially renowned in the Arab world as the master of the Arabic short story.

Idris was born into a traditional Sunni Muslim family in the village of al-Bayrum in the Nile Delta. As he recounts in a rare and brief sketch of his life,[48] his father worked on land reclamation projects, a job that required him to be constantly on the move, away from his family and far from city life. Yusuf, his eldest son, was sent at the age of six to live with his grandparents in their village, so that he could attend primary school. Poor and illiterate, the grandparents' living conditions were harsh and their mentality coarse. For the young boy, this was an extremely painful transition: not only was he torn away from the bosom of his family, but he also found himself compelled to live in poverty. Lonely and homesick, he craved warmth in a household full of rough adults and dominated by his maternal grandmother, a strict and unaffectionate woman. The school was far away from his grandparents' house, and he had to walk two hours back and forth every day. Underfed, inadequately clothed, and ill-equipped with school items, he was often punished with the cane by his teachers for the slightest offense. Only as an adolescent did he return to live with his parents, joining his younger siblings, five brothers and two sisters. Idris speaks of his unhappy childhood with great anguish, declaring that the forced separation from his home scarred him for life: "It took me away from my family forever and deposited me in an entirely different community and atmosphere. From now on, I had to live as a stranger among strangers, an orphan whose parents were still living, yet totally out of reach. And from this point on, I remain for most of my life in a state of profound nostalgia, needing a family of my own, a father, a mother, a brother, or a sister" (p. 8).

Idris portrays his mother as cold, distant, and "mean with money" (p. 9). His relationship with her lacked the warmth and affection that normally bind mother and child. By contrast, Idris was strongly attached to his father and missed him terribly. As he movingly recounts: "My love for him was so great that I used to burst into tears whenever I remembered him. Even though he was large and sunburned and his wrinkled face always wore a serious expression, he was the kindest and most loving man I have ever known" (p. 7). Twice married before, the father craved a son, whom his previous wives were unable to produce for him. Idris's mother was much younger than his father, but poor, and to marry her he had to write his entire estate over to her name. Resentful of his mother, Idris says that her preoccupation with material security did not abate after the marriage. All the household effects, clothes, and jewelry that she demanded were brought to her by a husband "who absolutely adored her and who was now humiliating himself in the process" (p. 8).

Despite his mother's shortcomings, Idris experienced his departure from home at such a young age as a severe psychological crisis. He suddenly fell from the heights of being the "crown prince" to the pits of being an orphan or an outcast. He tried to run away from his grandparents' house, but was caught and given a severe beating. He writes that he managed to cope with this crisis thanks to two avenues of escape: "The first is the fact that I would daydream all the time" (p. 11); "The second of these things was the tales that my great-grandmother told" (p. 12). Thus the creative impulse in him was born. Although his great-grandmother was 90 years old, Idris felt that she was closer to him and to his childhood world than any other person in the household. The void left by his parents' absence, then, was partially filled with a surrogate relationship with his great-grandmother.

In his unforgettable memoir *Angela's Ashes*, Frank McCourt says: "When I look back on my childhood I wonder how I survived at all. It was, of course, a miserable childhood: the happy childhood is hardly worth your while."[49] This sentiment is echoed in Idris's reflections on his childhood. While he acknowledges that without this childhood he would never have become a writer, he emphasizes that it is such a painful chapter in his life that he will never write about it:

> The mere notion of recalling my scattered childhood memories made me physically sick. My childhood can be regarded as the innermost nuclear oven of my existence.... I see no point in actually going through the furnace and reliving it all over again. I will never write about my childhood; it is inhumanely painful to do so. In the meantime, I have to admit that without this childhood I would never have become a writer. And so, my thanks to it, but damn it for all time! You can take my career and prestige, even if I were to be the best writer in the entire history of humanity, and give me instead a moment, just one moment, of my lost childhood. I would accept it without the slightest hesitation.... What is the use of hell, even if its role is to create paradise? It still continues to burn, and the heat it gives off still causes intense pain. (pp. 12–13)

It is no accident that while all of Idris's works were written in Arabic, the sketch of his childhood was written in English. As he explains in his introductory note to this piece of writing, he resorted to his "second language" in order to distance himself from the painful memories of his childhood and enable him to feel as if he was writing about somebody else (p. 5).

Idris is aware that the parental deprivation that he experienced as a child might have resulted in an entirely different sketch of his life as an adult: "It's the same kind of sketch that might be written if you traced the life history of a criminal or a genius. I was lucky because I became a writer. But that's just a matter of luck" (p. 13). That he was able to overcome his childhood deprivations and become a successful physician and a writer is a tribute to his exceptional personality, the core of which was formed before he was separated from his parents. Interestingly, while Idris's short stories frequently depict intimate personal relationships, especially between husbands and wives, they rarely portray a father-son relationship. Apparently, the topic was too painful for him to deal with even in his fiction. (One exception is the story "The Journey," which is discussed in the next chapter).

Conclusion

In all the works examined above, the authors compare the personalities of their parents. The comparison reveals that the cultural prototypes of a nurturing mother and an authoritarian father in Arab families are not always realized. Al-Hakim and Idris experienced their mothers as cold and remote and had a strained relationship with them, whereas Jabra and Naimy experienced their fathers as kind and caring and had a close and loving relationship with them. Intriguingly, both Jabra and Naimy belonged to Christian families. Except for these two authors, a conflicted father-son relationship characterizes the majority of the autobiographical texts in this sample. It is encountered in varying degrees of severity in the narratives of Zaydan, Amin, Said, al-Hakim, Mina, and Choukri. These authors complain of paternal tyranny, repression, deprivation, rejection, or downright abuse. Their rebellions are motivated by the need to establish their own identities, express their individualities, and shape their own destinies. On a symbolic level, the liberation of the son from paternal control is equated with the liberation of society from autocratic rule.

The question of whether there is a difference in the portrayal of family life between the Arab East (Mashreq) and Arab West (Maghreb or North Africa) has been raised. It has been suggested that Arab Christian fathers are less brutal and more humane than Arab Muslim fathers and that Levantine fathers are less brutal and more humane than North African fathers.[50] These assertions, however, cannot be supported or refuted on the basis of this small sample. In this study as a whole, tyrannical fathers appear in male texts from both the Mashreq and the Maghreb. Further, the village-city dichotomy does not appear to be a determining factor in the interactional dynamics between fathers and sons. Said and al-Hakim belonged to urban families, whereas Mina and Choukri belonged to rural families. They all had conflicted relations with their fathers, who were unaffectionate and unnurturing. Class, on the other hand, does appear to play a decisive role in family life. Poverty leads to degradation and dehumanization; the father who cannot meet his economic obligations toward his family tends to vent his frustrations on the wife and children who are dependent on him. This is borne out in the case of Mina and Choukri but not in the case of Naimy and Jabra. The difference is probably due to the individual personalities involved. While poverty may be the cause of paternal abuse and neglect, wealth is not necessarily a guarantee for a caring and loving style of parenting, and wealthy fathers are not always good fathers. As Said's and al-Hakim's

narratives illustrate, a father's disappointment over unmet expectations on his son's part may spoil the relationship between them. In
this respect, education is not always a determining factor either. Some
uneducated fathers, like Naimy's and Jabra's, may be compassionate
and supportive, while others, like Mina's and Choukri's, may be cruel
and abusive. Conversely, some educated fathers, like Amin's and al-
Hakim's, may be extremely authoritarian and strict. Once again, in
such cases the individual personality seems to be the key factor in
determining the father's style of parenting and his mode of interaction with his son.

All these autobiographical accounts illustrate, in the words of
Kimmel and Messner, that "men are not born; they are made. And
men make themselves, actively constructing their masculinities within
a social and historical context."[51] We see how the sons' identities as
men are developed through a process of interaction with their social
environment, be it the home, the neighborhood, the school, or the
workplace. While their primary role models are their fathers, some
sons grow up without caring fathers or lose their fathers and seek
surrogate father figures or other male mentors to emulate, an older
brother (Jabra), a wise teacher (Amin), or a friend (Zaydan). That the
home is not always the ideal place for constructing one's masculinity
is evident from the fact that all the sons in these narratives leave home
and embark on a journey of self-discovery in which they continue to
learn the gender scripts and try to modify them to their individual
needs. Sometimes the journey is from the village to the city or from
the town to the capital city within their own country, sometimes from
their country to another Arab country, and sometimes from an Arab
country to Europe or America. They blossom away from home, and
their exposure to other role models, values, and ways of life contributes to their inner development and the establishment of autonomous
and authentic selfhood. In this respect, the journey away from home,
though fraught with dangers and hardships, serves as an indispensable rite of passage for the sons.

Furthermore, these autobiographical accounts show that the
experience of masculinity is not uniform among the narrators and is
subject to variations by family composition (specifically the father's
presence or absence), the pecking order (e.g., being the eldest son
or the only son), age (boyhood to adulthood to old age), class, education, religion (Muslim or Christian), setting (Bedouin, rural, or
urban), historical period, and geographic location. A striking example of how masculinity is attained differently by class is that of Said
versus Choukri. For the upper-class Said, pursuing various forms of

sport—tennis, rugby, horse riding—was the path to masculinity. For the destitute Choukri, it was the pursuit of sex and petty crime in the backstreets of Tangier. Moreover, these autobiographical accounts reveal variations in masculinity: Naimy and Choukri, for example, did not get married and did not have children, thus departing in a significant way from the hegemonic model of "man-the procreator-protector-provider." Given that hegemonic masculinity in most of these autobiographical accounts was associated with fathers who were unaffectionate, uncaring, unkind, terrifying, and even violent, it is no wonder that some sons chose to distance themselves from it so as to avoid its negative attributes.

Finally, we see how masculine practice varies within the culture over time. The older generation—the grandfathers and fathers—made use of the male privileges of polygamy and divorce to produce many children, especially sons (e.g., al-Hakim's grandfather, Idris's father), whereas the younger generation—the sons—were monogamous. The assertion that Arab masculinity is defined, among other criteria, by "the authority exercised over a woman and the maintenance of her inferior status"[52] is borne out by the marital relations of the fathers, but to a lesser degree by those of the sons who have been educated and exposed to foreign influences. Interestingly, the sons do not discuss their sexuality (except for Choukri, "l'enfant terrible") or marital relations in their narratives and it is mostly through indirect remarks that they make about differences in children's upbringing in the past and the present and about women's position in the West and Arab society that the reader can glean their attitudes. It appears that revelations about one's sexuality and marital relations are still considered a taboo, even for the younger generation of men.

Chapter 4

Fathers and Sons in Works of Fiction

The vicissitudes of the father-son relationship is a perennial theme in Arabic works of fiction, be they short stories, novels, novellas, or plays. As effective vehicles of self-expression and social criticism, these fictional forms enable Arab writers not only to explore the psyche of their protagonists but also to chronicle their struggles against the repressive social order and its institutions, foremost among them the family. In many of these works, the family embodies forces hostile to the protagonist's quest for autonomous and authentic selfhood. Indeed, the family is often depicted as a dysfunctional unit and as a central site of oppression. These literary works show how prevailing patriarchal values and practices weave their way into the fabric of family life and influence every aspect of it, including the father-son relationship. Frequently, this key family relationship is not only unnurturing but downright abusive. The father, as the center of patriarchal power, is the main obstacle to the son's efforts to define himself as an individual and pursue his dreams and ambitions. In many texts, the son's journey toward manhood is characterized by a series of clashes and conflicts with the father, who represents the past, tradition, and stasis. In the end, rebellion against the tyrannical father is the son's only way to attain freedom and independence.

Works of fiction depicting enlightened fathers who live up to the popular maxim "Bring up your son as a child and befriend him as a man" (Arabic: *in kabar ibnak khawihu*) are scarce. The literary representations of father-son relationships oscillate between a variety of opposite poles: love versus hatred, acceptance versus rejection, loyalty versus betrayal, oppression versus empowerment, bonding versus estrangement, admiration versus contempt, and so on. These dichotomous representations show that the father-son relationship is extremely problematic and far from the idealized view encapsulated in sayings such as "The womb does not bring forth an enemy" (*al-batn ma tigibsh 'aduw*) and "A man's wings are his children" (*janah al-shakhsh awladuhu*) of Arabic proverbial lore.

Paterfamilias: Naguib Mahfouz's *Trilogy*

Any discussion of father-son relationships in Arabic fiction must begin with Naguib Mahfouz's Cairo Trilogy, the magnum opus of this Nobel Prize Laureate (1911–2006).[1] The literary scholar Sabry Hafez calls Mahfouz's Trilogy "the patriarchal novel par excellence," pointing out that its hero, the charismatic al-Sayyid Ahmad, "is both the father of the family and the pivot of the narrative world. From his loins all the protagonists emerge, and from his social and business activities other characters are brought into being. He is the prime mover of the text and the source of its life and every character in the novel is hierarchically placed in relation to him. Narrative structure, characters' motivation and spatial presentation are all mobilized to reflect and enforce the patriarchal order."[2]

Mahfouz's Trilogy was written in the 1950s, spanning the period between 1917 and 1944 in three voluminous parts. It provides an intimate portrait of father-son relations over three generations of an Egyptian family against the background of a society in transition from British colonial rule to independence and modern statehood, thus illuminating the connection between the psychosocial and the political factors, as well as between the personal and national levels. In the first volume of the Trilogy, the patriarch is depicted as the absolute authority in the family. He rules over his wife and children with a heavy hand, severely punishing any form of disobedience. He prays and fasts as ardently as he drinks alcohol and commits adultery, compartmentalizing his sin and devotion. This duality is a central theme of the narrative, as the patriarch "enforces puritanical discipline in his home, indulges his large appetites for wine, women, and song on his houseboat, and prays in the mosque, all with equal intensity."[3] His veiled and secluded wife Amina is confined to the domestic domain, where she dutifully fulfills the traditional roles of homemaker and mother. "It had occurred to her once, during the first year she lived with him, to venture a polite objection to his repeated nights out. His response had been to seize her by the ears and tell her peremptorily in a loud voice, 'I'm a man. I'm the one who commands and forbids. I will not accept any criticism of my behavior. All I ask of you is to obey me. Don't force me to discipline you'" (1:4). Since she lacks intimacy and companionship with her husband, she turns to her children to satisfy her emotional needs. The sons, Yasin (the patriarch's eldest son by his former wife), Fahmy, and Kamal, though different individuals with different personalities, are united in their overwhelming fear and awe of the father. A strict disciplinarian, al-Sayyid Ahmad beats Kamal with a stick and even threatens him with castration: "He had even made circumcision itself a means for terrifying the boy" (1:50). Criticizing his father in an interior monologue, Kamal says: "What have you done besides hurt and punish us with an ignorance your good intentions do nothing to excuse?...We've known you as a tyrannical dictator, a petulant despot" (2:372–73). Not surprisingly, each of the sons eventually rebels against the father. Yasin seeks self-gratification in sexual escapades, causing scandal after scandal; Fahmy secretly joins the struggle for national liberation from British occupation; and Kamal finds escape from the oppressive home atmosphere in reading books about science and philosophy, some of them regarded as heretical. These different rebellions have different outcomes for each son. Yasin settles down after his third marriage and his wild behavior improves, thanks to his wife, who tames him. More important, when he becomes a father, he does not want to replicate the patriarch's parenting style: "[He] had never wished to play the cruel role with [his children] that his own father had with him. The idea of creating in [his son's] heart the feelings of terror and fear he had felt for his own father was deeply abhorrent to Yasin" (3:53). Fahmy's life comes to a tragic end when he is killed in one of the demonstrations against the British, causing his father such a great grief that he suffers a stroke. Kamal becomes an intellectual who rejects the tenets of Islam and the values of traditional culture, bitterly criticizing the whole social order. However, since he has deeply internalized these values at the hands of his father, he remains a conflicted individual throughout his life. It is no accident that Kamal never marries and does not move out of his father's house, but rather continues to depend on his parents even while rejecting their values.[4]

The Trilogy succeeds in showing the gradual erosion of the patriarch's authority over time. In the beginning of the narrative, he is the undisputed master of the household. "The only word that counts here," he bluntly tells his rebellious son Fahmy, "is mine. Mine, mine, mine" (1:425). He condemns Fahmy's participation in the popular movement against the hated British, declaring that "he alone would set [his children's] course for them, not the revolution, the times, or the rest of humanity" (1:422). Forbidding his son to be involved in the national struggle for liberation, he equates political rebellion with a personal rebellion against him: "The revolution should rage on the outside.... But the house was his and his alone. Any member of his household who talked himself into participating in the revolution was in rebellion against him, not against the English" (1:422). This shows that he grasps the connection between national freedom and personal freedom and is anxious to prevent his son from breaking away from him. The great power he has over his household is tempered only by the British colonial authorities, who humiliate him by forcing him to do a period of hard labor. Toward the end of the narrative, some 25 years later, the patriarch is but a shadow of his former self. He has suffered a stroke followed by a relapse in the wake of Fahmy's death, and his partying ways have finally caught up with him. Old, frail, and bedridden, it is he who is now confined to the house and totally dependent on his spouse who, in turn, is free to come and go as she pleases. This reversal of fortunes softens the father: he becomes more tolerant, sympathetic, and understanding. His death leaves a huge void in the lives of his wife and sons, who feel adrift without his guiding hand. Mourning over his father's passing, Kamal says: "How I feared him when I was young...but in his later years he revealed to me a totally different person, indeed a beloved friend. How witty, tender, and gracious he was...unlike any other man" (3:212). The narrative's focus then shifts to the third generation—the patriarch's grandsons, two of whom become revolutionaries, one a Communist and the other a Muslim Brother, and a third uses his charms to seduce an elderly Pasha and becomes a prominent figure in a right-wing monarchist party. Importantly, all the grandsons receive a more lenient upbringing from their fathers and their ties with them are markedly more relaxed and amicable than those of their fathers with the patriarch. Furthermore, the views they espouse about religion, politics, career choices, and marriage partners contrast sharply with those of their parents. Thus the passage of time, along with the societal changes it brings about, fragments the power of the patriarch—the Trilogy's very symbol of masculinity—and transforms the dynamics of interaction within the family.

The essence of the conflict between fathers and sons, as well as the connection between national and personal liberation, is captured in a revealing conversation between al-Sayyid Ahmad and his close friends. When the patriarch expresses his admiration for bygone times, they tease him:

"You're a reactionary. You always try to cling to the past....Don't
you insist on ruling your home by fiat and force, even in the age of
democracy and parliament?" Al-Sayyid Ahmad replied scornfully,
"Democracy's for the people, not the family." Ali Abd al-Rahim said
seriously, "Do you think you can rule the young people of today in the
old-fashioned way? These youngsters are used to demonstrating in the
streets and confronting the [British] soldiers." (2:398)

Mahfouz suggests that forces of repression are in constant struggle
with forces of freedom, be they in the family or in the wider society.
This struggle shapes not only the relations between the patriarch and
his sons but also between the Egyptian people and their rulers, be
they foreign or native.

The Authoritarian Father: Yusuf Idris's "The Journey"

"The Journey" by Yusuf Idris (1927–91), one of the most influential
and innovative short story writers in the Arab world, takes the form of
a monologue and uses the stream-of-consciousness technique.[5]
The narrative opens with a confession of love to a man. In the
beginning it is not clear who the speaker is, and the reader is tempted
to think that it is a woman addressing her lover. Only later, as the
monologue unfolds, does the reader discover that it is a son talking
to his father. The son tells his father about a secret journey that they
are going to undertake. He carefully dresses his father, helps him get
into the elevator, and then takes him to his car. Then they set off.
The son is elated at the presence of the father in the car. He reveals
all his feelings toward him and lapses into flashbacks of his childhood. Curiously, wherever they stop, people stare at them in terror
and complain of a terrible smell; they point at the father and scream of
a corpse. The son is so happy that he does not smell anything. Then,
little by little, he becomes aware of the stench. At first he ignores it
and attempts to continue the ride anyway, but later it gets so strong
that he is unable to put up with it any longer. Exhausted, he pulls up
and abandons the car on the roadside, with his father in it. Then he
continues the journey by himself.
From a psychoanalytic perspective, "The Journey" depicts a son
with a neurotic disturbance narrating a fantasy about his father. In
this fantasy, the existential aspect, in which there are some normal
elements, is interwoven with the sexual aspect, which is aberrant. The
first indication of its being aberrant is the fact that no woman at all

is mentioned in the fantasy, not a mother, sister, or even a girlfriend. The son talks about his brothers, but no reference is made to any female. What is being described in the text suggests an incestuous relationship of the son with his father. The son takes his father to the car, which serves as the setting for his activity, and has intercourse with him. Immediately afterward he is filled with a strong sense of shame and guilt—this is when he starts smelling the terrible stench. He then runs away from the scene of the crime, leaving his father buried in the car as in a grave.

Numerous clues in the story support this interpretation. In the beginning there is an intimate and erotic description of the father by the son: his clothes, his physique. The son touches the father, dresses him, and brushes his hair, constantly uttering reassuring words: "Don't be afraid. We'll set off immediately, far, far away, where no one will get either you or me....Don't be afraid, I've taken all the necessary precautions. Don't worry, everything will turn out as we want."[6] Another erotic description follows when the son recalls how he used to greet his father when he came home from work. Together with his brothers (there is no mention of a female figure) he would massage his father's toes, but he alone would attend to the *big toe*. In psychoanalysis the big toe is a phallic symbol.[7]

Then the son reveals how much he loved physical contact with his father, often faking sleep in order to be carried in his arms. Within traditional psychoanalytic theory, this is considered a normal feeling with a child if he also has emotional contact with his father, if he has tender loving care and understanding. In such a case, the child will develop normally. But if physical touch is the only contact between father and son, and the father is a harsh, strict, and tyrannical figure, then the development of the son's libido is likely to suffer a neurotic disturbance, and this may later manifest itself in homosexual tendencies.[8]

The father in this story is exactly this type of oppressive figure. The son confesses that he was the only person in the world that he deeply feared. The father always argued with him and forced his opinions on him. Among other things, he didn't let his son smoke. In psychoanalysis, smoking is an important symbol for sex.[9] Inevitably, the son develops a rebellious spirit. He hates his father and at the same time he loves him very much. Such ambivalent feelings of love and hatred are distinctive signs of a neurotic disturbance.[10]

It should be noted that critics of traditional psychoanalytic theory argue that Freud focused on the *psychical* origin of homosexuality and failed to consider the *organic* factor in it. Some theorists regard

homosexuality as biologically determined, others as a social construction. The issue of "nature versus nurture" surrounding this topic has
not been resolved and continues to be hotly debated. The psychologist James Harrison advocates adopting a "both-and" rather than an
"either-or" approach: "The determinants [of homosexuality] for any
individual are likely to be an idiosyncratic mixture of various biological, cultural, and learning components."[11] In his view, the either-or
debate takes attention away from the more productive exploration of
the complexity and diversity of human existence.

   Given that nowadays traditional Freudian theory of homosexuality is considered outdated and controversial, the question that arises
is: Why does Idris draw on it to depict the son's behavior? The most
plausible answer is that he does so in order to *pathologize* the relationship between father and son. Indeed, the depiction of a disturbed
father-son relationship as the underlying cause of the son's homosexuality is crucial for the story's message. As a physician by training,
Idris's approach is medical-diagnostic, and he deliberately portrays
the son's sexual orientation as a "developmental arrest" or "sickness"
rather than as human difference in order to expose the "ills" of his
society.[12]

   The son, then, takes all the necessary precautions and finally succeeds in getting his father into his car—the vehicle that dominates
the narrative. Automobile symbolism, as studied by psychoanalysis,
appears frequently in dreams and fantasies and has a wide range of
meanings, mostly sexual. The British psychiatrist Charles Rycroft
explains: "Automobiles…are powerful machines rather obviously
capable of being used as phallic symbols.…I suspect that the relationship between a driver and his automobile has replaced the pla-
tonic image of the rider and his horse as the most apt and most used
metaphor for expressing the great variety of relationships that can
exist between a person and his passions."[13] Rycroft notes that "the
fact that cars are designed to have more than one occupant makes
automobile symbolism available for expressing ideas about the dreamer's relationship to those 'internalized' figures who may be experienced as disapproving or encouraging." He further points out that
"automobiles…often seem to represent the idea of a potency which
has been acquired inauthentically, the dreamer arrogating to himself
potency which in fact belongs to the car…so that he appears to be
active and dynamic when in fact he is being passive."[14]

   These comments are all applicable to "The Journey." The sexual
overtones of the car ride in the narrative cannot be overlooked. They
are apparent in the passionate confessions of love and exclamations of

tremendous pleasure uttered by the son. The son feels so high he can almost fly. In the car, all the disagreements and arguments between father and son vanish, and they become one, completely united. The car is their island. People surround them with hostility because they do not approve of such an act—incest. It is pathological and against the moral code. They threaten them, they want to drown them, devour them. The policeman, like the traffic light, is a symbol of the social order. It is his job to keep order, and he is suspicious. He takes a sniff at the air and almost discovers the truth, but in the end the son manages to deceive him.

All along, the son fears the end. Apparently he has been there before. The beginning is the best part, the end is the worst. The sobering up after the sexual experience, filled with a sense of shame, guilt, and remorse, is shattering. Suddenly the fear of the consequences becomes a fear for his life. He panics and runs away, leaving his father behind. In his flight there is pain, but also a sense of relief. He is free now…until the next time.

At a deeper level, "The Journey" is a story of strong social and political criticism. Idris points out the generation gap: the son belongs to the generation of the car and of freedom, whereas the father belongs to the generation of the train and of slavery. The society described is patriarchal; the authoritarian figure of the father serves as its representative. Significantly, the story was first published in June 1970—the third anniversary of the Six-Day War with Israel, which ended in a humiliating Arab defeat. The main attack is on Nasser, who, in spite of the calamity of the war which he brought on Egypt, remained in power.[15] Nasser is represented by the father in the story, the powerful patriarch who has total control over his son. The oppressed son represents Egypt or the Egyptian people. The message is that Nasser brings death to them, the stench of a decaying corpse. He wears a *red* tie, an indication of his strong affiliation with the then Soviet Union. The relationship between father and son, which has known some tender and affectionate moments, gradually develops a morbid pattern. It takes the son a long time to realize that there is something wrong with his father, namely, to sense the stench. At first he even denies there is a stench, and only after it almost suffocates him does he realize that he must get rid of its source, or else die. There is simply no other choice. The father's life must come to an end so that his own life can begin, and, however painful, this end is inevitable. So he buries his father in the car and runs away, breathing the fresh air with a new sense of freedom.

That Idris was one of Nasser's opponents is well known. As a staunch supporter of social change, he initially stood by the revolutionary and charismatic figure of Nasser, the "father" of the Egyptian republic. However, the pace and direction of the revolution brought him into conflict with this much-admired leader. In 1954 Idris was arrested and imprisoned for one year, apparently for his open sympathy and involvement with the extreme left. The Six-Day War of 1967 caused a final break with Nasser, whom he viewed as responsible for the Egyptian debacle. In 1969 Idris wrote the play *The Striped Ones (Al-Mukhattatin)*, which was banned by the censor on account of its biting criticism of Nasser's regime. Following the publication of "The Journey" in *Al-Ahram*, Idris was fired from his post with the newspaper, but was later reinstated, thanks to Sadat. For better or worse, Nasser had, by Idris's own account, always been a source of inspiration for him.

What gives "The Journey" its Arab coloring is the name *Abdallah*. Abdallah is the doorman who helps the son get his father into the car. It is the only name mentioned in the story, therefore it is significant. *Abdallah* means "the servant of God." Why would Idris give the only name in the narrative to the doorman, and of all common Arab names choose this one, with its religious connotation? The answer is that he probably did so to create Koranic allusions.

In the Koran, the theme of the Day of Judgment occupies a central place. On the Day of Judgment, all the dead will be resurrected and brought before the Almighty to stand trial. The righteous will be rewarded; the evildoers will be punished. God's servants, the angels, will assist him in conducting the trials.

In Idris's story, the dead father is resurrected. He is dressed up, moved out of his abode, and taken on a journey. The journey is the trial. At the end of it he is found guilty and sentenced to doom. This is when he is dumped in the car.

Surat Qaf in the Koran, which deals with the Day of Judgment, says: "And the trumpet is blown. This is the threatened Day. And every soul cometh, along with it a *driver* and a *witness*" (50:20–21); "The day when they will hear the (Awful) Cry in truth. That is the day of coming forth (from the graves). Lo! We it is Who quicken and give death, and unto Us is the *journeying*" (50:42–43).[16]

The words *driver, witness,* and *journeying* are significant. In Idris's story the son serves as his father's driver. He takes him on a journey. All along the way they encounter witnesses who raise an accusing finger at the father. This is the day of reckoning.

Thus Idris's journey takes place at four levels: the personal, the psychological, the sociopolitical, and the religious. These are skillfully layered one beneath the other. As a result, Idris manages not only to explore the complex motivation that underlies human behavior but also to reveal his shrewd understanding of his society and its changing values.

The Martyr Father: Yahya Haqqi's *The Saint's Lamp*

The image of the father as a "martyr" to his sense of duty and devotion to his son features prominently in *The Saint's Lamp*, a novella by the pioneering Egyptian fiction writer Yahya Haqqi (1905–92).[17] In this narrative the protagonist, Ismail, is the focus of his family's life: "Only when Ismail went to bed would the whole family feel that their day was over and begin thinking about his needs for the morrow. The life of the whole family, their every movement, was aimed at providing for his comfort; a whole generation was wasting itself so that one single individual might have the chance to develop" (p. 3). The father, a small shopkeeper in the vicinity of al-Sayyida Zaynab (Umm Hashim) mosque in Cairo, spares no effort to give his son a good education. Pinning all his ambitions on Ismail, he sends him to a government school with the hope that he will graduate with high grades that will allow him to enter the Faculty of Medicine. However, Ismail does poorly on his final examinations and finds the doors of this faculty closed to him.

The father's acquaintances expect that he will be satisfied with the amount of education that his son has received and will now try to get him a job that will relieve him of the need to support him and thus lighten his burden. But they are mistaken. The father is so determined to fulfill his son's—and his own—dream that he goes around asking for advice and is told to send his son to study abroad. This solution presents him with a tough dilemma. First, he does not know if he can finance his son's travel, tuition, and living expenses abroad for several years. It would mean that the rest of the family would have to live in deprivation. Second, the father wonders whether he or his wife can bear parting from their beloved son for such a long time. In the end, he decides that his son's future comes first and foremost. He raises all the money he can, and the mother sells her jewelry, and with the proceeds they pay for their son's travel abroad. Ismail goes to England, where he stays for seven years and studies medicine without any financial worries. He is so self-absorbed that he never bothers to ask his father where the money comes from. In fact, "although [the father's] financial resources had dwindled he still regularly deposited in the bank the necessary money for his son. He never mentioned his troubles to his son or wrote to him to ask him to hurry with his studies and come home" (p. 24). He tenaciously bears his hardships, displaying total self-sacrifice and self-denial for his son's sake.

The father is finally rewarded for his efforts when Ismail returns home as an eye doctor. He receives his son "with a quiet smile on his face. He had gone grey, but his back was still straight. In his eyes there was a look that denoted a mixture of patience and exhaustion, of an easy conscience and with it the awareness of bearing a heavy burden" (p. 24). However, Ismail's homecoming soon turns into a family crisis. During his stay in England he has come under the influence of Western culture and science, and his view of traditional Arab culture and values has changed. He is unable to reconcile himself to the ignorance, superstitions, and crude customs of his family members and the people of his quarter. When he sees that his mother treats the eyes of his cousin Fatima, who suffers from trachoma, with oil from the lamp in Umm Hashim's mosque, he is outraged. He snatches the bottle and smashes it, then goes to the mosque and smashes the lamp, only to be attacked by the angry crowd of worshipers, and narrowly escapes with his life. And so, on the night of his arrival, instead of rejoicing and celebrating his homecoming, the family assembles around him to mourn the loss of his reason: "The mother beat her face from grief, the father moaned and suppressed his anger and pain" (p. 30). In the following days, Ismail's parents avoid him and cease to object to the things he does, fearing for his health. Eventually, Ismail finds a compromise between modern science and religious faith, which allows him to restore his equilibrium and return to practice medicine. He marries his cousin Fatima, who bears him 11 children, and dedicates his life to the treatment of poor patients from the city and the village. This *Bildungsroman*, or novel of apprenticeship, ends on a positive note with the protagonist finding his place and role in the world.

The image of the father as a martyr is depicted with wry humor in a vignette titled "Dialogue" by Naguib Mahfouz. In this short text, the father returns home and finds his sons waiting for him. He sullenly takes out his wallet and mutters, "The father in this age of ours is a martyr." The sons say nothing. Then they disperse in the manner that martyrs do.[18] This cameo portrait captures the weakening of family ties in contemporary Arab society, a transformation that is a feature of modern life and that is in sharp contrast to how family ties used to be in the past. In this vignette, the only reason the sons go to see their father is that they are hard up for money. They have no intention of spending time with him: their visit is brief and utilitarian. The father, who guesses why they have come, does not rejoice at their sight. He sees himself as a martyr to his sense of responsibility toward his sons and as being saddled with a never-ending obligation to support them. The manner in which they part, that is, as "martyrs," suggests that they do not expect to see each other again. Ironically, while the text is titled "Dialogue," there is no conversation at all between the father and his sons and no demonstration of love or affection. This may well suggest that their ties are loose or distant.

The Alienated Father: Zakaria Tamer's "The Family"

The fictional world of Zakaria Tamer (b. 1929), one of Syria's most prominent short story writers, is one in which the normal logic of life and reality is absent. In "The Family,"[19] the protagonist, Abdullah, goes home to discover that he cannot enter his house because he does not have the key, that the woman who opens the door for him does not look at all like his wife, that his grown up son and daughter squabble about a ball like little children, that his son brutally kills his sister in a fit of rage, and that his slain daughter suddenly opens her eyes and begins to laugh at him. Shocked and disoriented, he collapses on the floor and closes his eyes, only to hear voices whispering:

> "He died and has brought peace to himself and to others."
> He heard his son say: "He's left us nothing but debts."
> He heard his daughter say: "What shall we do now?"
> He heard his wife say: "We must hurry up and bury him."
> He heard his son say: "I'll dig a grave." (p. 36)

Sobbing silently, Abdullah does not resist when he is wrapped in a shroud and placed in a grave: "He did not attempt to call for help but gave himself up to the earth which, dark and heavy, was piled upon him" (p. 36).

This narrative recounts a nightmare of profound personal alienation. The father, Abdullah, suffers from a severe identity crisis. He goes home hoping that there, amid his family, he will find his real self and sense of belonging. The fact that he gives "a sigh of relief" when he reaches his house indicates that he is in a state of anxiety and distress. However, he is unable to find the key to open the door, unable to recognize his wife, and unable to control his children—all clues indicating that he fails to regain his sense of identity and belonging

at home. The family, which is supposed to be a haven of peace and
safety, turns out to be a dysfunctional unit, uncaring, conflicted, and
all the more alienating. The disintegration of family ties and values is
reflected in the senseless slaying of the daughter by the son, the disobedience and disrespect that both of them show toward the father,
and the indifference displayed by the mother. Abdullah's desperation
increases when he realizes that he has no authority and no role to play
in his family. Isolated and emasculated, he withdraws into himself
and disengages from his surroundings. His death comes as a relief
to himself—and to his family members. No one mourns over him.
The son's final words, "He's left us nothing but debts" and "I'll dig
a grave," are devoid of sympathy or affection for the father. Tamer's
style of combining elements of dream with reality, innocence with
madness, and satire with tragedy is highly effective in demonstrating that, in the words of Ibrahim Muhawi, "there is a malaise at the
core of the traditional Arab psyche, perhaps at the core of Arab culture itself, that accounts for the aberrant behavior of many of [his]
characters."[20] When the atom of society—the individual—is dysfunctional, so is the society at large.

The Failed Father: Fathy Ghanem's *The Man Who Lost His Shadow*

The character of the "failed" father is a salient feature of male-
authored narratives of childhood and coming-of-age. Most often, the
father's failure is depicted in socioeconomic terms: he can't provide
for his family and can't protect them; he is lazy, weak, corrupt, unreliable, or incompetent; he has a weakness for women, drugs, or alcohol.
However, even wealthy fathers may be portrayed as failures if they
neglect their sons and deny them the emotional support and guidance that they need as children.[21]

The "failed" father figures prominently in *The Man Who Lost His
Shadow* by the Egyptian novelist Fathy Ghanem (1924–98).[22] The
novel consists of four parts narrated by four different characters, two
women and two men, each of whom describes the events from his or
her point of view. The last of the four—and the hero of the novel—is
Yusuf Abd al-Hamid, a young and ambitious Cairene journalist. He
is first seen through the eyes of Mabruka, the peasant servant girl
who marries his widowed father, then through the eyes of his mis-
tress Samia, an aspiring film actress whom he rejects, then through
the eyes of Muhammad Nagi, the aging editor of the daily newspaper
Al-Ayyam, whom he ousts from his post, and lastly Yusuf tells his own

story as he sees it. The narrative of each member of this quartet elaborates on the information provided by the others. This technique of
multiple narrators or viewpoints, new to Arabic writing at the time, is
considered Ghanem's major contribution to the Arabic novel.

The novel offers a panoramic view of Egyptian society from shortly
before World War II until a few years after the Egyptian revolution of
1952, addressing issues such as poverty, prostitution, illiteracy, corruption, opportunism, and abuse of power. The novel's intriguing
title suggests that the hero has lost his real self—his innocence, identity, and moral integrity—in the relentless pursuit of his ambitions. As
Yusuf admits in a moment of truth, "How was it I grew up, acquired
knowledge, fame and fortune, yet lost myself?" (p. 238).

Yusuf's troubled relationship with his father begins as a little boy.
The only child of Abd al-Hamid Effendi, a poor primary schoolteacher, he is deeply attached to his mother, who is gentle, doting,
and loving, and resentful of his father, who is cold, distant, and stern.
His childhood is marked by isolation and deprivation: his father forbids him, as the son of a teacher, to mix with the children of the
neighborhood, saying that they lack "breeding or manners" (p. 242).
A revealing scene in the narrative is that of Yusuf peering secretly
from the window of his apartment at children playing in the street
and imagining that he is one of them (p. 243). The father also forbids
him to buy sweets or snacks from street vendors, telling him that
these foods are poisonous. Filled with anxieties and phobias, Yusuf
is taught to look up to the Ratebs, his father's rich and aristocratic
distant relatives, as his ideal.

Abd al-Hamid Effendi is impatient with his timid and introverted
son and uses derogatory names to scold and humiliate him: "You're
behaving like a donkey" (p. 241); "Don't stand there like a lump of
wood" (p. 263); "When we got home my father told my mother that
her son had behaved like a girl and had disgraced him" (p. 241). Yusuf
submits to his father's authority and does not defy him, except when
he mistreats the mother: "If my father spoke coldly to my mother,
I'd scream: 'You're terrible, Father. I don't love you'" (p. 239). He
begrudges the father for not being at home the day he was born,
regarding his absence as a sign of rejection and disapproval.

Yusuf becomes motherless at the young age of nine when his
mother suddenly dies of a heart attack. The loss of the mother leaves
father and son alone in their apartment for many years. However, they
do not develop close ties and their relationship remains distant and
shallow. The older Yusuf grows, the more aware—and ashamed—
he becomes of his father's poverty and lowly position, especially in

relation to the rich Ratebs, whose son Medhat the father tutors to supplement his meager income. As a student at the College of Law, Yusuf looks down on his father after seeing the company he keeps and the squalid café he frequents: "The place reeked of drink and the lavatory. A midget called Mikhaili served the drinks. It was a disgusting place. My father was the familiar of these degraded people, some of them alcoholics, all of them vulgar" (p. 271). Yusuf's view of his father as an all-time loser is reinforced when he learns that his grandfather owned an estate but lost a law case with the government for failure to pay the tax. His lawyer was no other than Saad Zaghloul, who later became the leader of the nationalist movement, and the documents, which were written in his handwriting and had a historical and financial value, were carelessly kept by his father in a biscuit tin, where the mice might get them (p. 271).

The breakup between father and son comes after Abd al-Hamid Effendi retires as a schoolteacher and takes Mabruka, a servant in the Ratebs' household, to work for them. Although Yusuf feels sexually attracted to the young maid and desires her, he is reluctant to cross the social boundaries between them. His lonely and aging father, on the other hand, becomes infatuated with the maid and has an affair with her. He is so jealous of his son's youth that he is afraid to leave her alone with him (p. 40). When Mabruka becomes pregnant he feels obligated to marry her, against the objections of Yusuf, who considers his father's marriage to a peasant servant girl a shameful scandal that can ruin his name and future. In protest, Yusuf moves out of his father's apartment, viewing himself as "hopeless, penniless, fatherless, motherless" (p. 286). While he despises his father for his disgraceful conduct, he acknowledges that he was too self-absorbed to notice the major changes in his father's life: "I failed to see that he was desperately lonely, that his world had collapsed, that he felt useless and old. He was, I now realize, screaming for help. And no one helped him" (p. 273). The remorseful father begs Yusuf to return home, saying: "I'm still your father. If I've done wrong, you become the father, but stay with me" (p. 289). Yusuf refuses, flatly rejecting his father. His mind is set: "I resolved I would be what my humble father had never managed to be. I would rise above poverty, tittle-tattle, scandal; to be Yusuf Bey, Yusuf Pasha—no £3 a month for me!" (p. 299). As it happens, he finds a job as a crime reporter for the daily newspaper *Al-Ayyam*, where he quickly becomes the protégé of Muhammad Nagi Bey, the editor in chief, whom he eventually replaces.

Nagi Bey is everything the father is not: rich, famous, influential. As a symbol of the successful man, he serves as a counterpoint to the pathetic figure of Abd al-Hamid Effendi. Yusuf regards Nagi Bey as a "noble warrior" (p. 297) who lives "like a king" (p. 301) and frequents the palace, in contrast to his father, whose haunt is "the abode of derelicts and drunkards" (p. 271). He looks up to him as his role model and mentor. As for Nagi Bey, he sees in Yusuf an ally in his world of social and political intrigue and becomes his guide, advising him about every aspect of his life, from his career to his friends to his love affairs. Yusuf, who is eager to avoid all the mistakes his father made, especially that of marrying the wrong woman (Mabruka), takes Nagi Bey's advice seriously and rejects the woman he loves, Samia.

The similarity between the fate of Mabruka and Samia on the one hand, and between the demise of Nagi Bey and Abd al-Hamid Effendi on the other hand, is striking. As Fatma Moussa-Mahmoud notes: "Nagi stands as a father-figure to Yusuf. He is the father whom Yusuf denies as he denied his own father. He marries Samia, the girl whom Yusuf should have married. He is obliged to do so when he discovers that she is with child, just as Yusuf's father did with Mabruka. It is part of the bitter theme of the quartet that the two women desired by Yusuf are finally married to the two spent old men, who stand in a position of father to the hero, one his real father and the other his tutor and chief."[23] Both Abd al-Hamid Effendi and Nagi Bey die of a sudden heart attack induced by the stressful circumstances of their lives.

In the relentless pursuit of his ambitions, Yusuf destroys the lives of the other three characters. A ruthless social climber, he steps over "the dead bodies of kin and foe" to attain his goal.[24] In the end, he discovers that life at the top is lonely and dreary. His concluding words reveal that he has achieved a measure of self-knowledge: "To my woe, to my joy. I know that I'm a child. My words are the words of a child. Now I know! It was the child who taught me. Because he's remained with me. He didn't go, he didn't desert me. My darling child, Yusuf Abdul Hamid: You were hidden, you mischievous child, inside me" (p. 352).

Living Vicariously: Mu'nis al-Razzaz's "Abu Richard"

The short story "Abu Richard,"[25] by the Jordanian fiction writer Mu'nis al-Razzaz (1951–2002), is a compelling portrait of a father and son who live vicariously through each other. The story consists of two scenes. The first scene depicts the father, who has a paralyzed leg, the result of a wound he suffered while fighting with the

Jordanian army in the 1948 Arab war, sitting with a friend on the pavement of a deserted alleyway. He can't talk about anything else except his son Rashad. Boasting that he is a medical student at George Washington University, he expects him to graduate soon and return home as a qualified doctor to cure his leg. The friend tries to disabuse Abu Rashad of his false expectations, telling him bluntly: "I don't reckon Rashad's coming home at all. He left nine years ago and he's never once been back or even written home" (p. 149). But Abu Rashad continues to fantasize about his son, describing every aspect of his life, until the friend angrily yells at him: "You are nothing but a day-dreamer. You don't live your own life; you're living Rashad's. You get on my nerves. You never stop telling me about Rashad's life, as if you were his shadow: studying, eating, sleeping, you tag along with him like a ghost" (p. 149). The friend advises Abu Rashad to stop living his son's life and focus on the present and his own reality. But Abu Rashad refuses, saying: "I live in the future. I loathe and detest the present" (p. 151).

The second scene in the story depicts the son, Rashad, in the United States, in the company of a hippy girl, completely stoned. The girl tries to talk some sense into him: "Look, Richard, you are far too heavily into drugs, and you go on far too much about what a hero your father used to be, way back" (p. 151). The irony of the situation is heightened by the fact that the failed son, much like the father, is desperately trying to escape from the present. His escape is twofold: first through drugs, and second through reveries about his father's heroism in the 1948 Arab war. However, unlike the father, who escapes into the future, the son escapes into the past. As his girlfriend rebukes him: "You are living in the past, Richard! It wouldn't be so bad if it was your own past. But it's your father's past" (p. 152). In this cameo portrait, both father and son are captives of their expectations of each other: while the father lives with the ghost of his son, the would-be great doctor, the son lives with the ghost of his father, the had-been great fighter. As a result, they can't face reality—or each other.

Child Neglect: Alaa al-Aswany's
The Yacoubian Building

The father may be an educated, successful, and wealthy man who provides his son with all the comforts of life, and yet the son may regard him as "deficient" and "failed" if he does not meet his emotional needs for attention, affection, and guidance. In *The Yacoubian*

Building,[26] by the Egyptian novelist Alaa al-Aswany (b. 1957), Hatim Rasheed, one of the major characters, complains of child neglect and lack of paternal supervision and tender loving care. The novel is set in one of Cairo's main boulevards, where its namesake was built. Each of the inhabitants of the building, from the poor squatters on the roof to the ruthless businessman whose stores occupy the ground floor to the impoverished aristocrat and the frustrated pious son of the building's doorkeeper, embodies a facet of Egyptian society. Hatim, who is an intellectual and editor in chief of the French-language newspaper *Le Caire*, is gay. The only son of a French mother of humble origins and an Egyptian father who was a great scholar and dean of the College of Law in the 1950s, Hatim blames his parents, especially his father, for his homosexuality. He believes that his sexual orientation is the result of his flawed upbringing, which was marked by emotional deprivation and lack of supervision and guidance. His recollections of his father are filled with anger and resentment:

> He would say to himself that if they had made a little time to look after him, he would never have sunk this low but they were preoccupied with their professional ambitions and had devoted themselves to achieving wealth and glory so they left him and his body to the servants to play around with. He never blames Idris [his servant] or doubts for one moment that he loved him truly but he longs to see his father, Dr. Hassan Rasheed, rise from his grave just once so that he can tell him what he thinks of him....He wouldn't be afraid of him at all and he would say to him, "Great scholar, since you'd dedicated your life to civil law, why did you get married and have children? You may have been a genius at law but you certainly didn't know how to be a real father. How many times in your life did you kiss me? How many times did you sit down with me so that I could tell you about my problems? You always treated me as though I were a rare art object or painting you'd acquired because it had taken your fancy; then you'd forgotten about it, and from time to time, when your crowded work schedule permitted, you'd remember it, look at it for a while, and then forget about it again." (p. 181)

Hatim's explanation of his homosexuality fits in with traditional Freudian theory and echoes Yusuf Idris's account of the son's homosexuality in "The Journey." By attributing his failure to achieve manhood, as defined by the traditional code of Arab masculinity, to a disturbed father-son relationship, Hatim highlights his total victimization on the one hand, and his inability to assume personal responsibility on the other hand.

Hatim has no fond memories of his mother either. He feels deep contempt for her as an unfit mother, an ungrateful wife, and a woman of loose morals:

> You were just a barmaid at a small bar in the Latin Quarter. You were poor and uneducated and your marriage to my father was a bigger social leap than you'd ever dreamed of. Despite this, you spent the next thirty years despising my father and blackmailing him because he was Egyptian and you were French. You played the role of the cultured European among the savages. You kept grumbling about Egypt and the Egyptians and treating everybody coldly and haughtily. Your neglect of me was part of your hatred for Egypt. I think you were unfaithful to my father more than once; in fact I'm sure of it…You were just a whore like the ones anyone could catch by the dozen in the bars of Paris simply by sticking out his hand. (pp. 181–82)

While Hatim condemns his mother for being immoral, he himself shows no scruples in his own pursuit of pleasure and sexual gratification. He exploits the poverty of Abduh, an unemployed and uneducated young man with a wife and a child, to turn him into his sexual toy. When Abduh decides to leave him and return to his wife, Hatim refuses to let him go, hurling threats and abuse at him. Enraged, Abduh loses his self-control and attacks him, beating him to death. Hatim's sordid end shows that the neglect and abuse that he endured as a child have impaired his moral judgment, his functioning, and his ability to manage his life.

Child Sacrifice: Yusuf al-Qa'id's *War in the Land of Egypt*

War in the Land of Egypt,[27] by the Egyptian novelist Yusuf al-Qa'id (b. 1944), is set in the Egyptian countryside, where the author was born and raised. The narrative unfolds against the backdrop of the 1973 October war with Israel. It is told by six characters (the umda, the broker, the night watchman, the friend, the officer, and the investigator), each of whom tells part of the story, rather than all of it, in a monologue. This modified use of the technique of multiple narrators (or viewpoints) enhances the story's dramatic impact by eliminating repetition and creating suspense in the progression of the plot.[28] A young man has been drafted into the army. His father, the umda (village mayor), persuades a poor night watchman to send his own son as a substitute. The impersonation plan goes horribly wrong when the night watchman's son is killed in action and the deception discovered. The police launch an investigation to determine who should bury the body and receive the death benefits, but the investigation is stopped on orders from a top government official.

There are two sets of father-son relationships in the narrative. The first is that of the umda with his son. The umda is a rich landowner who has three wives and five sons. The one who was called up for military service is his youngest, by his third, newest wife. The umda has a low opinion of this son, a spoiled boy and an utter failure who has not even earned his preparatory school certificate. When the call-up papers for this son arrive, the umda feels conflicted: "On the one hand I wanted my son to go into the army and learn some discipline. How much longer was he going to be pampered? I wouldn't be around to look after him for his whole life; one day he'd have to fend for himself. Yet on the other hand I couldn't bear to think of being parted from him, even for a day" (p. 11). The real reason for the umda's dilemma is that he cannot have any more children. He fell ill after this boy was born, and the doctors had to remove his prostate. As a result of the operation, the umda became impotent, a predicament that he was determined to keep secret at all costs: "Loss of the prostate meant loss of my manhood, and if the people in the village got wind of it they might say I was no longer fit to be their umda, because the umda has to be a complete man" (pp. 11–12). The only person who knows this secret is his third wife, in whose room he sleeps every night. The son in question is her only child, and the umda fears that she will disclose his secret if he lets him be taken away from her and sent to the front, where he might be killed. With the help of the broker, a petty criminal known for fixing other peoples' problems by means of bribery or forgery, the umda talks the retired night watchman into sending his son into the army in place of his own son.

The night watchman is a poor man who farms a small plot of land, the size of three feddans, which was confiscated from the umda under Nasser's Agrarian Reform of 1954. A new law passed by the Sadat regime decreed the restoration (within certain limits) of property nationalized under Nasser, and the night watchman, like many other poor peasants in the village, finds himself having to return the land he leased from the Land Reform Agency to its former owner, the umda. This spells disaster and ruin for the night watchman: without the land—his source of livelihood—he cannot support his large family, a wife and six children, who already live in abject poverty, having barely enough food and clothing. What is he to do?

The night watchman's son, the only character with a name in the narrative (but not a voice, for he is not one of the narrators), is called Masri. The name, which means "Egyptian," is symbolic, alluding to the multitude of peasants in the country. Known throughout the village for his intelligence and high grades at school, Masri is admired by everyone, including the umda, who feels jealous and frustrated, for the way life deals with people, "it gives the earring to the person with no ear" (p. 29), as a popular saying runs. Both the umda's son and the night watchman's son were born in the village on the same day, but because Masri is the only boy among five girls, he is exempt from military service.

The second father-son relationship in the narrative is that of the night watchman with Masri. Unlike the umda, who looks down on his youngest son and is exasperated with him, the night watchman looks up to his son in amazement, unable to explain his great talent. "How can a poor man's son be so brilliant?"; "Where does he get his intelligence?" (p. 88). Even Masri's mother is astonished, quoting the old saying, "It's a strange sight, a cake in an orphan's hand" (p. 88). The night watchman has great respect for education: "After all, education's the best thing there is, and people like me have always longed for one of our sons to come home one day as an educated man, an effendi" (p. 88). He quarrels with his son about his future, believing that the best job in the world is to be a primary teacher at the village school. But Masri has higher aspirations: he wants to graduate from the Faculty of Law or Arts. His dreams are shattered by his family's dire poverty. He cannot continue his studies, even though he has earned his preparatory school certificate with distinction, because his father cannot afford to send him to a secondary school, available only in the district town.

Giving up his education is the first sacrifice that Masri is required to make for his family's sake. He has to stay at home and help his father farm the land, which the night watchman believes will one day belong to them. "The land will be yours," he promises his son, "and that'll be compensation for not continuing your studies" (p. 90). A model of filial duty and obedience, Masri accepts his father's decision, but resolves to continue his studies independently at home. Then comes the blow of the new government's decree to restore the land to its former owner, the umda. The night watchman's dream of ever owning the land collapses, and his source of livelihood is threatened.

The corrupt umda offers the destitute night watchman an economic transaction: Masri will go to the army in place of his son and in return the night watchman can keep farming the land on a share-cropping basis. The emerging parallel between sons and land is striking. As Fedwa Malti-Douglas notes: "Land and sons are both related to fecundity: the umda will trade his land for his son because he cannot create another son—he is impotent."[29] Initially, the night watchman's response is to refuse: "Right from the start I didn't want to have anything to do with the whole thing, because the world and everything in it isn't worth the dust under Masri's feet, but as you can imagine, it wasn't easy to forget the umda's promises—especially about the land" (p. 91). Ultimately, hunger drives him to accept the hideous offer. As he admits: "I was hungry and the umda's offer meant bread to fill my mouth, and the mouths of all my family as well" (p. 91). Hunger is the night watchman's constant enemy: "All my life I've been hungry all day long: hungry for sleep, hungry for bread, hungry for clothing, hungry for rest— a lifetime of hunger. I tried to stop thinking about it but I just couldn't" (p. 86).

When the night watchman approaches his son about the umda's offer, he rejects it, but is pressured to agree. As he later confides in his close army friend:

> My father agreed to this—as a matter of fact the whole family was delighted with the bargain—but I refused to have anything to do with it. I wouldn't even discuss it. Anyway, the people in my village don't know what discussion means. The way my family looked at me, I knew they thought I was refusing to do it because I was too selfish to make a sacrifice. They couldn't even see why I should call it a sacrifice. We needed some way out. And then I thought, well, maybe we might find it if I accepted the offer and left the village—who knows?...So I agreed to go, but from that day I've been in a daze. (p. 108)

After a few months in the army, the October 1973 war against Israel breaks out, and Masri's unit is sent to the Canal Zone. By this time, he feels hopelessly trapped. "'Masri is lost,' he'd say" (p. 109). His feeling of despair stems from two reasons: first, he learns that the umda has not kept his promise to his father about the land and continues to exploit and oppress him; second, he realizes that he has lost his real self, his identity has been subsumed into that of the umda's son. Seeing no way out of his predicament, he volunteers to be in the front line and shortly afterward dies on the battlefield. Masri's final actions reveal that he came to the conclusion that only death can liberate him from this hellish trap. The fact that on his declaration for the army authorities he refused to name the beneficiary of payments owed to a fallen soldier and instead wrote the ambiguous words, "the legal heirs," suggests that he had ambivalent feelings toward his father, perhaps even resentment.

Masri's death leads to the discovery of the identity fraud. The police launch an investigation to determine who should be punished and who should bury Masri's body and receive his death benefits, but just when the investigation is about to be concluded it is stopped on orders from a top government official whose help the powerful umda has managed to enlist. In the end, Masri's father is denied his son's death benefits, which are awarded to the umda as the deceased's "legal heir." To prevent unrest in the village, the government authorities bury Masri's body in a secret location, thus denying his father even the comfort of going to his grave to perform the traditional rites. Altogether, Masri's sacrifice has been in vain: his family ends up without the land, without their only son, and without his death benefits.

Masri died a heroic death at the age of 24, his life cut short and his promise unfulfilled. His tragic story raises many questions about fate and free will (including the notion of socioeconomic determinism), the meaning of patriotism, and the limits of paternal authority and filial obedience. A comparison with the Koranic story of Abraham and Ishmael springs to mind. Surat al-Saffat recounts the story of Ishmael's binding: "We gave him news of a gentle son. And when he reached the age when he could work with him, his father said to him: 'My son, I dreamt that I was sacrificing you. Tell me what you think.' He replied: 'Father, do as you are bidden. God willing, you shall find me steadfast.' And when they had both submitted to God's will, and Abraham had laid down his son prostrate upon his face, We called out to him saying: 'Abraham, you have fulfilled your vision.' Thus do We reward the righteous. That was indeed a bitter test. We ransomed his son with a noble sacrifice and bestowed on him the praise of later generations" (37:101–105).[30] Like Ishmael, Masri is obedient and compliant, the perfect model of the perfect sacrifice. He gives his explicit consent to his father to sacrifice him. But unlike Ishamel, he is not ransomed in the last minute and is not rewarded with any blessing. The novel's ultimate question remains: For whose sake was Masri's life sacrificed? Was it for the sake of the rich, namely, the umda, or for the sake of his country and the Egyptian people?

War in the Land of Egypt is a novel of strong social criticism. Al-Qa'id exposes the ills of contemporary Egyptian society, from class divisions to the oppression of the poor by the rich to the corruption of government authorities and the incompetence of the bureaucracy. Not surprisingly, the novel was originally banned in Egypt: written in 1975, it was not published until 1978 in Beirut and 1985 in Egypt.

The Lost Father: Ibrahim al-Koni's *Anubis*

The novel *Anubis* is deeply rooted in Tuareg folklore and Ibrahim al-Koni's (b. 1948) childhood landscape, the Tuareg Libyan desert.[31] The Tuareg are pastoral nomads who live in the Sahara and speak Tamasheq, a Berber language also related to ancient Egyptian. Traditional Tuareg society is characterized by caste divisions between nobles, vassals, blacksmiths, and slaves. Tuareg men are famous for wearing veils. Women do not normally wear veils but have headscarves.[32]

The narrative is a modern retelling of the ancient Tuareg legend about Anubi, the archetypal son of an unknown father who sets out to search for that father and through this, his identity. The journey of the figure of the title, Anubis, through immense trackless desert to find the father he remembers only as a shadow from his childhood consists of a series of life-threatening tests and tribulations, including isolation, thirst, incest, patricide, animal metamorphosis, and human sacrifice. Tragically, Anubis unknowingly encounters his father and kills him. The cycle is then repeated as his own son starts following the selfsame path of searching for the father he does not know, and when he finally stumbles upon him he fails to recognize him and kills him.

Anubis's longing to find his father is awakened when he asks his mother where he came from. "Same as everyone," she replies. "From a mother and a father." He then asks, "You're my mother...Why don't I see my father nearby?" His mother says, "Because absence is the destiny of fathers" (p. 13). Anubis is troubled by his mother's prophecy and struggles to understand the meaning of her aphorisms: "The father wants to be worshiped, not loved" (p. 13), and "We worship fathers but love mothers" (p. 14). Gradually, the longing for his father turns into a passion and an obsession that keeps him from sleeping or eating, until he leaves his home and ventures into the desert to learn the truth. While some tribesmen advise him to "beware of searching for a father in the desert. This brings nothing but calamities" (p. 15), others admit that "it's futile to attempt to dissuade a man from something that is part of his destiny" (p. 15).

Anubis pays a costly price for his departure: he loses his mother. She sacrifices her life to liberate him from the reign of metamorphosis that transformed him into a creature with a gazelle's body and a man's head when he got lost in the desert and almost died, having saved himself by drinking the urine of a gazelle. Anubis resolves to avenge his mother's death by punishing the priest who shed her blood on the altar. When he finds him he kills him, only to be told later by his sister that the man he slayed was actually his father. Incredulous, Anubis asks, "How can I have searched for my father throughout the world when he was within arm's reach?" His sister replies, "All the things we search for in faraway places are actually within arm's reach" (p. 45). Shocked by this revelation, Anubis decides to flee at once from the tribe and roam through the desert. "Perhaps I could free myself from my destiny" (p. 47).

Anubis's tragedy calls to mind another famous myth, that of King Oedipus. The two legends have many features in common. Both heroes have unknowingly encountered and killed their fathers. Anubis's self-imposed wandering and suffering in the desert parallel King's Oedipus self-inflicted blindness and exile after he discovers that he has committed patricide and incest. Anubis, too, is guilty of incest, for he has unknowingly taken his sister for a wife and had a son by her. Both heroes are driven by a compulsive obsession to unravel their identity/origins, and in their relentless pursuit of the truth they violate the laws of moral conduct. Furthermore, both heroes are aided in their quest by prophecies: Oedipus consults the Greek oracle and Anubis is guided by the maxims and prophetic revelations of the shadowy figures, specters, and jinns of both sexes that he encounters on his way. "These maxims direct the path that Anubis should follow, nurture his sense of duty and responsibility, even of guilt, and guide his relation with the world."[33] Some of these fascinating maxims are grouped together at the end of the novel.

During his meanderings in the desert, Anubis accidentally discovers the lost oasis of Targa. For a while he becomes the leader of this oasis and reconciles with the laws of the tribe that he has abandoned before. But eventually he falls victim to conspiracy and plotting by new settlers who want to seize power and wage wars of aggression against peaceful tribes in order to enslave them. The conspirators cluster around his sister-wife-priestess, who betrays him. He is exiled from the oasis and finds himself once again alone in the desert. At this level, the narrative reads like an allegory of human civilization, especially of the encroachment of urban life on the traditions of the desert.

The hero's exile from the oasis means separation from the son that he has fathered there. He sadly realizes that this fulfills a prophecy:

I was not surprised when [the nobles] kept me from seeing my son, preventing me from sharing stages of his development as he grew, matured, and explored the desert, where he learned to hunt, grew tough, and discovered how to be a man. I found myself alone, isolated, and abandoned, just as I had always been. I grew ever more certain that the fate of men in this desert is always Anubi's. I was born in the desert like Anubi, live in the desert like Anubi, and will leave the desert one day the way Anubi did, for anyone whose father has ever left him will have Anubi's destiny as his eternal fate. (p. 146)

Eventually, father and son do encounter each other. The encounter lasts briefly and ends violently as the son, failing to recognize his father and fearing that he would disclose his secret, kills him. Before Anubis breathes his last, he asks his son: "Is the son destined to slay his father?" The son replies: "Each of us, master, is created to slay his father. Who among us does not seek his father? Who among us does not wish to slay his father?" (p. 167). The father recognizes a prophecy/truth in what his son says. His dying words are: "We must slay our father in order to search for our father. We must slay our father in order to find our father" (p. 168).

The novel is not an easy read on account of its cryptic dialogues and disjointed sequences. The descriptions of the desert, which is as much a character in the novel as the hero, are the author's point of strength, vividly evoking its expanse, desolation, and mystery. The novel's primary concern is to "unravel the complexities of obligation and customs that delineate how relationships are made between father and son, mother and son, then brother and sister, and man to woman" in a tribal society.[34] Many of the prophetic revelations and maxims spoken by the characters that inhabit the fictional world of the novel provide insights into these complex ties, especially between fathers and sons. Some intriguing examples are: "Absence is the destiny of fathers" (p. 13); "Fathers, like lords, are not really fathers unless they distance themselves" (p. 13); "[The father] wants to be worshiped, not loved" (p. 13): "The father is spurious, the mother is always authentic" (p. 118); "Fathers must die, since a father is always a shadow. A father is always a specter" (p. 117). Anubis's sister-wife says to him, "You've wasted your life chasing after your father and have reaped nothing but the wind" (p. 117). Anubis admits that he has failed in his quest: "I had always lost my way to my father and had found myself isolated, forsaken, and lost whenever I thought I had grasped the reins of my truth" (p. 119). Nevertheless, he declares that this quest is not only inevitable but necessary: "Children who do not search for their true nature by tracing their paternal ancestry have little to recommend them. There is no point to a creature that does not seek out its efficient cause. Searching for a father, however, is

dangerous. If my son had set out on this path, alas for him, considering all the terrors of the road" (p. 162). Thus, even though "Anubi's
fate was atrocious" (p. 119), the tradition must continue: "Each of us
searches for his father. A son who does not search for his father is not
worth much. A son who does not search for his father will never be
successful" (pp. 154–55).

The novel has several layers of meaning: personal, allegorical, and
universal. A chase across the desert is also a metaphorical quest for
knowledge. However, knowledge does not necessarily bring happiness, as the verse from Ecclesiastes, which al-Koni quotes in the
final part of the novel, states: "In much wisdom is much grief; and
the greater a person's wisdom, the greater his sorrow" (1:18). In the
author's note at the beginning of the novel, al-Koni writes that he
devoted a long time to investigating the legend of Anubi, believing
that he was motivated by intellectual curiosity, until he realized that
the story echoed his own: "I discovered in the story of our forefather
Anubi aspects of my own story (and of the story of any person who
thirsts for truth)...I felt certain that Anubi's journey is nothing other
than man's journey through this desert that people call 'the world,'
that Anubi's tribulations in searching for the answer to his riddle are
mankind's tribulations in search of our riddle's answer, and that the
tribe of Anubi is, actually, the human tribe, which has yet to discover
its secret truth, although we have searched for this since primeval
times."[35]

Conclusion

Critical portraits of father-son relationships are common to male-
authored works the world over. Complaints such as child neglect,
child sacrifice, and living vicariously are not unique to Arabic fiction, nor are themes such as the alienated father, the martyr father,
or the lost father. Still, the relationship between fathers and sons in
Arab families is affected by a number of culture-specific factors that
have no parallel in the West. The various customs and traditions
that impact this relationship in Arab families and can pit fathers and
sons against each other have been discussed in detail at the outset
of this study. Based on the myriad texts presented in this chapter
and the preceding one, it is fair to conclude that the predominant
quality of the father-son relationship that is singled out for special
criticism by Arab writers is paternal authoritarianism. This is most
evident in the first volume of Mahfouz's Trilogy, where the patriarch
yells at his rebellious son Fahmy: "The only word that counts here

is mine. Mine, mine, mine" (1:425). As a number of Arab scholars have pointed out, the authority relationship extends from the family to the classroom, the workplace, and the religious and political spheres.[36] "Each political leader, employer, and teacher," observes Halim Barakat, "behaves and is conceived of as a father."[37] The Syrian writer Zakaria Tamer is noted for his allegorical depictions of the paradigms of authority and submission in the family and the society. In his short story "The Thunderbolt,"[38] for example, which is set in a classroom, the teacher is the prototype of paternal authority, all-powerful, repressive, and fearsome, whereas the pupil is the prototype of the subordinate son, frustrated, resentful, and defiant. The tremendous tension and hostility that build up between the teacher and the pupil inevitably result in an explosion of rage and violence. A particular detail in the story, which describes the shape of the teacher's head as triangular, alludes to the former Syrian leader Hafez Assad, who was known for his high brow and angular face. Thus, through the figure of the teacher, Tamer denounces the authoritarian nature of the Syrian regime.

Significantly, even when the authoritarian father is gone from the family, his power and influence over his son's mind persist. This is illustrated in Mahfouz's Trilogy, Idris's "The Journey," and Choukri's *For Bread Alone*. The idea of the "paternal yoke within," which the son carries, corresponds to the notion of the "harem within," which the daughter carries.[39] This similarity indicates that the patriarchal socialization of the son and the daughter is so deeply internalized by them that they are unable to get rid of its legacy.

The predominance of negative portraits of the father figure in Arabic works of literature, especially those coming from North Africa, has prompted the Moroccan writer Abdellatif Laabi, in his novel *Rue De Retour*, to defend the image of the Arab father by declaring that he experienced his own father, and thus his childhood, completely differently:

> From circle to circle you reach back to your childhood. You rummage through your memory and paradoxically you don't find anything. Obedience? Unknown. Your father was not one of those paterfamilias who haunt many stories set around the edge of the Mediterranean and the Arab world. The dictator in his room, the indestructible kernel of the family and solid unit around which gravitate all economic activity, the dominant ideology, arranged marriages, divorce by decree, religious rituals and festivals. The trunk of a genealogical tree and the hand of Providence in everything. He was a good-natured small craftsman who left each day to go to work at six o'clock in the

morning and came back at eight in the evening. Except on Fridays. A highly precise machine at work in our own apparently drifting and lethargic society, turning its back on productive work. This small artisan had managed to send all his children to the "French-Muslim" school so that they might learn the language of power of those days and understand the mystery of that power.

No, you do not remember obedience at that level. Therefore you never experienced any revolt against your father, something which perhaps explains why you never had any desire to write one of those edifying autobiographies which were a kind of initiatory test in the literature of the colonized.[40]

Laabi's positive image of his father brings to mind similar positive portrayals in Naimy's *Seventy* and Jabra's *The First Well*. His intriguing conclusion points to a similar phenomenon in Arab women's literature, where negative depictions of the mother figure served as an "initiatory test" for female authors in the first stage of feminist writing.[41]

Still, the fact that negative portraits of the father figure abound in male texts, both autobiographical and fictional, calls for some comment. First, the father represents traditional Arab culture and way of life. Second, the father is the center of power in the family and thus the son's main antagonist.[42] Both of these aspects make him the prime target of criticism in works that revolve around the son's rebellion against family control and his quest for freedom. As Tetz Rooke remarks, "since the structure of the Arab family is patriarchal . . . freedom often becomes synonymous with freedom from the rule of the father."[43] Needless to say, the image of the patriarchal family is not idealized in these texts.

As can be expected, criticism of "the father" does not go unpunished by the censor or the authorities. This is attested by scores of writers in the Arab world who have been jailed or whose work has been banned from publication.[44] The Moroccan author Mohamed Choukri speaks of his own bitter experience: "There is, in Moroccan society, a more conservative faction. Those people judge my works as depraved. In my books, there's nothing against the regime. I don't talk about politics or religion. But what annoys the conservatives is to notice that I talk about my father. The father is sacred in Arab-Muslim society."[45]

Of all the texts discussed in this chapter, Mahfouz's Trilogy shows most effectively how the meaning of masculinity varies within the culture over time and over the course of an individual's life. At the beginning of the narrative, the patriarch, al-Sayyid Ahmad, is the epitome of traditional Arab masculinity, embodying the roles of "man-the-procreator-protector-provider." Gradually, these roles are undermined by his sons' acts of rebellion, the British colonial authorities, sickness, and old age. With the erosion of his masculinity comes the fragmentation of his authority, and at the end of the narrative he is no longer the center of power in the family. Furthermore, over the span of three generations, different versions of masculinity have evolved, along with different rites of passage and different masculine practices: the son Fahmy becomes a freedom fighter, his younger brother Kamal a confirmed bachelor; one grandson is a Communist, another a Muslim Brother, and yet another is "queer" or gay. Whether these individuals attain/manifest their masculinities by fighting in a war, engaging in a revolutionary activity, pursuing an alternative sexual orientation, or rejecting marriage and fatherhood, their actions challenge hegemonic masculinity and show that it is under pressure from socioeconomic changes in the environment.

The turbulent history of the Arab Middle East, with its numerous struggles for national liberation, promoted the theme of becoming a warrior as a path to manhood. Almost invariably, in texts that are set in the colonial period (e.g., Mahfouz's Cairo Trilogy, Mina's trilogy), the enemies are the British or the French, whereas in texts that are set in the postcolonial period (e.g., al-Razzaz's "Abu Richard" and al-Qa'id's *War in the Land of Egypt*), the enemy is Israel.

It is interesting to examine Dialmy's observations about Arab sexuality in the light of all these texts. His assertion that Arab masculinity is essentially equated with virility is illustrated by the patriarch's eldest son Yasin in Mahfouz's Trilogy on the one hand, and by the umda in al-Qa'id's *War in the Land of Egypt* on the other hand. Yasin is a philanderer who finds in his conquests confirmation of his virility and thus masculinity, whereas the umda, who lost his virility due to the removal of his prostate, is terrified that the village people might discover that he is not a "complete man" and thus deem him unworthy of being their mayor.

Most intriguingly, despite the taboo on the topic of homosexuality, it is depicted in Mahfouz's Trilogy, Idris's "The Journey," and al-Aswany's *The Yacoubian Building*. It should be noted that homosexuality is considered one of the gravest forms of *zina* (illicit sex) in Islam. From the patriarchal perspective, it is seen as a direct attack on manhood and as a sign of femininity. The intent of these authors is not so much to question old patterns of virility as to portray a state of anomie and malaise in society. Their approach to homosexuality is thus psychoanalytical, and they employ the theme of "aberrant sexuality" to highlight the "ills" of their society. A society that produces distorted personalities and discrepant male identities and sexualities is a dysfunctional society in need of reform. The psychologist James Harrison points out that even from a social constructionist perspective, homosexuality can be criticized, for one may say: "If homosexuality is a social construction, then what has gone wrong with society that it has created conditions under which persons of the same sex may establish intimate relationships?"[46] Not surprisingly, the depictions of homosexual relations in these texts are negative: like all social relations, they too are predicated on the paradigms of domination and subordination and entail the abuse of the young by the old, the poor by the rich, and the weak by the mighty. These sexual relations are characterized by depravity, exploitation, coercion, and violence rather than love, nurturance, equality, and freedom. Hence they serve as a powerful symbol of the ills of society.[47]

Chapter 5

Fathers and Sons in Poetry and Politics

The Father-Son Nexus

The great Arab poet and philosopher Abu al-ʿAla al-Maʿarri (AD 973–1057) was known for his pessimistic outlook on life. Blind from an early age, he regarded procreation as a sin and universal annihilation as the best hope for humankind. True to his views, this unconventional thinker never married: he shut himself in his house, adopted ascetic practices, and passed the greater part of his life in relative seclusion. It is said that he wished that the following verse should be inscribed on his grave:

> This wrong was by my father done
> To me, but ne'er by me to one.[1]

Nearly a millennium later, Saʿd Darweesh (b. 1923), a modern Egyptian poet, published a long poem with the title "I've Committed No Such Crime!" and the subtitle "A Conversation with My Unborn Son," which he dedicated to his classical forerunner Abu al-ʿAla al-Maʿarri.[2] In this poem, Darweesh picks up the thread of al-Maʿarri's thoughts on fatherhood and develops it in detail. Composed in dual voices, one belonging to the lonely, frustrated father and the other to his yearning, unborn son, the poem reveals many of the core issues in the father-son relationship. The imaginary dialogue begins with the father's confession that he is tormented by feelings of guilt on account of his reluctance to bring his son into the world. His fears of becoming a father stem primarily from the heavy responsibilities that this role entails and the realization that he would not be able to protect his son from life's miseries. His own experiences were harsh: he had known many trials and tribulations, pains and sorrows, including betrayals in love. To stop the cycle of suffering from repeating itself, he decided to forego fatherhood. Not that he does not wish to see his name live on or fancy holding his son in his arms, but the thought that his son would one day cry "Father's crime!" namely, blame him for thrusting him into the cruel world, terrifies him. Giving up his son, then, is an act of compassion:

> To spare you all that I have seen,
> The losses I have sustained,
> I withstood the human impulse within.

The son begs his father to reconsider his decision, arguing that it is selfish and unfair. He desperately tries to change his father's bleak outlook by highlighting the many blessings of fatherhood. He also pledges his unconditional love, loyalty, and devotion to his father. He even promises to share the burden of responsibilities with him. But all his entreaties are in vain, for the father refuses to reverse his decision. The poem concludes with the son's pleading words:

> O Father dear, I long to see you still,
> I crave the warm thrill
> Of your embrace,
> I long to see your face;
> And I will wait,
> May the waiting be not long.
> Like the leaves vernal
> Of a green perennial
> The heart of a poet will quiver
> Even to a morning whisper,
> And so I shall see you,
> I know,
> My waiting can't be long![3]

This poem captures the problematic nature of the father-son relationship. It is a relationship fraught with ambivalence: love and aggression, acceptance and rejection, admiration and resentment, nurturance and deprivation, attachment and alienation, to name but a few dichotomies. A father is simultaneously flattered and threatened by his son's existence; he feels both fear for his son and fear of his son. A son admires his father and looks up to him as a role model. At the same time he resents his authority and struggles to attain autonomy and express his individuality. The intense and mixed feelings between father and son are further compounded by the expectations and demands that they have of each other. Life-cycle stages and transitions produce additional tensions and strains in the dynamics between father and son, who have to redefine their relationship in response to their changing needs and abilities. Some men are frightened by the obligations of fatherhood and refuse to assume the role. They feel a variety of acute anxieties as a result of their own unhappy childhood or of real-life struggles.[4] Other men flee from the role as a way of asserting their social protest against the problems of the increasingly complex world. Considering the many stresses that impact the experience of fatherhood and the interaction between fathers and sons, it is no wonder that the father-son relationship has been described in the social science literature as "the most challenging of all family relationships."[5]

Arabic poetry has a long tradition, extending from pre-Islamic times to the modern era. Called *diwan al-arab*—"the register of the Arabs"—Arabic poetry is not only the record of their history, battles, and great deeds, but also the repository of their values, cultural ideals, greatest aspirations, and traditional wisdom. As such, it provides a wealth of information on the topic of this study. The following selection of Arabic poems illustrates various images of Arab masculinity, challenges prevailing ideas about the father-son relationship, and offers intriguing insights into the forces that shape the dynamics between them in both the personal and the political sphere.[6]

The Ethos of Masculinity

According to Jazia al-Hilalaite, Bedouin poet of the Maghreb, the ethos of masculinity comprises three essential qualities: bravery-courage, hospitality-generosity, and chivalry-prudence. As he sums it up: "Men worthy of tears and lamentations are of three kinds: a man who is ready to face peril to put out the flames of war; a man who entertains his guests in famine years and offers them water in days of thirst; and a man of spirit and intelligence who, with the power of his mind and eloquence, is able to secure his own rights and defend others'. The rest are not men but males who can only multiply their own kind of mortals. They deserve no tears or mourning, and a blind person who cannot look at them will miss nothing worth seeing."[7] The distinction between real *men* and mere *males* is here sharp and categorical; the great respect expressed for the former is contrasted by the utter contempt shown for the latter. Crucially, the virtues described by al-Hilalaite endow a man with honor, the all-important component of his personality that he must defend at all costs. "He who has no honor has no religion" (*illi ma lahu sharaf ma lahu din*) runs a popular Bedouin proverb, affirming that men who behave dishonorably are not good Muslims.[8]

The virtues that define manhood or masculinity (*muruwwa*, *rujula*) for the Bedouins are regarded by many Arabs, in both the villages and the cities, as moral imperatives and as the most highly prized personal qualities. As Jacques Berque observes, "The emotional intensity of the desert dweller has imposed its ideal on the opulent cities."[9] In a poem titled "Choice," the Yemeni poet Abd al-Aziz al-Maqalih reflects on the meaning of manhood. For him, a man's destiny and glory lie in the brave deed—the courage to fight against any form of disgrace, injustice, or oppression:

> Between grief on my knees and death on my feet
> I choose death:
> between a safe silence and a voice that's bloodied
> I choose the voice:
> between a slap and a bullet
> I choose the bullet:
> between the sword and the whip
> I choose the sword:
> This is my destiny and my glory,
> this is the longing of man.[10]

That it is not easy to live up to such lofty ideals is a recurrent complaint. In "Getting the Hell out of It," the Moroccan poet Abdulilah Salhi laments:

> We were men
> and we failed to prove it
> opportunities fizzled out
> and often changed costumes
> or numbers.
>
> Men—
> we are still men on paper
> somewhere at the bottom of the page
> between brackets
> with our Greek sandwiches
> and an urgent need not to forget anything.
> Sex, alas,
> remains a high sincerity zone.[11]

The feeling of frustration arising from not measuring up to the prescribed code of masculinity can be debilitating. In "Untitled," the

Egyptian poet Mohamed Metwalli expresses the sense of shame, worthlessness, and despair that he feels as a "failed man" by referring to himself as a "straw doll." In the epigraph of his poem, he acknowledges the influence of T. S. Eliot's famous poem "The Hollow Men" and quotes its opening lines:

> We are the hollow men
> We are the stuffed men
> Leaning together,
> Headpiece filled with straw.

Metwalli's innovative poem, which combines passages of prose with verse, is a disparaging self-portrait of an unmanly conduct. He begins his poem and ends it with the lines:

> We are two straw dolls,
> My friend and I, wearing
> Elegant evening clothes
> And shining shoes.[12]

The word "dolls" is highly charged. Dolls are closely associated with the female sex: it is mostly little girls who play with dolls, which are usually small models of female figures. Attributing the quality of femaleness to an Arab male is considered the gravest insult. It implies that he has lost his superior status as a man and has become weak and helpless like a woman, an "inferior" human being. Regarded as one of Egypt's angry voices, Metwalli's poem speaks of his being co-opted by the ruling political system, of having become servile, like a puppet, to a corrupt master. Failing to act out his masculinity by taking risks, verbalizing defiance, and resisting subjugation makes him feel emasculated and effeminate.

As mentioned earlier, Arab masculinity is closely intertwined with virility and fertility, especially with the procreation of sons, who are valued above daughters. The more sons the head of a family has, the more prestige he gains in the eyes of his relatives and friends. That it is difficult for the individual male to meet his obligations as "man-the-procreator-protector-provider" is a recurring poetic theme. A father is expected to make many sacrifices for his son's sake, even to deny his own needs while providing for him, only to discover, when the son grows up, that he does not possess him, that the son has a mind of his own, and that he wants to establish his independence from his father. The toil and hardship associated with fatherhood are a topic of complaint in a poem titled "Adam" by the Syrian poet Adonis. Featuring the progenitor of humanity, the poem voices Adam's deep sense of grievance over the fact that the burden of fatherhood has deprived him of the bliss of paradise:

> Choking quietly
> with pain,
> Adam whispered to me,
> "I am not the father
> of the world.
> > I had
> no glimpse of paradise.
> Take me to God."[13]

Similarly, the Iraqi poet Hashim Shafiq expresses profound disillusionment with his life as a man in a poem revealingly titled "Mirage":

> Nobody told me when I was born
> that my life would be harder than my father's and son's lives.
> Nobody told me when I was a child
> that life was full of pits and tunnels and trackless labyrinths.
> Nobody told me when I was a youth
> that my homeland was not a homeland
> and that my enemy and friend are aligned against me
> and my lover would be as fickle as a chameleon.
> Nobody, except Brecht, told me when I was a young man
> that exiles are shoes,
> and only Sartre told me
> that political parties are religions,
> and only Abu al-Atahiah[14] told me that mankind is a curse.
> And when I became an adult,
> I did not tell myself: Beware of tomorrow.[15]

The poet describes his journey from child to youth to man as fraught with disappointments and rude awakenings that left him feeling bitter, depressed, and hopeless.

The Child Is Father of the Man

Wordsworth's insightful observation "The Child is father of the Man" captures the intimate link between the experiences that a boy encounters in his childhood and the kind of man that he turns out to be in his adulthood. The influences that contribute to the formation of a child's personality endure through life. The father, who serves as

the son's primary role model and mentor, represents a major formative influence for him during the childhood years and beyond. In
fact, the quality of the father-son relationship determines to a large
extent the son's childhood recollections as happy or wretched. Given
the lifelong repercussions of childhood, it is no wonder that it is the
subject of countless works of prose and poetry and a constant preoccupation with writers who are concerned with self-knowledge.

Many Arab poets pay homage to their childhood as the happiest
period in their lives. They look back on it with nostalgia, yearning for
its magic and innocence. In an ode to childhood, titled "Celebrating
Childhood," Adonis writes:

> I still follow the child
> who still walks inside me.

Adonis declares that his childhood continues to enchant him and be
a source of inspiration for him, mysteriously coming to life "in the
palms of a light" whose name he does not know and which names
him. In his view, the imprint of childhood on a person's life is as
indelible as that of a village. People are captives of their childhoods
just as they are captives of their villages: they are unable to cross the
boundaries of either one. He concludes his poem with a vivid analogy
between a womb, a village, and childhood:

> I was born in a village,
> small and secretive like a womb.
> I never left it.[16]

In another poem, titled "Beginning Speech," Adonis reflects on
the many transformations that he has undergone since his childhood.
He sadly acknowledges the gulf separating his younger self from his
older self:

> That child I was
> came to me once
> an unfamiliar face
>
> He said nothing—we walked
> each glancing in silence at the other
> One step
> an alien river
>   flowing.
>
> Our common origins
>   brought us together

and we separated
a forest written by the earth
and told by the seasons.

Child that I once was, advance,
What now brings us together?
And what have we to say to each other?[17]

Like Adonis, the Palestinian poet Anton Shammas, in his poem "I Have a Drawer," yearns to unlock the door to the magical realm of his childhood:

I have a drawer full
Of lullabies. It's locked. I stand before it
And grow, hoping one day to reach
The key my mother hung
On her death peg.[18]

The image of the father figures prominently in childhood recollections. Some poems depict the father in a favorable light, while others (as illustrated in greater detail in the following sections) are critical. In "The Inheritance," the Iraqi poet Sami Mahdi paints a loving picture of a father who welcomes his newborn son into the world:

Between the earth and the sky
I draw a map for a newcomer.
Before I die
I give him his inheritance:
the glow of love
a ladder
and a living room full of friends.[19]

In this poem, the three gifts that the father bestows on his son are love, virility (symbolized by the ladder), and companionship.

An equally charming depiction of a father's affection for his son is presented in a poem titled "My Son" by the Kuwaiti poet Khalid Saud al-Zayd. The father in this poem describes the infinite joy he derives from watching his little boy play, listening to his sweet voice, and indulging his whims and wishes. He is elated to see a reflection of himself in his son:

My image is imprinted on his face, if only he knew
And in his eyes flash echoes of my roots.

When the son calls "Papa!" the father hastens to reply "Yes, heart of my heart," and rejoices to see him smile and swell with pride. He regards his son's little fists, which the boy uses to punch anyone who provokes his father, as "protectors for my dreadful old age" and readily admits:

> I toil just to bring him joy
> And clown to make him laugh.[20]

While the preceding poem is written from the father's perspective, what follows is written from the son's perspective. Composed by Adonis as an elegy to his father's memory, the poem depicts his figure in striking images of "a tomorrow" and "a sun" that signify what the father meant for his son:

> My father is a tomorrow
> that floats down toward us,
> a sun.

Adonis mourns the loss of his father, whose passing is foreshadowed by the appearance of dark clouds above his house, and affirms his deep love and admiration for him:

> I love him, his decaying bones and mud.[21]

In contrast to this sympathetic portrayal, in "The Flower of Life and My Father's Black Heart" the Lebanese poet Abbas Beydhoun speaks of his father in negative terms: instead of empowering him, he saddled him with his "black heart" and "a pack of lies" that doomed all his efforts and ambitions to failure:

> We ate live secrets,
> the flower of life
> and my father's black heart.
> I ate them;
> they had no taste
> except that my hands
> tossed away a heap of lies
> that never flowered.
> My hair grew empty and seedless
> and I threw a fistful of names
> to the birds
> but they did not care.[22]

Many Arab poets pay tribute to their mothers, rather than to their fathers, tenderly portraying them as the most important force in their lives. In a poem titled "My Mother, in Memoriam," the Iraqi Fadhil Assultani writes:

> You are here in my little room,
> the closest point in the universe to the heavens.
> All night I hear your last prayers,
> I touch your forehead as it bows to God.
> Your spirit, here in my little room,
> the closest point in the universe to life.[23]

For Assultani, the mother was a sustaining force on both the existential and the spiritual level. Naguib Mahfouz expresses similar sentiments about his mother in his reflections on his life. In "A Mother's Love," which he composed on the occasion of her death, he writes: "I was lucky enough to get my fill of my mother's affection and tenderness, for God allowed her to live until I was in my fifties. During all the times when one really needs a mother and the special quality of the love only she can give, my mother was there for me. I can't imagine what it must be like to grow up without that kind of tenderness—one must feel an aching void all one's life." Mahfouz admits that when he was 25 he experienced a great loss when his father died; however, he was much closer to his mother and felt like an orphan only with her passing: "With her gone, I came to feel that I was truly alone in the world."[24] Mahfouz's words echo the idea encapsulated in a popular Tunisian proverb, "Orphaned of his mother, the child has the threshold as his pillow; orphaned of his father, he still has his mother's lap."[25]

The Quest for Freedom

Arabic poetry abounds with poems that portray the father-son relationship. At times sorrowful and plaintive and at other times angry and accusatory, these outspoken poems reveal not only the gulf between the idealized view and human experience but also the complex and multifaceted nature of this male relationship.

Different factors enter into the father-son relationship and influence the interactional dynamics between them. Not infrequently, the father's perspective on life, especially how his son should live his life, collides with the perspective that the son develops for himself when he reaches adulthood. This is depicted in "Belonging to a New Family" by the Moroccan poet Mohammad Bennis. In this poem, the son questions the validity of what his father has taught him and rejects his views and attitudes:

> My father recommended safety
> fearing to contradict law and order
> he memorized the legal code, advised me:
> if you're wise, stay out of politics
>
> But how crowded courts and prisons have become
> how gallows have swung, bullets whined
> how much blood shed, enveloping castles with anger and mutiny
> down through the ages!
>
> How this question turns colorless, emptied of meaning
>   whether I dream or wake?
> How the silence that reigns behind numb curtains
> slips away in the absence, pierces walls
> and becomes tablets of wrath? How such curtains reveal
> voices spreading on flame to bring us to the massacres of history?
>
> How can we sit on chairs, strapped down by advice
> recommending safe submission?
> How return?
>   Without taking action
>   words lie dead on library shelves
>   canned in manuscripts, newspapers, books.[26]

Here the father represents traditional values: conformity, silence, passivity, and submission to authority. The son cannot reconcile these values with the oppressive social reality, which calls for revolutionary action and change. Hence he rejects his father's advice and refuses to follow in his footsteps.

The opposite of filial rejection is acceptance. Sometimes the young son internalizes his father's message so deeply that he feels obligated to carry on his work after his death. In "My Father's Dream," the Iraqi poet Sargon Boulus depicts the impact that his father's mystical vision had on him as a child:

> One night
> my father saw a saint in his dream
> He saw a tall saint
> who spoke to him
> with eyes burning like two embers
> in a voice full of authority
> very sure of being obeyed

In the morning
my father went out
to knock on village doors
one after another
to tell his dream
. . . .
He kept knocking on the doors
one after another
the sack of burlap on his back
filling up as evening advanced
with loaves of bread, the village's
black rice, tea, and salt
whenever he told his dream
which he did more than fifty times
till I knew it by heart

He had taken me along
to carry the sack when he got tired.[27]

The son's sympathetic portrayal of his father's devotion to his calling
shows that he identified with him and shared a close bond with him.
At the same time, he experienced his father's legacy as a heavy burden
that he had to carry on his shoulders since his childhood.

The desire to get rid of the paternal yoke, whether physical or
psychological, and live in freedom is a dominant poetic theme. The
Saudi Ahmad Qandeel expresses his quest for freedom in a poem
whose title, "A Scream," signifies a desperate cry to be heard:

Don't bind my steps
With what you call
Traditions, or a system of life

Don't wipe away my tears
With all your gifts
of advice

Don't fell my will
With what you insist
is rationality and commitment

Don't belittle my escapades
With what you readily number
As sins or mistakes

Let my feet walk freely on the path
my sighs exhale bitter sorrows
and my ideas decide the verdict clearly

Give me the right to do things openly
He who lives in chains is not alive in the world
Birds have their wings, rocks have their solidity
Water goes stagnant when it's blocked by dams
We were born for the flow and ebb of life.[28]

Here the son rebels against the constraints of family and society,
seeking to chart his own course in life and learn from his own
experiences, be they failures or successes. The desire to become
"his own man," to define his own goals, and to live on his own
terms is depicted as central to his journey of self-discovery and self-
attainment.

In "Tales about My Father," an innovative poem consisting of
three stanzas, each with its own subtitle, the Iraqi poet Abd al-Karim
Kassid depicts the expectations that father and son have of each other
as the cause of conflict and tension between them:

Protest:

Once he asked me:
How is it that these return after a few years
with titles and white collars
and slimly built...?
And when I answered him tersely
he shouted at me:
But you read night and day
night and day.

History:

I said to my father one day:
There are many who enter history
as a whore enters the bed.
There are even more who exit history
as a whore leaves the bed.
But he did not understand.

After the burial:

Between one day and the next
he would sit in his usual corner
shaving with old implements he acquired—perhaps before I was
    born.
And when he died
and I carried him with these two hands
and buried him under the earth
where my mother calmly knelt as though addressing one alive

> I returned to find him in the house
> in front of his small mirror
> shaving, still shaving
> with his old implements
> his implements he acquired before I was born.[29]

The son in this poem has disappointed his father by failing to obtain the diploma that he expected of him. His failure is deeply felt by the father, who regards him as an extension of his ego and personalizes whatever credit or discredit he earns. The son feels rejection and contempt on the part of the father, whom he regards as a representative of the past, symbolized by the old shaving implements that he uses. The mutual sense of disappointment and resentment between father and son is reflected in their terse exchange. Significantly, even after the father's death the son still feels his oppressive presence in the house. He is especially haunted by the image of his father shaving with his old implements. Most probably, this ritual, which is performed with a razor blade, triggers the fear of castration in the son's mind.

By contrast, for Anton Shammas the death of his father diminishes the emotional distance that existed between them. In "No Man's Land," he writes:

> My father died in the summer, and the barrier
> Between us has since been crumbling.
> Now, in the fall, he stands like a door
> At the edge of the no-man's-land of my life—
> The border before him.
> Thus I tell the child
> Trampled in me,
> Thus I tell the child
> Standing before me.
> My father stands like a door,
> And one of us three goes in.[30]

Intriguingly, the dead father appears in his son's dreams as a door. Since the door gives access, it signifies the antithesis of a wall or a barrier. The father stands on the edge of an unknown chapter in his son's life, serving as the threshold to a new experience or journey. The son sees his younger self (the child trampled inside him), his older self, and his father's self as three components of his identity in need of harmony. It is probably his reconciled sense of self, having resolved this inner tension, which goes through the door.

The Master-Disciple Dialectic

In his work *Master and Disciple: The Cultural Foundations of Moroccan Authoritarianism*, the anthropologist Abdellah Hammoudi argues that at the heart of Moroccan culture lies a paradigm of authority that juxtaposes absolute domination against absolute submission. Rooted in Islamic mysticism, this paradigm, which he calls "master and disciple," has been transferred from Sufi life to political life, and it informs all major aspects of personal, political, and gender relations in Moroccan society. Hammoudi believes that the influence of the master-disciple paradigm, which is enshrined in daily discourse and practices, is so pervasive that it reinforces and perpetuates the authoritarian structure of the Moroccan government. He highlights the similarities between the master-disciple relationship and the father-son relationship:

> The way a disciple relates to his master is not radically different from the way a son relates to his father. It entails the same kind of submission interspersed with outbreaks of disobedience, which may lead to heartrending separations. (Near-lethal fistfights between son and father are common events, especially in the countryside.) Moreover, both groups impose a double standard and expect two different types of behavior: agreeable and modest in the father's (or master's) presence; virile and domineering in relation to others, in particular women and boys of the same generation.[31]

Hammoudi emphasizes that the paradigm of authority seen in the master-disciple dialectic shapes not only the superior-subordinate relationship that forms the backbone of modern bureaucratic and political order but also the configuration of power in the family and the workplace. In his view, as long as the master-disciple dialectic remains the dominant paradigm of power relations in Arab societies, male authoritarianism will prevail as the dominant political form.[32]

The Syrian sociologist Halim Barakat shares this view. He traces political authoritarianism in Arab societies back to familial authoritarianism or patriarchal family organization: "Political socialization takes place in the home, resulting in the congruency of political orientations among members of the family. Also, rulers and political leaders are cast in the image of the father, while citizens are cast in the image of children. God, the father, and the ruler thus have many characteristics in common. They are shepherds, and the people are the sheep: citizens of Arab countries are often referred to as *ra'iyyah* (the shepherded)."[33] Barakat supports his statement with popular Arabic sayings such as "A father's satisfaction is part of God's satisfaction" (*rida al-ab min rida al-rabb*) and "A father's anger is part of God's anger" (*ghadab al-ab min ghadab al-rabb*). He points out the striking similarities between the concepts of the father and of God: "*Rabb al-usra*, the lord of the family, became *rabb al-'amal*, the lord of work (a term that survives with reference to the employer), which in turn became *rabb al-kawn*, lord of the universe or of existence."[34] These similarities indicate that God is perceived as an extension or abstraction of the father.

Arabic poetry is replete with poems that reflect these attitudes. "The Murder of the Moon," by the Egyptian poet Amal Dunqul, illustrates the conception of the leader as a father, the nation as his family, and the citizens as his children. The poem calls for some introductory remarks. The moon is an important symbol in Arab culture. First, the worship of the moon god was prevalent in pre-Islamic Arabia. Second, the crescent moon is the symbol of Islam. Furthermore, the lunar cycle is important to the Arabs (and to all Muslims), who reckon their ritual schedule by it. For example, the fast of Ramadan begins with the first appearance of the crescent moon on the night of Shaaban 29 (the eight month of the Muslim year), and ends with the appearance of the crescent moon on the First of Shawwal (the tenth month of the Muslim year). In the hot climate of the Arab region, especially the desert, the moon influences people's daily activities, particularly in the summer when moonlit nights allow them to walk and work in cool temperatures. Needless to say, the spellbinding effect of the moon's silver rays inspires romantic love in the hearts of young men and women everywhere. Interestingly, although in Arabic the word "moon" (*qamar*) is masculine in gender, it has traditionally been used as a metaphor for female beauty, specifically a woman's face, which is glorified when it is round, full, and radiant like the moon's.

Dunqul's poem begins with the terrible news of the moon's murder spreading like a wildfire through the city:

> "The moon has been killed!"
> They saw him crucified, his head dangling from the trees!
> Thieves had stripped the costly diamond breastpin
> from his chest,
> and left him in the branches
> like the black legend in the eyes of a blind man.
> My neighbour said:
> "He was a saint, why did they kill him?"

In these lines, the moon is personified as a martyr and a saint. The moon's slaying shocks the people in the city, who, "like orphans," feel a deep sense of grief and bereavement:

> Tears streamed from every eye.
> Like orphans, like the moon's own children
> they offered their condolences, and walked away.
> The moon had died, like anyone else!

The narrator goes to the countryside and informs the people of his village about the dreadful death of their "father":

> People of my village, your father is dead!
> They killed him in the city—shed the tears
> of Joseph's brothers over him, then fled,
> leaving his corpse on the asphalt
> in the blood and fury of their streets.

The villagers, however, refuse to believe the narrator's words. In the following lines, the symbolic meaning of the moon as a father, leader, or god is used interchangeably with its literal meaning as a planet or a heavenly body:

> My brothers: Your father is dead!
> —What? Our father can't be dead!
> Yesterday, he was up all night
> telling us his sad tale!
> —My brothers: With my two hands I held him;
> I closed his eyelids for you to bury him!
> They said: Enough;
> you must be raving.
> I said I was only telling the truth.
> Wait, they said, an hour or two
> and he'll come by.

In the poem's concluding lines, the moon suddenly reappears at night. Apart from the simple explanation that climatic change may have enhanced visibility and thus allowed the moon to be seen by the naked eye, this miraculous event may symbolize the resurrection of the fallen leader or, alternatively, his immortality in the hearts and minds of the people:

> Evening fell
> and the moon appeared

with dapper smiles and diamond beams.
—My brothers: Here is your father,
in the flesh!
Who can it be stretched out on a city street?
A stranger, they said,
whom people took for the moon
and killed and wept over,
repeating: "The moon is dead."
Our father couldn't possibly die.
No; never![35]

The poem may be a veiled criticism of the personality cult surrounding Arab leaders in autocratic regimes.

Criticism of Arab leaders abounds in Arabic poetry, which has
traditionally been closely connected with public life, especially the
political sphere. In "From Exile to Exile," the Yemeni poet Abd-
Allah al-Baraduni denounces the leaders of his country as tyrants who
oppress the people and hold them in bondage:

My country is handed over from one tyrant
to the next, a worse tyrant;
from one prison to another,
from one exile to another.
It is colonized by the observed
invader and the hidden one;
handed over by one beast to two
like an emaciated camel.

Al-Baraduni finds no escape from the vicious circle of oppression,
exile, and alienation:

My country grieves
in its own boundaries
and in other people's land
and even on its own soil
suffers the alienation
of exile.[36]

Oppression often goes hand in hand with lies and deception. In
"Legend," the Saudi poet Abdallah Salih al-'Uthaymeen exposes the
myths and falsehoods propagated by the leaders of his country, the
elders, who misguided the people and set them on the path of ruin.
As a boy, he listened to old legends told by his grandmother; as an

adult, he listened to new legends told by the elders. These legends led him to join the wars against Israel, only to be defeated time after time. After each defeat, the elders came up with newer legends to explain the military disaster:

> And once again I listen to the elders
> Revealing to people the secret of the defeat
> With words that concealed
> half the truth
> One day they would say: treason
> the next day they called it: intervention
> Recently they mentioned casually
> that I am off to an honorable battle
> assuring for future generations
> dignity, a glorious victory
> reclaiming the land and justice for my scattered people.

Al-'Uthaymeen complains bitterly about the elders' shifting position and the discrepancy between their words and actions:

> Yesterday they said:
> No peace
> With the enemies of the Arabs
> Today I sing
> the praises of
> the peace proposals
>
> Yesterday they said...
> Yesterday they said...
> Everything said yesterday has changed
> All the things they said
> Were only legends retold
> And I
> am forever submerged,
> caught between
> my grandmother's legends
> from my boyhood
> and the elders' new legends for today
>
> All that has changed is
> that once upon a time
> I listened to legends enchanted
> And now
> I listen to legends
> with dismay.[37]

A similar denunciation of Arab leaders is voiced by the Palestinian poet Kamal Nasir. In "The Leaders of My Country," he declares:

> When I write the history of my country
> with tears and ink,
> I will reserve a dark page
> for disgrace,
> a page wearied by nights of tattered mourning,
> a page that exposes the secrets of corruption
> and deceit in the course of our long struggle.
> I will speak openly
> to the perplexed millions in my country
> about our leaders.[38]

The sharpest indictment of Arab leadership is expressed in the poetry of the Syrian Nizar Qabbani. In a long poem titled "Marginal Notes on the Book of Defeat," he condemns the Syrian regime for oppressing the people so cruelly that it cost them the crushing defeats in the 1948 and 1967 wars with Israel:

> If someone would grant me dispensation—
> If I could meet with the Sultan,
> I would say to him: My master Sultan,
> . . . .
> You have lost the war twice
> because half of our people have no tongues.
> And what is the worth of a voiceless people?
> Half of us
> are besieged like ants and rats
> inside the walls.[39]

Authoritarian leaders rely on coercive measures to rule. They repress their people and discourage them from rebellion by means of persecution, surveillance, imprisonment, torture, and assassination. Deprived of civil liberties and paralyzed by fear, the citizens are rendered mute and powerless. In "The Ruler and the Sparrow," Qabbani paints a grim picture of a police state where freedom of speech is nonexistent, creative literature is heavily censored, and the recital of poetry is forbidden:

> I travelled in the Arab homeland
> To read my poems.
> I was convinced
> Poetry was the public's bread.

Qabbani finds himself tossed about by police stations and soldiers when all he has done is carry "a sparrow" in his pocket:

But the officer asked
For the sparrow's passport.
The word in my country needs a passport.

Qabbani mocks at the notion of "one Arab nation" and "one Arab homeland," where an Arab can travel freely from one country to another. Staring at sandbags at a checkpoint, he anxiously waits for a pass, only to be cast off at his country's gates "like broken glass."[40]

In a police state, the feeling of fear is instilled deeply in the hearts and minds of the people in order to obtain their submission and compliance. In a poem titled "Fear," the Yemeni poet Abd al-Aziz al-Maqalih depicts a hellish reality of living in a constant state of fear:

I walk behind its voice
It walks behind mine
At times I become its shadow
At times it becomes mine.

The fear that resides in his blood and keeps him awake at night has no boundaries: it extends from "yesterday's ashes" through "today's sands" to "tomorrow's frost," and penetrates the most private recesses of his life. Robbed of his joy of living and peace of mind, he is fixated on a single thought—his fear. It consumes him and he consumes it. Hopeless, he asks, "When will we part?"[41]

The sense of fear that haunts the individual in Arab societies is so intense that the Syrian poet Muhammad al-Maghut, in a poem revealingly titled "The Tattoo," cries out in despair:

From whom did I inherit this terror?
this jittery blood like mountain panther?
Whenever I glimpse an official paper on the threshold
or a helmet from the crack of the door
    my bones rattle,
    tears race, and my terrified blood
    jolts in all directions
    as if an eternal legion of police
    chased it from vein to vein.

Al-Maghut gloomily concludes that this profound sense of fear must have been transmitted to him in the womb:

Somehow I was not tied to the womb
by the umbilical cord
but by the noose![42]

These somber thoughts are shared by the Egyptian physician and writer Nawal El Saadawi. In discussing the link between democracy, creativity, and Arabic literature, she writes:

People in our countries are nurtured on fear. They feed on it the moment they are born. Fear of the Father, the Ruler, of God, are all combined. From a very early age, children are taught to fear punishment or Hell, or the father's displeasure, which can end in their being thrown out of the home. Women fear divorce, fear to be left alone without shelter, or a future, or security of any kind. Students fear their professors' whims and are taught to cringe lest they be failed, or given bad marks or refused access to higher studies. Writers are afraid of being dismissed from their jobs, for in developing countries the establishment rules with a heavy hand over all areas of intellectual and artistic creation. Obedience is considered the highest of virtues everywhere, in the family, at school, in religion, morals, administrative systems, and political institutions.[43]

El Saadawi observes that as a result of this situation, writers are driven to indulge in hypocrisies, take refuge in silence, or go into self-exile. All these reactions have a detrimental effect on their creativity and Arab intellectual life.

The Demigods: Arab Leaders, Rulers, and Despots

In describing the crisis of civil society in the Arab world, Halim Barakat emphasizes the authoritarian character of Arab political systems: "Arab governments tyrannize over society and deny the Arab people their basic human rights." Moreover, "authoritarianism is not merely an attribute of the political system. Interpersonal and social relationships are also characterized by authoritarian tendencies." Barakat traces the roots of these tendencies to the "dominant patriarchal system and related practices."[44] He points out the fundamental difference between foreign occupation and indigenous despotic rule: "It is much easier to mobilize people against the former than against the latter. Indigenous despotic rule, resulting from the struggle for independence, has managed to silence people in the name of national and popular goals."[45] This distinction explains the mass participation in uprisings in the pre-independence period, and the demoralizing resignation afterward.

Hence, he argues: "It is wrong to expect that the Arabs will as easily [as the East Europeans in the former Soviet Union] depose their rulers and dismantle the indigenously established order."[46]

It is interesting to examine the recent history of the Arab region in the light of these assertions. It is especially pertinent to learn what kind of relations contemporary Arab rulers had with their fathers on the one hand, and with their sons on the other hand. Did they have a close and nurturing father-son relationship or a troubled and conflicted one? How has the father-son relationship evolved over three generations, from grandfather to father to son? And lastly, how can the phenomenon of "hereditary presidency," where leadership of an Arab republic is passed from father to son, be explained?

Saddam Hussein (1937–2006), the ruthless dictator who ruled over Iraq from 1979 until 2003, when he was deposed by a coalition of countries led by the United States and England, was an orphan. He was born in the village of al-Awja east of Tikrit in northern Iraq to Subha Tulfah al-Musallat. His father, Hussein al-Majid, was absent at his birth and presumed dead. Little is known about the father's life or where he is buried. Some accounts say he was killed; others say he abandoned his family. Saddam himself was silent on the subject of his father for most of his life. His mother, an illiterate but forceful village woman, soon married another cousin, Hassan Ibrahim, and bore three more sons, half-brothers to Saddam. The Jordanian journalist Said Aburish, who penned a biography of the man who came to be known as "the butcher of Baghdad," sees a striking similarity between Saddam's family and Stalin's: "Stalin had a strong-willed servant mother whom he revered and with whom he corresponded, but his father was a drunken cobbler who died young and about whom little was said."[47] Although Saddam stated that being fatherless left no bitterness in him, some accounts assert that the absence of a father figure made him the butt of other children's cruelty. It is undisputed that his stepfather, a poor and illiterate villager, was a brutal man who abused the young Saddam verbally and physically. Aburish believes that the combination of being fatherless, of living in poverty, and of suffering abuse at the hands of his stepfather left an imprint on Saddam's psyche. He became *ibn al-aziqqa*, or "son of the alleys," someone who is rough and lacks civility or good manners. At the age of eight or ten, Saddam left home to live with his maternal uncle, Khairallah Tulfah, a teacher and a former army officer, so that he could go to school and become literate. This step is generally regarded as his first rebellion. At his uncle's house he met his cousin and future wife Sadija, and the nationalist army officer Ahmad Hassan al-Bakr.

A first cousin of his uncle, al-Bakr eventually participated in the coup that overthrew the Iraqi monarchy in 1958 (and in the coups that followed it), assuming absolute power over Iraq in 1968. Acting on Khairallah's advice, al-Bakr took Saddam under his wing and made him his second in command and heir apparent. As Aburish reports, Khairallah was "a firm believer in the use of relations instead of party members or ideologues to run a government. 'Blood is thicker than ideology,' he is supposed to have told al-Bakr when he prevailed on him to depend on someone as young and inexperienced as Saddam."[48] Several years later, in 1979, Saddam forced the ailing al-Bakr to resign and formally assumed the presidency.

All of Saddam's half-brothers were rewarded with high office when he came to power. In fact, the Iraqi regime was very much a family affair. Saddam's immediate relations and clansmen held influential posts throughout the army, intelligence, and the Ba'ath party. Saddam named his younger son, Qusay, as his successor. His other son, Uday, had control of newspapers, television, and the main Iraqi sports business. Both were known for their brutality and corruption. Although Saddam indulged his sons and relatives, he inspired the same fear in them as in the Iraqi masses. He punished them severely if they disobeyed him and never forgave those who betrayed him. Purges within Saddam's clan claimed many lives, including two of his own sons-in-law, who were also cousins and senior officials.

Analyzing Saddam's public persona through his depictions in photographs, statues, and monuments, the Lebanese journalist Hazim Saghieh observes that Saddam's machismo is expressed in his wearing military uniform in family pictures, although such a grouping generally implies a relaxed dress code. In these pictures, "we are reminded of the first task entrusted to the totem: to protect his square and the immediate circle before all else."[49] In other pictures, Saddam is shown living in his goat-hair tent, on a shooting trip, hunting deer, visiting soldiers in the army or children in kindergarten. These pictures illustrate how the traditional characteristics of Arab masculinity were utilized for political expedience. Saghieh points out the similarity between Saddam's tactics of magnification on the one hand and intimidation on the other hand, and the tactics used by other totalitarian leaders: "Just as Stalin in photos carried his little daughter, Svetlana, and Hitler had many delightful pictures taken with children presenting him with bouquets, Saddam has been photographed carrying his daughter while wearing his revolver at his waist."[50] Saghieh explains that "the little boy or girl represents, in each case, the extreme need of the vulnerable for protection exercised by an all-powerful father."[51]

He notes that the image of an Arab leader carrying his little girl is not recorded in the work of artists of earlier times but is tied to the modern era. "In our present context, humility—and even brokenness—before a child enhances the 'manhood' of a man rather than reducing it. For he is not humbling himself or breaking down before another man, who by implication is equal in stature and strength. Rather, he uses this modern value of 'tender' fatherhood to strengthen and serve another value which is centrally bound up with the notion of real manhood as power."[52] Altogether, the monolithic image of Saddam was intended to secure the masses' acceptance of all manner of myths that legitimized his leadership, especially in times of war and severance from tradition.[53] Describing the Iraqi president as "a self-appointed divinity," Saghieh's conclusion is that "we are faced with something resembling a modern tyrannical paganism in which the totem becomes a meeting place for fathers whose capacity for fatherhood is restricted by force. For he is the man and the god: unconcerned with winning the hearts and minds of his servants, he crushes them, caring only that they are prevented from any attempt at resisting his worship."[54]

Hafez Assad (1930–2000) was the president of Syria for three decades. He was credited with bringing stability to Syria, which endured decades of military coups and countercoups before succumbing to what appears to be a hereditary dictatorship. At the same time he was criticized for repressing his own people, especially for ordering the Hama massacre of 1982 and countless extrajudicial executions against opponents of his regime. His life story is exceptional, coming from a poor peasant family named *wahhish* ("savage") who changed their name to *asad* ("lion") and who belonged to the Alawite minority sect, which represents only 12 percent of the total predominantly Sunni population in Syria.

As with most political figures in the Arab world, much is known about Assad's rise to power and his public life, but relatively little about his family life, which, regarded as the private domain, is traditionally closed to scrutiny or disclosure. It is frequently Western scholars who shed light on the personal aspects of these leaders' lives. Patrick Seale, one of Assad's biographers, writes that Assad's father, the patriarch Ali Sulayman, was "a dignified, rather austere, figure who on special occasions such as on visits to the French authorities in Latakia wore a fez and a tie. In traditional Arab fashion, Ali Sulayman was not only loved by his children but also, and perhaps more so, respected and obeyed. The boys would kiss his hand in the mornings, would not sit down in his presence and as they grew up would not dare to smoke in front of him. Assad's mother, Na'isa, much younger than her husband, was a strong-minded woman in her own right who came increasingly to be the dominant parent—with particular influence over her two youngest sons, Jamil born in 1933 and Rif'at born in 1937."[55]

Ali Sulayman married twice and had eleven children, eight sons and three daughters. He was already 55 when Hafez was born, the fourth child of his second marriage, and must have seemed an old man to him. As one of the few literate people in the mountain village of Qurdaha (southeast of Latakia), the father was highly respected. He appreciated book learning and was determined to give his younger sons an education. His first eight children had no schooling because none was available in the village at the time. In the 1930s, when the French authorities opened a primary school in Qurdaha, the father was able to secure Hafez a place, thus making him the first of his children—and of the village children—to start a formal education. Assad attended secondary school in Latakia, then joined the Military Academy of Homs, and finally went to the Air Force Academy in Aleppo. Influenced by his father, Assad showed a lifelong interest in books, poetry, and the Arabic language. Throughout his years as president, his public speeches were noted for his accomplished use of classical Arabic.[56]

According to Seale, Assad's education and vigorous personality were the reason he was seen as the heir to Ali Sulayman. The father was so old—80 by the time Assad was 25—that his outstanding son soon came to assume certain family responsibilities. "In particular, he helped his mother with his two younger brothers, Jamil and Rif'at who, being less serious and single-minded, regarded him as a somewhat stern father-figure whose approval they sought but whose authority they liked to challenge."[57]

In 1958, Assad married Aniseh Makhluf, a distant relation. Remarkably, it was a love match rather than a traditionally arranged marriage. Even as a bachelor, Assad had no record of wild escapades, rough behavior, or bad language. "Apparently uninterested in sexual experiment, he had from an early age seemed to be looking for a stable, intensely private marriage relationship which would free him for a life of professional achievement."[58] As Aniseh came from a more affluent and more prominent family than that of Assad, the marriage helped him rise to a higher social level. She lived in his shadow and bore him one daughter and four sons, all of whom attended Damascus University. Unlike the children of some notables who preferred foreign universities, Assad insisted that they complete their education in Syria. The Assad couple lived in simplicity, and the ethos of the family was rather puritanical. They resided in a modest villa, which, though comfortable, had "none of the Arabian Nights splendour of the palaces of kings and presidents in other states of the region."⁵⁹ Assad, who had kept the bed he slept on as a defense minister and the chair he used when he first took office, was more interested in power than its trappings.

By Seale's account, the Assad children were aware of their duty to set a good example. At college they worked hard, wore the prescribed military-style uniform, and were noted for their good manners—unlike some of the sons and daughters of the regime's top men, who wore fashionable clothes, quarreled with their teachers, and drove wildly in the streets of Damascus. The Assad children were intensely loyal to their father, although they saw very little of him growing up. As Basil, the eldest son, recounted: "We saw our father at home but he was so busy that three days might pass without our talking to him. We never had breakfast together or dinner and I can't remember our ever lunching together as a family, or only once or twice, on formal occasions. As a family we might spend a day or two together in Latakia in the summer, but even there he worked in his office and we didn't see much of him."⁶⁰

Despite his austere personal life, Assad encouraged a personality cult around him, promoting himself as a historical leader of the stature of Saladin and Nasser. According to *Middle East Insight*, "in no other country in recent memory...not Mao's China, nor Tito's Yugoslavia, has the intensity of the personality cult reached such extremes. Assad's image, speaking, smiling, listening, benevolent or stern, solemn or reflective, is everywhere. Sometimes there are half a dozen pictures of him in a row. His face envelopes telephone poles and trucks, churches and mosques. His is the visage a Syrian sees when he opens his newspaper."⁶¹ The historian Moshe Ma'oz writes that in the media and myriad publications, Assad was variously described as the boss (*al-mu'allim*), the president (*al-ra'is*), the general, (*al-fariq*), the comrade leader (*al-rafiq al-qa'id*), the historic leader (*al-qa'id al-ta'rikhi*), and Syria's Asad (*suriyya al-asad*).⁶²

When Hafez Assad died of heart failure in June 2000, his son Bashar succeeded him as Syria's president. The first father-to-son succession in an Arab republic was received with a great deal of cynicism around the world. The Egyptian intellectual Saadeddin Ibrahim was inspired to merge the Arabic words for republic, *gumhuriya*, and kingdom, *mamlaka*, into *gumlukiya*.⁶³ Bashar, aged 34 at the time, was not his father's first choice as a successor. His elder brother, Basil, was groomed for the job. When Basil was killed in a car accident in 1994, Bashar, who was a medical resident training to become an ophthalmologist in London, found himself thrust into politics. This turn of events earned him the epithet "the accidental autocrat."⁶⁴ Despite his promise to bring reforms to Syria, Bashar did not make any economic or political changes. In the early months of 2011, young Syrians, tired of waiting and inspired by the revolutions in Tunisia and Egypt, protested and demonstrated in the streets. Bashar chose to preserve his father's repressive style of rule and sent his troops to quell the dissent. In the brutal civil war that ensued between pro- and antiregime forces, thousands of Syrians lost their lives. At this time, the final outcome of this long civil war is still unclear.

Gamal Abdel Nasser, the charismatic leader of Egypt's 1952 revolution and Egypt's president from 1956 until his death in 1970, was the foremost Arab leader of his time. His detractors stress his police-state methods and dictatorial regime, as well as his disastrous foreign policies, which involved Egypt in a war with Yemen (1962–67) and brought about the humiliating defeat in the Six-Day War with Israel (June 1967). Others praise his internal reforms and see him as the man who abolished the monarchy and led Egypt to secular independence in the 1950s. Nasser was born in Alexandria in 1918 to a postal worker of peasant stock with roots in Beni Murr, a village in Upper Egypt. His family moved frequently as his father was transferred to different parts of the country. Nasser lived in many different towns and houses, often away from his family, and went to many different schools. When he was eight years old, his mother, Fahima Hamad, died after giving birth to his third brother. At the time, Nasser was living with his uncle in Cairo so he could attend primary school there. He learned of her death only when he arrived for a holiday at his family home. According to his biographer Robert Stephens, Nasser remained deeply wounded by the loss of his mother, to whom he was strongly attached: "His mother's early death must have added another element of insecurity to a disturbed childhood in which he was constantly parted from his family and never had the feeling of a real home. The experience of life away from his family in early years may have helped to produce that combination of restlessness, suspicion, tension and passion with patience and ability to conceal his real feelings, which was among his later characteristics as a private conspirator and public figure."[65] Nasser himself described his mother's death as "a cruel blow that was imprinted indelibly on my mind," admitting that for years afterward he had kept himself apart from his family.[66] Another biographer, Jean Lacouture, writes that things became even worse when less than two years after the mother's death his father remarried. Nasser did not get along with his stepmother from the start and eventually became estranged from his father: "He would never really forgive the postal clerk for having begun a new life so fast; and never again would he reestablish a real family life with his father and his three brothers at home."[67]

In an interview for *The New York Times* in March 1969, Nasser was asked about his "dreams for twenty-five years hence." He reportedly said: "I have no personal dream. I have no personal life. I have nothing personal."[68] Several months earlier, when the journalist Emmanuel d'Astier asked Nasser about his parents and childhood, he could only extract a few fragments of confidential statements: "For an Arab, that is a difficult question... Yes, my grandfather was a peasant... I do not remember my mother... we were a very large family."[69]

Nasser married Tahia Kazim, who bore him two daughters and three sons. Lacouture writes that though Nasser was proud of his children, he never made any plans for his sons, repeating that it was for them to choose their own future. "But the good father was not a very affectionate son," he remarks. "Relations between father and son were often stormy."[70] Nasser resented his father for having been an unkind husband to Fahima and remarrying too soon after her death. He hated to see his father's photograph in the newspapers, telling an editor in chief who thought he would please him by publishing it: "I do not want, for my father or my brothers, any publicity which might corrupt them. I want them to live like ordinary citizens."[71]

When Nasser died suddenly in 1970, he was succeeded by *Anwar Sadat*, his vice president and one of the Free Officers group who overthrew King Farouk and removed the British. Sadat was the first Arab leader to sign a peace treaty with Israel (1979), after restoring Egypt's honor in a surprise joint attack with Syria on Israel in October 1973. Winner of the Nobel Peace Prize, he allied his country with the West, but was less popular at home than abroad. His failed economic and domestic policies led to the 1977 food riots. When attacks on his policies intensified, he censored the press, jailed many of his opponents, and passed the Law of Shame (1980): an authoritarian decree that severely restricted public criticism of his person and policies and placed a heavy punishment on offenders. Although he valued his roots as a peasant, he gradually gave up his simple lifestyle and let some of his friends and relatives use their connections for personal gain. Economic and social problems, his peace treaty with Israel, and his opulent lifestyle all contributed to his assassination in 1981 while reviewing a parade on the anniversary of the October War.

Sadat wrote his autobiography, *In Search of Identity*, while still in office. The book chronicles his intellectual and political development from a village boy to a head of state, covering his education, his imprisonment by the British, his role in the July 1954 revolution, Egypt under Nasser, the 1967 and 1973 wars with Israel, and the road to peace paved by his historic visit to Jerusalem in 1977. While the book is candid and provides many details about Sadat's public life, it hardly offers any glimpses into his personal life. Of peasant stock, Sadat was born in 1918 in the village of Mit Abul-Kum in the Nile Delta to an Egyptian father, who was an army clerk, and a Sudanese mother. He does not say much about his childhood except that it was happily spent in the village. He pays tribute to his paternal grandmother, who ran the household and supervised the family's land while his father was away: "How I loved that woman! She had a very strong personality and enjoyed a rare wisdom—a natural innate wisdom, matured through lifelong experience. Throughout my childhood in the village she was the head of the family, as my father was away working for the army in the Sudan. She looked after us and supervised the work on the two and a half acres my father had acquired."[72] With respect to his father, Sadat says that he was one of the few literate people in the village and that he encouraged his education, although he was poor. As for his mother, he mentions that she used to recite to him the ballade of Zahran, a local hero of the battle against the British. Except for these few remarks, he offers no information about his family life or his relationship with his parents.

Camelia Sadat's memoir, *My Father and I*, is remarkable for its rare glimpses into the man behind the public figure and for the exceptional candor with which it depicts the father-daughter relationship. Camelia is the youngest of Sadat's three daughters by his first wife, Ikbal Madi, a traditional Muslim woman from his native village. Sadat divorced Ikbal in 1949 to marry the young, westernized Jihan. As a Muslim father, he had custody over his daughters, so when Camelia was ten he took her, along with her older sister Rawia, to live with him. Camelia says of her father: "He was very traditional. When he met one of his parents he would take a hand and kiss it as a sign of respect before conversation. When he was seated and elders entered, he would rise to honor them. He did not smoke in front of others, or crossed his legs, and he did not try to gain advantages over others."[73] Camelia writes that her father guarded his public reputation jealously, raising hell when a blood relation was rumored to be involved in corruption. He had two of his own brothers jailed for several months on a capricious accusation. "Father, honest and exceptionally strict, seemed to feel that when something touched his family he had to be the toughest. Although he was not the eldest male in his family, he used to punish close kin who made mistakes....He showed no mercy and would not listen to opposing views."[74] As for her father's relationship with her, she admits: "Father's behavior had alternated between indifference and indulgence for many years now and I longed for him to be consistent."[75] For example, on the one hand he married her off when she was 12 to a man 17 years her senior, and on the other hand he supported her decision after her divorce to travel by herself to the United States to study for a master's degree at Boston University. Camelia emphasizes the influence of village life on her father, noting that its interdependence was a lasting model for him. In his speeches, "he often referred to Egypt as a large village. And as president, he would hear complaints from the students at Cairo University with the patience, skill, and humor of a village *omda*, or mayor."[76] As for the army, he showed paternal attitudes toward the soldiers. On Eid al-Fitr (The Feast of Breaking the Fast), he would not go to the village to celebrate it with his family; instead, "he would always visit 'his children,' meaning Egyptian citizens in the armed forces who were on active duty, and would travel to various places where they were stationed to be with them."[77]

Following Sadat's assassination in 1981, *Hosni Mubarak*, his vice president, became Egypt's president. Under his leadership, Egypt continued to be an authoritarian state and a single-party government. The issue of hereditary succession arose with him. After 30 years in power, the elderly (b. 1928) and ailing Mubarak was ambitiously grooming his son Gamal to succeed him. Fed up with the corrupt and oppressive regime, and inspired by the Jasmine Revolution in Tunisia, which ousted its despotic president Zine el-Abidine Ben Ali after 23 years of rule, thousands of Egyptian protesters and democracy activists took to the streets in February 2011, demanding that Mubarak step down. The most unusual aspect of this uprising was that the army, the bedrock of the political system, remained neutral. Its tanks and soldiers stood on the sidelines as demonstrators clashed with the police, and refrained from intervening. After several weeks of massive protests, Mubarak announced his resignation. Egypt's autocratic regime came to an abrupt end and a new era of social change, though as yet undefined, was begun.

Conclusion

The foregoing account of the personal histories of several Arab "demigods" shows that their regimes were conducted very much like a family affair. Lifelong presidency, hereditary rule, and nepotism were characteristic features of these regimes. The father-son relationship was hopelessly conflicted in some cases (e.g., Saddam and his stepfather, Nasser), and formal and remote in other cases (e.g., Hafez Assad, Anwar Sadat). The mode of exercise of power by all these supreme leaders was authoritarian and predicated on the use of force and repressive measures to control their people (or their own family members). Projecting the image of the father was central to their public persona, especially in the case of Saddam Hussein, in order to enhance their manhood and secure acceptance by the masses.

The degree to which the image of the ruler as the father is internalized by the ordinary people is vividly depicted in the best-selling novel *The Yacoubian Building* by the Egyptian author Alaa al-Aswany. In this narrative, set in modern-day Cairo, Taha el-Shazli, the pious son of the building's doorkeeper, is denied admission to the Police Academy because of his father's poverty and lowly occupation. The humiliated Taha decides to write a letter of complaint to the president of Egypt, detailing his unfair treatment by the head of the Police Academy and asking for justice. In his letter he writes: "I ask you, Mr. President, to look into this complaint with the eye of a loving father who will never agree that injustice be done to one of his sons." He signs his letter with the words: "Your sincere son, Taha Muhammad el-Shazli."[78] These words are meant to evoke in the president feelings and behavioral expectations that characterize the father-son relationship, specifically compassion, support, and protection. Taha's appeal is denied. Disillusioned and angry, he joins an Islamist movement and adopts their jihadist views. He dies as a martyr during an assassination attack on a top government official.

In 1967, the Syrian poet Nizar Qabbani denounced in his poem "Marginal Notes on the Book of Defeat" the despotic Arab regimes for the crushing defeat in the Six-Day War with Israel, seeing the only hope for the liberation of the Arab nation in a new generation of Arab children:

> We need an angry generation.
> We need a generation that ploughs the horizons,
> excavates history from its roots
> and thought from the depths.
> We need a future generation
> with different features—
> one that does not excuse mistakes, does not forgive,
> does not bow down
> and has not learned to prevaricate.
> We need a giant
> Generation
> to lead us.[79]

Qabbani's words proved to be prophetic. Forty-five years later, the Arab Spring was led by an angry and restless generation unwilling to put up with the corruption, ruthlessness, and incompetence of their rulers. Called the "Internet generation" and the "Facebook revolutionaries," these young men and women possessed communication tools and skills that were unavailable to their parents and grandparents. They tirelessly organized demonstrations and marched in protests, unwilling to "bow down" until their demands for regime change were met. The "youthquake" that they launched has changed the political landscape of the Middle East and redefined the relationship between the ruler and the ruled.

The tide of Arab revolutions began in January 2011 in Tunisia, a small country in North Africa. Then the protests spread to the largest Arab country, Egypt, toppling a regime that was firmly entrenched. Suddenly street protests appeared everywhere in the Arab region, challenging the rule of autocrats and monarchs who have been in power for decades. In Libya, pro-change forces rebelled against Muammar Gaddafi, the eccentric dictator who held the country in his grip for 41 years, since he overthrew King Idris in 1969. Gaddafi was openly grooming his son Saif al-Islam as his successor. Unlike the peaceful revolutions in Tunisia and Egypt, Gaddafi refused to step down, sending his troops to suppress the revolt. A bloody civil war erupted, stretching over ten months, at the end of which the rebels, aided by NATO and the United States, were able to defeat Gaddafi's forces and free Libya from his rule. In Yemen, President Ali Abdullah Saleh, in power for nearly 34 years, agreed to leave office after enduring almost a year of protests and fighting. But in Syria, Bashar Assad, unwilling to relinquish power, cracked down on the rebels, killing and displacing thousands of civilians, men, women, and children. His brutality toward his own people led to Syria's suspension from the Arab League.

These dramatic events support Halim Barakat's assertion that "it is wrong to expect that Arabs will as easily [as the East Europeans in the former Soviet Union] depose their rulers and dismantle the indigenously established order."[80] The deposition of autocrats was not easy at all—the Arab Spring came about only after decades of social unrest and movements of different kinds. Many people lost their lives, and the violence continues at present in various parts of the Arab world along sectarian, tribal, or regional lines.

Despite these setbacks, the Arab Spring proves that Arabs, like people everywhere, aspire to live in a free society that protects their civil rights, ensures social justice, and provides them with opportunities for employment and prosperity. All the revolts were led by young Arab men and women using modern tools, such as social networking sites on the Internet and texting over mobile phones, to organize and amplify their protests. Significantly, in almost every Arab country, more than half the population is currently less than 30 years old. Increasingly aware, informed, and connected, this young generation prefers the freedom that comes with democracy to the dubious stability of political autocracy. Their actions show that rebellion against the authoritarian regime, much like rebellion against the patriarchal family, is the only way to liberation.[81]

Traditionally, the patriarchal family has been the strongest state institution. In Arab monarchies, this may be because no other institutions were allowed to develop; in Arab republics, because other institutions have been systematically undermined.[82] The tide of revolt that swept through the Arab region in 2011 shows that the power of the patriarchal family, along with the authority of the father, has eroded. Empowered by new information technologies—satellite television, mobile phones, computers, and the Internet—and motivated by unfulfilled political and economic aspirations, the youth of the Arab world is no longer willing to wait for change. They reject the old order and demand the right to choose their leaders and create forms of government that are in tune with their needs and with modern times. Their main strategy of using civil disobedience and noncooperation debunk the old narrative according to which the only outlet for youthful anger and discontent is Islamic extremism and violence. This young Arab generation has shown that it has come of age. It remains to be seen whether they can hold on to the gains they have made and create a durable democratic political system in their countries.

Chapter 6

Conclusion: Embattled Selves and the Dream of Liberation

The Trap of Masculinity

In his book *The Hazards of Being Male*, Herb Goldberg writes: "Cultural mythology has it that the male is in a favored position. After all, it does appear as if he has more options, more choices, more power, and greater freedom than the female. If all of this is in fact true, then he is paying an incredibly high price for being 'top dog' because the facts of his reality are frightening indeed."[1] This observation is particularly applicable to the male in Arab societies, where patriarchal culture and Islamic laws "indulge" men by giving them a higher status than women and numerous privileges that are denied to women. As noted earlier, relationships within the traditional Arab family are organized hierarchically by age and gender: the young are subordinate to the old and females to males. In traditional milieus, the subordination of women is reflected in veiling, seclusion, and sexual segregation. Women are absent from public life, which is the exclusive domain of men, and confined to the private domain of the home. Muslim family law discriminates against women in matters related to marriage, divorce, child custody, and inheritance. Specifically, a man is permitted to marry up to four wives at any one time but women must be monogamous; the husband has a unilateral right to repudiate his wife, but a woman's right to divorce is severely limited; child custody laws favor the husband, who almost always receives custody of the children; and a male heir is entitled to twice the share of a female heir when dividing an inheritance.[2] As the provocative title of a short story by the Moroccan writer Mohamed Choukri declares, "Men Have All the Luck."[3] But do they?

A close examination of the male condition in Arab societies reveals that men, the apparent beneficiaries of all these privileges, are in reality paying heavy penalties for them. The institutions of polygamy and repudiation, for example, create a structural instability in the family unit and undermine marital relations. Given the prospect/threat of polygamy and repudiation, both husband and wife are less inclined to invest emotionally in each other and as a result the marital bond is weak. Traditionally, the weak marital bond is compensated by a strong mother-son relationship, a situation that produces intense rivalry, jealousy, and animosity between the son's wife and his mother, who often interferes in her son's marital life. The mother-son-wife triangle has adverse effects on the emotional climate in the family and on child development. The vulnerability of Arab masculinity is manifested in its inability to resolve the tensions between mother and wife, who make conflicting claims to it.[4]

Moreover, certain paradoxes that are embedded in the traditional code of masculinity are the underlying causes of many dark side behaviors in men. The sensitive concept of honor and the related practices of ritual murder and blood revenge are prime examples. As previously noted, while honor in its nonsexual connotation is termed *sharaf*, a woman's sexual honor is called *'ird*. The *sharaf* of the man depends almost entirely on the *'ird* of the women in his family. This concept puts the man in a highly precarious position: he is judged *not* by his own actions but by someone else's actions, and a woman's to boot. Commenting on the absurdity of this situation, the Moroccan sociologist Fatima Mernissi does not mince words: "That is the great tragedy of the patriarchal male: his status lies in irrational schizophrenic contradictions, and is vested in a being whom he has defined from the start as the enemy—woman."[5] Consequently, in traditional Arab families a girl's virginity is a highly guarded property. To lose her virginity to anyone but her husband is the gravest sin she can commit. Correspondingly, the greatest dishonor that can befall a man results from the sexual misconduct of his daughter, sister, or cousin.[6] When a girl brings dishonor on her family by losing her virginity before her marriage, it is incumbent on her paternal relatives—her father, brother, or uncle—to avenge the family honor by severely punishing her. In conservative circles, this means putting her to death. Ritual murder is considered the only way to cleanse the stain inflicted on the family honor.[7] Even if a father (or brother or uncle) does not wish to kill his daughter (or sister or cousin) for losing her virginity, the pressure of public opinion may force him to do so against his will.

Nawal El Saadawi's short story "She Is Not a Virgin" depicts such a situation.[8] The moral dilemma arising from the practice of ritual murder can pit fathers and sons against each other. Yusuf al-Qa'id's novel *News from the Meneisi Farm* portrays the tragedy of a rural family torn apart by an honor killing committed by the brother against his sister.[9] Yusuf al-Sharuni's story "Blood Feud" dramatizes the heavy toll in human lives exacted by the custom of blood revenge in two neighboring village communities.[10]

The opposite side of virginity is virility, which is "one of those overriding qualities which a man will uphold even if he must in the process sacrifice other values."[11] As mentioned earlier, the act of defloration, which is one of the most important rites of passage for both genders, testifies to the virginity of the bride and the virility of the groom. Traditionally, the groom is expected to consummate the marriage on the wedding night, with family members anxiously awaiting outside the bedroom the proof of the bride's virginity: the bloodstained sheet. This ritual puts undue pressure on the male to perform, resulting in anxiety and wedding night impotence.[12] Alifa Rifaat's short story "My Wedding Night" demonstrates how stressful this expectation can be for the groom, who fails to perform and breaks down in tears. A crisis is averted only thanks to the bride, who handles the situation with empathy and sensitivity.[13]

Viewed as the essence of Arab masculinity, virility encompasses sexual prowess, multiple sexual partners, and fertility, all of which redound to a man's honor. Given the ease with which an Islamic marriage can be contracted and dissolved, the sanction of polygamy, and the practice of temporary marriage (*mut'a*), the Arab male, in the words of the Tunisian sociologist Abdelwahab Bouhdiba, "is and remains a Don Juan who has found his dearest ally in the *fiqh* [Islamic jurisprudence]."[14] But does having a harem of women at his disposal make him really happy?

In a poem titled "Schahriar's Tears" (a variant spelling of the name of the cruel king, Shahrayar, in the frame story of *The Thousand and One Nights*, who would slay a virgin girl every night after having sex with her), the distinguished Syrian poet Nizar Qabbani confesses that living up to the male image of virility by pursuing multiple sexual relations gives him neither happiness nor satisfaction but rather produces feelings of loneliness, emptiness, and alienation in him:

> What's the use of arguing
> if you, my beloved, are satisfied

that I'm the heir of Schahriar
slaying every night
thousands of concubines
rolling breasts like fruits
melting in acid every woman
that sleeps by my side.

No one understands me.
Sex is an escape
an anesthetic
we sniff night and day
a tax we pay without election.
Your breasts, kneaded with spice
are my guillotine
my suicidal rock.

My friend!
I'm weary of trading concubines
weary of my vessels
and my seas.

I feel ugly and seasick
when I return from the harem
shrunk like a conch
when all lips
become like thorns in the heath
when all breasts
throb monotonously
like wall clocks.

You'll never understand me.
When a thousand women
sleep by my side
I feel as if no woman
sleeps by my side.[15]

In another candid poem titled "I Am Accused of Being like Shahrayar," Qabbani depicts in vivid detail his predicament as an Arab male:

I am accused of being like Shahrayar
By my friends
And by my enemies,
Accused of collecting women
Like stamps
Like empty matchboxes
That I pin up

On the walls of my room.
They accuse me of being narcissistic,
Sadistic,
Oedipal,
Of being disturbed
In order to prove
They are educated
And I am deviant.

Nobody, my love,
Wants to listen to my testimony.
The judges are biased,
The witnesses are bribed,
I am pronounced guilty
Before I testify.
Nobody, my love,
Understands my childhood,
I belong to a city
That does not love children,
That does not recognize innocence,
That has never in its life
Bought a rose or a book of poetry.
I belong to a city whose hands are rough
Whose heart and emotions are hard
From having swallowed nails and pieces of glass.
I belong to a city whose walls are made of ice
Whose children have frozen to death.
. . . .
I want to say
If only this one time
That I am not a disciple of Shahrayar,
I am not a murderer
And have never melted women in sulfuric acid.
Rather, I am a poet
Who writes in a loud voice,
Who loves in a loud voice.
I am a child with green eyes
Leaning on the gates of a city
That does not recognize childhood.[16]

In this poem, Qabbani attributes his pursuit of love affairs to a deprived childhood lived in a cruel city that "does not love children" and "does not recognize innocence," a city "whose hands are rough" and "whose walls are made of ice." His multiple sexual relations are at once a compensatory mechanism for, and a form of escape from, his harsh social reality. The unnamed city is most likely Damascus, the seat of the despotic regime in Syria, where people live in constant fear and privation. The cruel city may also be a metaphor for a prison or a place experienced like a prison, such as the patriarchal family or a conservative society.

Fertility is the third component of virility. In a culture that places much emphasis on procreation and whose code of masculinity equates having children, especially sons, with being a man, an infertile male faces a crisis of enormous magnitude. He is regarded as "weak" and "incomplete," not a "real man," a perception that calls into question his sexual and gender identities and threatens his whole personhood. The condition is so stigmatizing that he is tormented by feelings of shame, inadequacy, and self-loathing. Such emotional and psychological suffering is the price an infertile male pays for not living up to normative masculinity.[17] On the other hand, the fertile male who proves his virility by having many children must carry the heavy burden of providing for them in a region suffering from a high level of unemployment, poverty, and overpopulation. Yusuf Idris's short story "The Cheapest Nights" dramatizes the vicious circle between poverty and large families.[18] While a Muslim Arab whose wife is infertile can divorce her or take a second wife—with even greater economic responsibilities—a Christian Arab does not have these options.

It should be noted that the core values of Arab culture are shared by all segments of Arab society, regardless of religious denomination or sectarian affiliation. Arab cultures, whether Muslim or Christian, are patriarchal. As Marcia Inhorn states: "Patriarchal ideologies cut across social classes, religious boundaries, and household types."[19] Suad Joseph, for example, examined the mother-son relationship in a Christian village in Lebanon and found that it conformed to the traditional cultural model in being close and powerful, thus affirming that "the norms of Muslim communities have influenced the minority Arab Christian communities."[20] While Arab Muslims and Arab Christians share many norms, customs, and attitudes, the predicament of childless Christian men is worse than that of Muslim men because they have no recourse to divorce or polygamy, both of which are forbidden by the church to Maronite Catholics, Roman Catholics, Coptic Orthodox, or Greek Orthodox. A compelling example of the tragedy resulting from being trapped in an unproductive marriage is Andrée Chedid's novel *From Sleep Unbound*. The narrative tells of a childless Coptic husband who, unable to divorce his wife, abuses her and slowly drives her into madness, until she explodes and shoots him to death.[21]

As for the subordination of women—one of the defining criteria of masculinity in Arab societies—enlightened Arab men have long recognized that the status of women is inseparably tied to the status of a nation. More than a century ago, the Egyptian lawyer Qasim Amin (1863–1909), in his landmark book *The Liberation of Women* (1899), argued that when the status of a nation is elevated, reflecting progress and civilization, the status of women in that country is also elevated, and when the status of a nation is low, reflecting an underdeveloped condition, so is the status of women there.[22] Men do not benefit from the subordination of women but rather are crippled by it: "In every society women constitute half the population on average. To condemn them to be ignorant and inactive occasions the loss of half the society's productive potential and creates a considerable drain upon the society's resources."[23] The French ethnographer Germaine Tillion, in her classic work on the oppression of women in Mediterranean society, *The Republic of Cousins*, expresses a similar view:

> The female veil became a symbol: a symbol of the enslavement of half the human race....Widely plundered despite legislation, sometimes sold, often beaten, coerced into forced labour, murdered almost with impunity, the Mediterranean woman is among today's serfs.
>
> Yet the disadvantages of this alienation are well known to all sociologists...and to most magistrates. For both are aware that it lowers the active potential of the nation and consequently weakens the State; that it paralyses all forms of collective and individual evolution, male as much as female, and consequently slows down or curbs progress; and that it causes multiple and irreparable injuries to children, and hence to the future. As for man, the supposed author and apparent beneficiary of this repression, at every period of his life—as child, as husband, as father—he is the direct victim of it; and the weight of bitterness that falls to his lot as a result is sometimes not very different from that which crushes his female companion.[24]

Thus behind the enduring facade of male privileges lie profound contradictions that are detrimental to Arab men. Inevitably, attempts to live up to unhealthy and unrealistic norms of masculinity warp Arab men and society. In "Being," the Kuwaiti poet Sulaiman al-Fulayyih expresses grave concern at Arab men's mode of being:

> Till when will we continue
> to engage in this madness?

Urging his countrymen to transcend the fetters of social convention, al-Fulayyih demands to know:

> When will we strive, my friend, to be
> not as others imagine us
> but as we wish ourselves
>   to be?[25]

The consequences of the crisis in Arab masculinity and the resulting state of malaise and societal dysfunction are bluntly depicted by Dhabya Khamees, a woman poet from the United Arab Emirates, in a poem revealingly titled "Schizophrenia":

> Because things are not alright
> Death—and escape from death—
> Are the only professions of the East.[26]

An equally bleak view of Arab societies is expressed by the Iraqi poet Sami Mahdi in his poem "Abel's Brothers," written in the wake of the 1991 Gulf War:

> In every generation there is a slayer and a slain
> And a legacy of fear and suspicion.
> It is the story of Cain
> As he mends his criminal cloak
> Fearing punishment.
> It is the story of Abel
> Searching for his wound
> Between nail and tooth.
> It is this pervasion of earth's laws
> This desolation.
>
> No way for Cain but madness
> No way for Abel but resignation
> No way for us for seven thousand years
> Except this.[27]

The Saudi poet Muhammad Hasan Faqi, in one of his most eloquent quartets, makes an urgent appeal to his fellow Arabs to put aside their feuds, relinquish their dreams about past glories, and unite so that they can shape a better future for themselves and their societies:

> Brother, here is my hand,
> Clasp it in yours.

My future, should you question,
Is tied to yours.
The fate of all our brothers,
Hinges on yours.
I have abandoned dreams in my slumber-bed,
Therefore, abandon them in yours.[28]

The foregoing account shows that the Arab male is compromised on many levels: he has to uphold an untenable sense of honor, virility, and family loyalty. He is caught in impossible binds that do not allow him to function optimally or to explore and express his humanity. Furthermore, some of the core values and practices of patriarchal culture pit fathers and sons against each other and form stumbling blocks in men's relation to men. Samira Aghacy, examining masculine identity in the fiction of the Arab East, observes that "patriarchal constructions of masculinity in Arab societies become constrictions, disrupting man's quest for self-autonomy and creating contradictions for individual men. Instead of generating autonomy and self-government, patriarchy exposes the male individual to a strong sense of personal inadequacy, ineffectuality, and failure to measure up to phallocentric masculine ideals."[29]

Male liberation calls for men to free themselves from all the gender role stereotypes and cultural straitjackets that limit their ability to develop a coherent sense of self, to fulfill their potential, and to contribute to the advancement of their society.

The Rap That Sparked a Revolution

The song "Ra'is Lebled" (meaning, President of the Republic), by the then-21-year-old Tunisian rapper known as El Général (his name is Hamada Ben Amor), was the battle hymn of the Jasmine Revolution that brought down Tunisia's president of 23 years, Zine el-Abidine Ben Ali, in January 2011. The song was then adopted by the demonstrators in Cairo's Tahrir Square who, a few weeks later, toppled Hosni Mubarak, Egypt's president of 30 years. From there the song was picked up by protesters in Libya, as rage against poverty and oppression spread through the Arab region from west to east. Soon the rap became the anthem of the Arab Spring—the wave of youth-led uprisings that swept across North Africa and the Middle East, dismantling several dictatorial regimes and challenging rulers and monarchs in countries such as Yemen, Syria, Jordan, Morocco, Algeria, Bahrain, and Saudi Arabia.

The lyrics of the sensational song that lit the fire of revolt are as follows:

> Mr. President, here, today, I want to say something to you
> It is on my behalf and on behalf of my people who are living in
>   misery
> 2011! Still people are dying of hunger!
>
> He wanted to work, he wanted to survive, but his voice is silenced.[30]
> Get to the streets and take a look
> People are turning mad, police are monsters
> Speaking only with their batons, tac tac tac, they don't care
> As long as no one is there to say no
> Our laws in the constitution are nothing but a decoration.
>
> Everyday, I hear of a new lawsuit
> Where the poor were set up
> Although they know he/she is a decent person
> I see snakes (powerful men) everywhere biting our girls
> Will you accept for your daughter to be bit?
>
> I know my words are so hard
> You are a father and you wouldn't allow that for your sons
> Thus, take my message as one from a son to his father
> I am speaking out of suffering
> We are living like dogs
> Half of the population is living in humiliation and misery.
>
> (Chorus) Mr. President, your people are dying
> People are eating rubbish! Look at what is happening
> Miseries everywhere, Mr. President
> I talk with no fear, although I know I will get only troubles.
>
> I see injustice everywhere
> How much longer? People are living in illusions.
> Where is freedom of expression?
> It is only in your speeches.
> The thieves are everywhere, you know who I'm talking about
> They stick to their positions, to their atrocities.[31]

This song is a damning indictment of a corrupt regime that has usurped its power and abused its own people who suffer from hunger, unemployment, exploitation, police brutality, lack of basic civil rights, and mass repression. Of particular interest is the reference to a father-son relationship in the lines "You are a father and you wouldn't allow that for your sons / Thus, take my message as one from a son to his father." These words are meant to generate in the president feelings and behavioral expectations that characterize the father-son relationship, such as trust, empathy, solidarity, support, and protection. The analogy that is drawn between father/ruler and son/citizen shows that paradigms of social interaction extend from the family sphere to the political sphere.[32]

The protests that spread like wildfire in Arab streets in 2011 were organized by a new generation of young men and women who had known little political freedom in their lives and were no longer willing to wait for it. Frustrated, disillusioned, and dispossessed, they voiced their rage at the aloof, ossified, and repressive regimes in their countries in massive demonstrations, demanding the basic rights to choose and change their leaders, have free and fair elections, put an end to corruption, and ensure employment opportunities, social justice, and economic reforms. Their actions inspired their parents' generation to join: when the older people saw the younger people go out in the street, they started to come out too. Thus fathers and sons were united in the pursuit of a common goal. In the course of one year, these popular uprisings brought down three long-time despots (the fourth, Yemen's Ali Abdullah Saleh, agreed to step down) and shook other autocratic regimes across the Arab region. In some countries, notably Syria and Bahrain, the protesters met with a fierce crackdown by brutal rulers determined to keep power at all costs. While the final outcome of several uprisings is still unclear, the actions of these protesters have already transformed the political reality in the Arab region and precipitated historic change.

In challenging, and in some places successfully dismantling, the old order, this young generation (in almost every Arab country more than half the population is under the age of 30) proved the old axiom that rebellion against the authority of the father/ruler is for the son/citizen the only way to liberation. Still, these events took the international community by surprise and turned several stereotypes about Arabs upside down. Central among them is the assumption that the only outlet for youthful dissent in the Arab world is Islamic extremism and violence. As noted earlier, the battle hymn of the rebels was not a verse from the Koran; it was rap. And the rebels were calling for freedom and democracy, not for the establishment of a theocracy. As for tools, the rebels' main strategy was to organize civil disobedience through peaceful demonstrations, strikes, marches, and rallies; they also used social media such as Facebook, Twitter, and YouTube to communicate and raise awareness. These nonviolent activities are a far cry from the stereotypical images of suicide bombing and other bloody acts of terrorism. Most importantly, the old narrative that Arabs "don't have the DNA for democracy," which is why they have remained mired in darkness and autocracy, has been debunked. The Arab Spring has clearly proven, as Michael Elliott aptly puts it, that "there is no 'Arab exception,' no iron rule that specifies that the desires that motivate human society anywhere—a right to choose your rulers, a hope that your children will lead better lives than you, a search for prosperity and happiness—are somehow absent from the Middle East. Why on earth should they?"[33] While the Arab men and women who called for regime change in their countries may not all had a clear vision of what kind of democracy they wanted, they did know that they preferred to live in a free, just, and modern society.

And yet, two years after it came about, the Arab Spring is not blossoming and seems to have ground to a halt. Some Middle East observers believe that this Arab Spring has been diverted from its original goals and hijacked from the younger generation by Islamist parties and tribal or sectarian forces. In Tunisia, the once-banned Islamist party Ennahda won in October 2011 the country's first democratic elections after President Zine el-Abidine Ben Ali was thrown out of office. Although Ennahda insists that its approach to Shari'a, or Islamic law, is consistent with Tunisia's progressive traditions, especially in regard to women's rights, its victory has caused concern among secularists. In Egypt, the groups that gained the most from Mubarak's ouster were the Islamists: the formerly banned Muslim Brotherhood won the largest number of seats in the parliamentary elections of January 2012, and the Salafis came in second. In the country's first free presidential elections, held in June 2012, the winner was Mohamed Morsi, the Muslim Brotherhood's leader. One year later, Morsi was deposed by a military coup for undermining democracy by writing an Islamist constitution. While Egypt's transition to civilian rule remains tenuous, the unrest and violence continue, with deadly clashes between Islamists and liberal activists. In post-Gaddafi Libya, tribal and regional loyalties played a stronger role than religion in the country's first free vote, held in July 2012, and the Alliance of National Forces, a coalition of liberal and secular parties, won the largest number of seats in the new parliament. However, the country remains split by feuding militias, and the continuous fighting threatens to break it up into two parts: the eastern region, where the oil is, and the western region. Can Libya survive as one country? In Syria, the raging civil war threatens to spill over into Lebanon, Turkey, Israel, and Jordan and cause regionwide conflagration. "One year after it captured the world's imagination," remarks the journalist Fareed Zakaria, "the Arab Spring is looking less appealing by the week. The promise of a new birth of freedom in the

Middle East has been followed by a much messier reality, particularly in Egypt, where there have been attacks on Christians, Western aid workers and women."[34]

Thus, while the Arab Spring has debunked one assumption about Arabs, it has brought two other ones to the fore: the resurgence of Islamism and the spread of violence. As the Lebanese journalist Hazim Saghieh opined before the first free Arab elections were held: "[The Arab uprisings] end this sense of the Arabs being a historic exception among the world's peoples. But in clearing old ground, they also highlight a new and twofold challenge. First, can Tunisia and Egypt, where the nation weighs more than the premodern loyalties (sects, tribes, ethnicities), build democratic republics without these falling into the hands of Islamists?...Second, can Libya, Yemen, Bahrain, and Syria, where the nation-state is fragile, avoid anarchy and civil war along sectarian or tribal or regional lines?"[35] As it happened, Tunisia and Egypt did fall into the hands of Islamists, and Syria is in the throes of a brutal civil war. While the future of the revolutions in the rest of the Arab region is unclear, the basic facts remain: Arabs are doing it for themselves, and they have been inspired by the example of fellow Arabs.[36] For Wael Ghonim, the Egyptian Internet activist who helped mobilize the massive street protests in Cairo, these fellow Arabs—heroic marchers and chanters—have proven a universal truth: "The power of the people is greater than the people in power." Ghonim rightly reminds his readers: "Revolutions are processes and not events, and the next chapter of this story is only beginning to be written." While admitting that Egypt is still a long way from a fully established democracy, he believes that Egyptians will never again put up with another Pharaoh: "Thanks to modern technology, participatory democracy is becoming a reality. Governments are finding it harder and harder to keep their people isolated from one another, to censor information, and to hide corruption and issue propaganda that goes unchallenged. Slowly but surely, the weapons of mass oppression are becoming extinct."[37]

The Changing Landscape of Men's Relation to Men

In a volume of candid reflections on events and situations in his life, Naguib Mahfouz, winner of the 1988 Nobel Prize for Literature, describes what the loss of his mother meant to him:

> It is true, as people say, that one only attains maturity with the death of one's mother. As long as she was alive, I depended on my

mother for many things—not for material things, but for emotional
support. With her gone, I came to feel that I was truly alone in the
world. I had friends, to be sure, and my own family: but the place
my mother had occupied was empty forever. Many young people
today leave their families as soon as they have finished school, and
assume full responsibility for their own welfare. In these cases, the
loss of a parent is not such a crushing blow. The world has changed
so much.[38]

Mahfouz's observation about modern life shows that the process
of social change currently in progress throughout the Arab region
has transformed many aspects of Arab family life. In the past, individual men and women found their economic and emotional support
within the traditional family structure. Today, a growing number
of young men and women are pursuing education and careers away
from their parents in urban centers, both within and outside their
home countries. State-sponsored education, employment, and welfare services have replaced some of the traditional responsibilities of
the family, thus reducing its function and power. Additional factors
such as industrialization, urbanization, the employment of women,
and exposure to foreign influences have precipitated changes in the
family structure. Trends include a shift away from the extended family toward the nuclear family, especially in the cities. Old patterns of
marriage and divorce are slowly being replaced by new ones, partly
owing to legal reforms in the areas of polygamy, repudiation, and
age of marriage. The economic pressures that have forced women
into the workforce have also sent men abroad as migrant laborers,
producing a rise in women-headed households. These structural
changes have undermined traditional roles, relationships, and values
within the family. New conceptions of the family, new attitudes to
gender roles, and new patterns of interactional dynamics have begun
to emerge.[39]

The most dramatic area of social change has been the emancipation of women. The old pattern of woman at home and man in
the workplace is breaking up. Although this is primarily due to
economic necessity rather than progressive ideology, it nevertheless
has far-reaching consequences. Working mothers and daughters are
redefining gender roles and male-female relations as they establish
their presence at school, on the street, and in the workplace. Their
contribution to the family income undermines the supremacy of the
male head of the family as the sole provider, thus weakening patriarchal control and facilitating the evolution of more egalitarian family
relationships.

The introduction of computers and the Internet into homes and workplaces, as well as a global satellite television culture, have been instrumental in empowering young men and women and changing traditional attitudes toward gender roles and male-female relations. Educated youth of both sexes tend to adopt more liberal views of marriage, seeking a relationship based on love and equality rather than on parental approval and male domination. Cell phones, social networking sites on the Internet, cyber cafés, and shopping malls facilitate direct contact between young adults and give them more opportunities to meet and form friendships, especially in urban centers.

These trends of development have promoted new forms of masculine practice, among them men's desire to date their future spouses before marriage, men's desire to live in nuclear residences with their wives and children, men's encouragement of daughters' education, and men's willingness to use means of birth control. These new forms of masculine practice in relation to women can be observed across the Arab region.[40]

Men's relation to men, particularly fathers to sons, is changing too. Increasingly aware, informed, and connected, young men are no longer willing to accept the tyranny of paternal authority and demand personal autonomy and freedom to shape their own futures. The anthropologist John Borneman, who lived in Aleppo in 2004 and spent much time among ordinary Syrian men, observing their everyday lives, writes: "The conditions of paternal authority in Syria have been severely compromised—in terms of an inability to procure jobs for their sons and daughters; an inability to reverse a trend in contemporary representation to reduce Arab men to terrorists, Islamic extremists, and ineffectual victims of Israeli politics; and an inability to assert any influence over the political sphere in their own country."[41] The crisis in the authority of the father is not unique to Syria but common to all Arab societies. In many families, fathers can no longer teach their children the skills or provide them with the resources they need to make decent lives in the modernizing world, a situation that undermines the traditional bases of their authority.[42] Borneman notes that most young men seek to understand the nature of paternal authority, the circumstances under which they should submit to it, and the cost of its inheritance, but they do not dare to break away from their families. As he explains: "For most men emotional dependence on the parents is too great to risk a break by questioning their authority or trying to establish much personal autonomy."[43] Thus, despite the many changes in Arab family life in recent decades, "what tends to remain constant and taken for granted until death is the relation with the father and mother, the former as source of authority, the latter as template for relations with women."[44] As Basil, a young Syrian man, affirms, "Fathers here have power over you until death."[45] Many sons in the Arab region face this predicament: "The precondition for freedom is also the father's death, for only upon his death can the son become his own source of authority, that is, to have authority over others and become subject only to himself: to choose his own wife, keep his own bank account, construct his own household. While the father is still living, the son can procreate as much as he pleases, but having children of his own does not release him of his duties and obligations to his father; only the father's death can free a son from this authority. So, young men are caught, needing the father to realize their freedom but unable to be autonomous until his death."[46] The autobiographical writings and works of fiction and poetry of male authors from across the Arab world reflect the inner conflicts in men's lives and daily experiences at a time of rapid social change when a close relationship between father and son can be a vital source of mutual stability, strength, and support.

Like other cultures, Arab culture is characterized by diversity, pluralism, and contradictions. As Halim Barakat states: "The Arabs have their own dominant culture (that is, what is most common and diffused among Arabs), its subcultures (those peculiar to some communities and classes), and its countercultures (those of alienated and radicalized segments of society)."[47] Owing to the struggle between these constituent cultures, and as a result of new inventions and resources, culture changes constantly. Thus, the thousands of ordinary Arab men who took to the streets in January 2011 introduced a new form of masculinity in Arab societies, "protest masculinity," whose rites of passage are marches and demonstrations. Similarly, the medical anthropologist Marcia Inhorn speaks of "emergent masculinities" in the Arab region in the era of biotechnology. These are infertile men, both Muslims and Christians, whose rites of passage to manhood consist of pervasive medical tests and procedures that they are willing to undergo to give their wives children. In so doing they defy the ban of Islam and the church on assisted reproduction. Inhorn believes that thanks to assisted reproduction, the issue of infertility is no longer the major crisis of masculinity it was once perceived to be, that many men do not view fatherhood as the be-all and end-all of masculinity, and that they value marital relations with or without children. Hence "reproduction, fatherhood, and manhood are in a state of flux—or what I shall call 'emergence'—in the Middle Eastern region as a whole. 'Emergent masculinities' bespeak not only the new

treatment options available for male infertility but also men's changing desires for a happy life."[48]

This state of flux, especially as it relates to the ties between fathers
and sons, is mirrored in the myriad themes and images that feature
in the works of Arab male writers. Intriguingly, the many voices and
testimonies assembled in this study reveal that while some sons are
oppressed by paternal authority, others are *adrift* without it. When the
Egyptian scholar Ahmad Amin, for example, looks back on his life,
he laments the strict upbringing, based on "fear and intimidation"
(p. 123), which he received at the hands of his tyrannical father. At the
same time he realizes that he has his father to thank for his education
and success in his studies, especially for instilling in him the qualities
of discipline, patience, and perseverance. This realization fills him with
appreciation for his father: "When I grew up and entered the Judicial
School and became free from his protection and severity, I began to
be aware of his merit. My fear of him turned to love and respect. . . . So
when he died I felt a painful heartache: a prop collapsed that was not
replaced, a vacuum arose that was not filled" (p. 141). Unlike Amin,
who became his own man, Yasin, the eldest son of the patriarch
al-Sayyid Ahmad in Mahfouz's Trilogy, remains helplessly dependent
on his father, both emotionally and materially. Yasin's pursuit of a life
of debauchery and sexual pleasures brings shame on the patriarch and
his family and causes repeated crises with his father. Yasin, however,
sees his rebellious actions as "natural expressions of his lust for life,
not as a desire to take over the patriarchal mantle."[49] He is unable to
measure up to his father and never feels self-assured, often wondering
why he has failed whereas his father has succeeded. After he marries
and becomes a father, his dependency on the patriarch is transferred
to his own son, Ridwan, who becomes a high-ranking official in the
same ministry that employs his father in a lowly job. This dependency,
which occurs concomitantly with the patriarch's aging and infirmity,
brings Yasin greater satisfaction and peace of mind, for he takes pride
in his son's accomplishments, regarding them as partly the product of
his own influence.[50]

The changing relations between fathers and sons, as well as the
link between personal and national liberation, are depicted in a candid conversation between al-Sayyid Ahmad and his close friends, one
of whom teases him for being a reactionary who clings to the past
and insists on ruling his home by force even in the age of democracy.
Al-Sayyid Ahmad replies scornfully, "Democracy's for the people, not
the family" (2:398). But his friend disagrees with him: "Do you think
you can rule the young people of today in the old-fashioned way?

These youngsters are used to demonstrating in the streets and confronting the [British] soldiers" (2:398). These words, written five decades before the Arab Spring, proved to be prophetic. The tide of revolutions that swept through the Arab region in 2011, when thousands of young men and women demonstrated in the streets against their despotic regimes, successfully bringing down dictators that have oppressed them for decades, reflects an irresistible impulse toward freedom and democracy. Needless to say, an egalitarian society promotes an egalitarian family and vice versa. Arab fathers and sons, as well as mothers and daughters, have awakened to a new dawn and a new sense of possibility. With luck, they may change the course of Arab history.

Notes

1 Introduction: Why Fathers and Sons?

1. Cited from Michael D. Coogan, ed., *The New Oxford Annotated Bible* (3rd ed. New York: Oxford University Press, 2001).
2. Carol Delaney, *Abraham on Trial: The Social Legacy of Biblical Myth* (Princeton, NJ: Princeton University Press, 1998), p. 6.
3. See Koran 37: 100–13. For a discussion of the influence of the story of Abraham on Arabo-Muslim culture, see Najat Rahman, "The Trial of Heritage and the Legacy of Abraham," in Lahoucine Ouzgane, ed., *Islamic Masculinities* (London: Zed, 2006), pp. 72–85.
4. Delaney, *Abraham on Trial*, p. 234. In the Arab region this is illustrated by various jihadist movements that employ suicide bombers as a means to achieve their goals.
5. Abdelwahab Bouhdiba, *Sexuality in Islam*, trans. Alan Sheridan (London: Saqi, 2004), p. 220.
6. Stephen A. Anderson and Ronald M. Sabatelli, *Family Interaction: A Multigenerational Developmental Perspective* (3rd ed. Boston, MA: Allyn and Bacon, 2002), pp. 54–56, 62–64.
7. Peter Blos, *Son and Father: Before and Beyond the Oedipus Complex* (New York: The Free Press, 1985), p. 6.
8. Robert J. Pellegrini, "General Introduction," in Robert J. Pellegrini and Theodore R. Sarbin, eds., *Between Fathers and Sons* (New York: The Haworth Clinical Practice Press, 2002), p. 2.
9. Leila Abouzeid, *Return to Childhood: The Memoir of a Modern Moroccan Woman*, trans. the author, with Heather Logan Taylor (Austin: The Center for Middle Eastern Studies at the University of Texas, 1998), p. iii.
10. Suad Joseph, ed., *Intimate Selving in Arab Families: Gender, Self, and Identity* (Syracuse, NY: Syracuse University Press, 1999), p. 9.
11. Ibid.
12. See the bibliography for relevant titles.
13. Lewis Yablonsky, *Fathers and Sons: The Most Challenging of All Family Relationships* (New York: Gardner, 1990), p. 13.
14. Ibid.
15. Ibid., p. 10.

16. Samuel Osherson, *Finding Our Fathers* (New York: Contemporary Books, 2001), p. viii.

17. Yablonsky, *Fathers and Sons*, p. 13.

18. See, for example, Nayra Atiya, *Khul Khaal: Five Egyptian Women Tell Their Stories* (Syracuse, NY: Syracuse University Press, 1982), p. 49.

19. Daniel Bates and Amal Rassam, *Peoples and Cultures of the Middle East* (Englewood Cliffs, NJ: Prentice-Hall, 1983), pp. 204–6. It should be noted that custom does not always reflect on-the-ground reality, which may vary according to individual circumstance, class, education, and geographical location.

20. Shelley Phillips, *Beyond the Myths: Mother-Daughter Relationships in Psychology, History, Literature, and Everyday Life* (London: Penguin, 1996), p. xvi.

21. Gerda Lerner, *The Creation of Patriarchy* (New York: Oxford University Press, 1986), p. 239.

22. Marcia C. Inhorn, *Infertility and Patriarchy: The Cultural Politics of Gender and Family Life in Egypt* (Philadelphia: University of Pennsylvania Press, 1966), pp. 3–4.

23. Soraya Altorki, "Patriarchy and Imperialism: Father-Son and British-Egyptian Relations in Najib Mahfuz's Trilogy," in Joseph, *Intimate Selving in Arab Families*, p. 232.

24. Davies Pryce-Jones, *The Closed Circle: An Interpretation of the Arabs* (Chicago, IL: Ivan R. Dee, 2002), p. 402.

25. Yablonsky, *Fathers and Sons*, p. 130.

26. Ibid., p. 133.

27. Anderson and Sabatelli, *Family Interaction*, pp. 42–44.

28. Albert Hourani, *Arabic Thought in the Liberal Age: 1798–1939* (Cambridge: Cambridge University Press, 1983), p. 1.

29. Ibid.

30. Halim Barakat, *The Arab World: Society, Culture, and State* (Berkeley: University of California Press, 1993), p. 33.

31. Ibid., pp. 32–33.

32. Ibid., p. 46.

33. William C. Young and Seteney Shami, "Anthropological Approaches to the Arab Family: An Introduction," *Journal of Comparative Family Studies* 28, no. 2 (Summer 1997): 1.

34. Ibid., p. 11.

35. See the bibliography for select titles.

36. I have used the same methodology in this study as in my previous work, *Mothers and Daughters in Arab Women's Literature: The Family Frontier* (Leiden: Brill, 2011).

37. This approach is adopted from Phillips, *Beyond the Myths*, pp. x, xix–xx.

38. To allow the Western reader who is not versed in the Arabic language access to this body of literature, I have indicated in the publication

data of each literary work whether it is available in English translation. If only an Arabic title is mentioned, this means that no English translation is yet available. If only an English title is mentioned, this means that the work was originally published in English (e.g., Edward Said's *Out of Place*, and Yusuf Idris's "A Sketch of My Life as a Child"). Many of the translations that I refer to in this work are my own labor of love.

39. For a discussion of the interaction between the novel and social science, see Morroe Berger, *Real and Imagined Worlds* (Cambridge, MA: Harvard University Press, 1977), pp. 1–11, 214–35.

40. While the field of Arab women's studies has enjoyed a surge of creativity in recent decades, the field of men's studies has lagged behind. It is actually thanks to the many new publications on Arab women's lives that men's lives and relationships have been illuminated and given more critical attention.

41. Among male authors who have been jailed for their writings are Yusuf Idris, Gamal al-Ghitani, Abdel Hakim Kassem, Hanna Mina, Sadiq al-Azm, and Mohammad Abdul-Wali. Among women writers who have been jailed for their writings are Nawal El Saadawi, Latifa al-Zayyat, Suhayr al-Tall, and Dhabya Khamis.

42. Stephan Guth, "Why Novels—Not Autobiographies?" in Robin Ostle, Ed de Moor, and Stephan Wild, eds., *Writing the Self: Autobiographical Writing in Modern Arabic Literature* (London: Saqi, 1998), pp. 146–47.

43. Trevor Le Gassick, "The Faith of Islam in Modern Arabic Fiction," *Religion and Literature* 20, no. 1 (Spring 1988): 97.

44. Barakat, *Arab World*, p. 210.

45. Ibid.

46. Ibid.

47. John Fowles, in the introduction to Naguib Mahfouz, *Miramar*, trans. Fatma Moussa-Mahmoud (Washington, DC: Three Continents Press, 1983), p. xv.

48. Barakat, *Arab World*, p. 210; see also pp. 207–8. It is important to recognize that there are limits to this reciprocal influence when we are looking at a society with a high degree of illiteracy. Nevertheless, through adaptations of short stories, novels, and plays for the cinema and television, as well as by setting poems to music, literature can reach many uneducated people.

49. Magda al-Nowaihi, "Constructions of Masculinity in Two Egyptian Novels," in Joseph, *Intimate Selving in Arab Families*, p. 235.

50. Edward W. Said, *The World, the Text, and the Critic* (Cambridge, MA: Harvard University Press, 1983), p. 5; see also pp. 8–15, 34–35.

51. Edward W. Said, *Orientalism* (New York: Vintage, 1979), p. 291.

52. Nancy Chodorow, *The Reproduction of Mothering: Psychoanalysis and the Sociology of Gender* (Berkeley: University of California Press, 1978), p. 32.

53. See, for example, Stanley H. Cath et al., *Father and Child: Developmental and Clinical Perspectives* (Boston, MA: Little Brown and Company, 1982); Ronald F. Levant and William S. Pollack, eds., *A New Psychology of Men* (New York: Basic Books, 1995); Salman Akhtar and Henri Parens, eds., *Real and Imaginary Fathers: Development, Transference, and Healing* (Lanham, MD: Jason Aronson, 2003); and R. W. Connell, *Masculinities* (2nd ed. Berkeley: University of California Press, 2005). See also websites such as www.menstudies.org and www.fatherhood.org.

2   The Voyage to Manhood: The Elusive Quest

1. Thomas De Quincey, *Autobiography*, in *The Collected Writings of Thomas De Quincey*, ed. David Masson (New York: Johnson Reprint Corporation, 1968), 1: 317–19; emphasis in the original text.

2. William S. Pollack, "No Man Is an Island," in Ronald F. Levant and William S. Pollack, eds., *A New Psychology of Men* (New York: Basic Books, 1995), p. 42.

3. Stephen J. Bergman, "Men's Psychological Development: A Relational Perspective," in Levant and Pollack, *A New Psychology of Men*, pp. 70–71.

4. Barry Richards, "Masculinity, Identification, and Political Culture," in Jeff Hearn and David Morgan, eds., *Men, Masculinities, and Social Theory* (London: Unwin Hyman, 1990), p. 162.

5. Chodorow, *Reproduction of Mothering*, pp. 141–58; Jonathan Rutherford, *Men's Silences* (London: Routledge, 1992), p. 33.

6. For example, Erik Erikson, Margaret Mahler, O. Kernberg, Nancy Chodorow, and Carol Gilligan.

7. Cited in Bergman, "Men's Psychological Development," p. 71.

8. Chodorow, *Reproduction of Mothering*, p. 169.

9. Ibid.

10. Ibid., p. 217.

11. Anthony Elliott, *Concepts of the Self* (Cambridge, UK: Polity, 2001), p. 109.

12. See, for example, Rutherford, *Men's Silences*, pp. 37–38.

13. See, for example, Hearn and Morgan, *Men, Masculinities, and Social Theory*, pp. 4, 97, 225.

14. Michael S. Kimmel and Michael A. Messner, eds., *Men's Lives* (2nd ed. New York: Macmillan, 1992), p. 9.

15. Ibid., p. 8.

16. Examples are: Suad Joseph, ed., *Intimate Selving in Arab Families* (Syracuse: Syracuse University Press, 1999); Mai Ghoussoub and Emma Sinclair-Webb, eds., *Imagined Masculinities: Male Identity and Culture in the Modern Middle East* (London: Saqi, 2000); Lahoucine Ouzgane, ed., *Islamic Masculinities* (London: Zed, 2006).

17. Mervat Hatem, "Toward the Study of the Psychodynamics of Gender and Mothering in Egyptian Families," *International Journal of Middle East Studies* 19 (1987): 287–306.

18. Mervat Hatem, "Underdevelopment, Mothering and Gender within the Egyptian Family," *Arab Studies Quarterly* 8, no. 1 (Winter 1986): 58.

19. Hatem, "Psychodynamics of Gender and Mothering in Egyptian Families," p. 302.

20. Abdessamad Dialmy, "Sexuality in Contemporary Arab Society," trans. Allon J. Uhlmann, *Social Practice* 49, no. 2 (Summer 2005). Available: http://www.berghahnbooksonline.com (accessed January 24, 2007).

21. Ibid., p. 2.

22. Ibid., p. 3.

23. Ibid.

24. Ibid., p. 4.

25. Ibid.

26. Ibid., p. 6.

27. Ibid., p. 12.

28. Ibid., p. 13.

29. Ibid.

30. Ibid., pp. 13–14.

31. Gary S. Gregg, *The Middle East: A Cultural Psychology* (New York: Oxford University Press, 2005), p. 359.

32. Young and Shami, "Anthropological Approaches to the Arab Family," p. 1; Margot Badran, *Feminists, Islam, and Nation* (Princeton, NJ: Princeton University Press, 1995), p. 124.

33. Gregg, *The Middle East*, p. 46.

34. Barakat, *Arab World*, pp. 97–107; Valentine M. Moghadam, *Modernizing Women: Gender and Social Change in the Middle East* (2nd ed. Boulder, CO: Lynne Rienner, 2003), p. 124.

35. For a discussion of Middle Eastern patriarchy, see Moghadam, *Modernizing Women*, pp. 113–50; Deniz Kandiyoti, "Islam and Patriarchy: A Comparative Perspective," in Nikki Keddie and Beth Baron, eds., *Women in Middle Eastern History* (New Haven, CT: Yale University Press, 1991), pp. 23–42; and Inhorn, *Infertility and Patriarchy*, pp. 2–10.

36. Gregg, *The Middle East*, p. 195; Bates and Rassam, *People and Cultures of the Middle East*, pp. 220–22; Raphael Patai, *The Arab Mind* (rev. ed. New York: Charles Scribners Sons, 1983), pp. 27–32.

37. Abdelwahab Bouhdiba, "The Child and the Mother in Arab-Muslim Society," in L. Carl Brown and Norman Itzkowitz, eds., *Psychological Dimensions of Near Eastern Studies* (Princeton, NJ: Darwin, 1977), pp. 128–29; Hisham Sharabi, "Impact of Class and Culture on Social Behavior: The Feudal-Bourgeois Family in Arab Society," in ibid., pp. 245–46; Gregg, *The Middle East*, pp. 182–83.

38. Gregg, *The Middle East*, pp. 228–30.
39. Hatem, "Psychodynamics of Mothering and Gender in Egyptian Families," p. 299.
40. Bouhdiba, *Sexuality in Islam*, p. 219.
41. Ibid., p. 221.
42. Bouhdiba, "Child and the Mother in Arab-Muslim Society," p. 131; Patai, *Arab Mind*, pp. 31, 35.
43. Hatem, "Psychodynamics of Mothering and Gender in Egyptian Families," p. 298.
44. Gregg, *The Middle East*, p. 199; Bouhdiba, *Sexuality in Islam*, p. 181.
45. Hatem, "Psychodynamics of Mothering and Gender in Egyptian Families," p. 298. See similar descriptions of the ceremony in Hamed Ammar, *Growing Up in an Egyptian Village: Silwa, Province of Aswan* (London: Routledge & Kegan Paul, 1954), pp. 116–17.
46. Ammar, *Growing Up in an Egyptian Village*, p. 116.
47. Ibid., p. 123. See also Gregg, *The Middle East*, pp. 208–9.
48. Bouhdiba, *Sexuality in Islam*, p. 183.
49. Nawal El Saadawi, *The Hidden Face of Eve* (London: Zed, 1980), pp. 33–43; Janice Boddy, *Wombs and Alien Spirits* (Madison: The University of Wisconsin Press, 1989), pp. 49–61; Nahid Toubia, "The Social and Political Implications of Female Circumcision: The Case of the Sudan," in Elizabeth Warnock Fernea, ed., *Women and the Family in the Middle East: New Voices of Change* (Austin: University of Texas Press, 1985), pp. 148–59. For statistics on female circumcision, see *UN Arab Human Development Report 2005: Towards the Rise of Women in the Arab World* (New York: United Nations Publications, 2006), pp. 117–18.
50. Bouhdiba, *Sexuality in Islam*, p. 182.
51. See *UN Arab Human Development Report 2005*, pp. 7–8, 77–87. See also Marilyn Booth, "Arab Adolescents Facing the Future: Enduring Ideals and Pressures to Change," in B. Bradford Brown, Reed W. Larson, and T. S. Saraswathi, eds., *The World's Youth* (Cambridge: Cambridge University Press, 2002), p. 224. She reports that the overall rates of illiteracy have declined in the Arab region in recent decades: from 1970 to 2000, they have dropped from 70.7 percent (56.1 percent for males and 85 percent for females) to 38.8 percent (27.1 percent for males and 51 percent for females). Although the gender gap in literacy narrows greatly from the older to the younger generations, gender disparities in education remain a problem.
52. Gregg, *The Middle East*, pp. 236–39.
53. Elizabeth Warnock Fernea, *Children in the Muslim Middle East* (Austin: University of Texas Press, 1995), p. 10; Gregg, *The Middle East*, p. 252.
54. Morroe Berger, *The Arab World Today* (New York: Doubleday, 1962), p. 136.

55. Booth, "Arab Adolescents Facing the Future," pp. 207–42.
56. Gregg, *The Middle East*, pp. 252–53, 258, 269–70.
57. Ahmed Abou-Zeid, "Honour and Shame among the Bedouins of Egypt," in J. C. Peristiany, ed., *Honour and Shame: The Values of Mediterranean Society* (Chicago, IL: The University of Chicago Press, 1966), pp. 245–59; Patai, *Arab Mind*, pp. 120–23.
58. Pryce-Jones, *The Closed Circle*, p. 37; Nawal El Saadawi, *The Nawal El Saadawi Reader* (London: Zed, 1997), p. 251. For statistics on honor crimes in the Arab world, see *UN Arab Human Development Report 2005*, pp. 116, 143–44, 198.
59. Barakat, *Arab World*, pp. 107–16. Progressive legislation in the areas of polygamy and repudiation varies from one Arab country to another. For a comparative view of Muslim family law, see *UN Arab Human Development Report 2005*, pp. 189–200.
60. Berger, *Arab World Today*, p. 137.
61. Ammar, *Growing Up in an Egyptian Village*, p. 126.
62. Bouhdiba, *Sexuality in Islam*, p. 219.
63. Fernea, *Children in the Muslim Middle East*, p. 10.
64. Joseph, *Intimate Selving in Arab Families*, pp. 9, 12; Patai, *Arab Mind*, pp. 282–83.
65. Barakat, *Arab World*, p. 100.
66. Soraya Altorki, *Women in Saudi Arabia: Ideology and Behavior among the Elite* (New York: Columbia University Press, 1986), pp. 71–74.
67. Bouhdiba, *Sexuality in Islam*, p. 220.
68. Hisham Sharabi, *Neopatriarchy: A Theory of Distorted Change in Arab Society* (New York: Oxford University Press, 1988), p. 41.
69. Sharabi, "Impact of Class and Culture on Social Behavior," pp. 244–45.
70. Sharabi, *Neopatriarchy*, p. 7.
71. Halim Barakat, "The Arab Family and the Challenge of Social Transformation," in Fernea, *Women and the Family in the Middle East*, pp. 45–46. An abridged version of this paragraph appears in Barakat, *Arab World*, p. 118.
72. Tetz Rooke, *In My Childhood: A Study of Arabic Autobiography* (Stockholm: Almqvist & Wiksell, 1997), pp. 237–38.
73. Gregg, *The Middle East*, p. 227. During my stay with a Bedouin family in a Jordanian village I have observed similar exceptions to the cultural prototypes of fathers and mothers.
74. Sabry Hafez, "Women's Narrative in Modern Arabic Literature: A Typology," in Roger Allen et al., eds., *Love and Sexuality in Modern Arabic Literature* (London: Saqi, 1995), p. 156.
75. Hussain Mohammed al-Amily, *The Book of Arabic Wisdom* (Northampton, MA: Interlink, 2005), p. 116.
76. Ibid., p. 18.
77. Ibid., p. 117.

78. Allama Sir Abdullah al-Mamun al-Suhrawardy, *The Sayings of Muhammad* (New York: Citadel Press, 1990), p. 103.
79. Paul Lunde and Justin Wintle, eds., *A Dictionary of Arabic and Islamic Proverbs* (London: Routledge, 1984), p. 122; Barakat, *Arab World*, p. 116.
80. See, for example, A. J. Arberry, *The Koran Interpreted* (New York: Macmillan, 1955), p. 321; and A. Yusuf Ali, *The Holy Qur'an* (Washington, DC: Khalil al-Rawaf, 1946), p. 742.
81. Berger, *Arab World Today*, p. 141.
82. Barakat, *Arab World*, p. 100; see also Nicholas S. Hopkins, ed., *The New Arab Family* (Cairo: The American University in Cairo Press, 2003).
83. See Zeinab Khedr and Laila El Zeini, "Families and Households: Headship and Co-Residence," in Hopkins, *The New Arab Family*, pp. 140–64; Homa Hoodfar, "Egyptian Male Migration and Urban Families Left Behind: 'Feminization of the Egyptian Family' or Reaffirmation of Traditional Gender Roles?" in Diane Singerman and Homa Hoodfar, eds., *Development, Change, and Gender in Cairo: A View from the Household* (Bloomington: Indiana University Press, 1996), pp. 51–79.
84. For example, in Algeria, Jordan, and Tunisia, women marry at age 24 or 25; in Egypt and Morocco, it is 21 or 22; even in a conservative Arab state such as Saudi Arabia it is 22; in Qatar and the UAE it is 23. The average ages of marriage for men are usually three to five years higher than those of young women. See Moghadam, *Modernizing Women*, pp. 138–40.
85. Fatima Mernissi, *Beyond the Veil: Male-Female Dynamics in Modern Muslim Society* (rev. ed. Bloomington: Indiana University Press, 1987), pp. xxii–xxix, 150–53; Eleanor Abdella Doumato and Marsha Pripstein Posusney, eds., *Women and Globalization in the Arab Middle East: Gender, Economy, and Society* (Boulder, CO: Lynne Rienner, 2003), pp. 1–22.
86. Booth, "Arab Adolescents Facing the Future," p. 212.
87. Barakat, *Arab World*, pp. 100, 102.
88. Moghadam, *Modernizing Women*, pp. 135–44.
89. Mernissi, *Beyond the Veil*, p. xxvii.
90. Barakat, *Arab World*, p. 118.
91. Ibid., p. 119.
92. Sharabi, *Neopatriarchy*, p. 23; see also pp. 3–8.
93. Andrea Rugh, *Family in Contemporary Egypt* (Cairo: The American University in Cairo Press, 1985), p. 81.
94. Ibid., p. 82.
95. Ibid., p. 84.
96. Ibid., p. 85.
97. Bouhdiba, *Sexuality in Islam*, p. 219.
98. Rugh, *Family in Contemporary Egypt*, pp. 80, 82.

99. Joseph, *Intimate Selving in Arab Families*, pp. 187, 188.
100. Barakat, *Arab World*, p. 100.
101. Ammar, *Growing Up in an Egyptian Village*, pp. 105, 121.
102. Bouhdiba, "Child and the Mother in Arab-Muslim Society," pp. 128, 129.
103. Mernissi, *Beyond the Veil*, p. 8.
104. Ibid., pp. 113–20.
105. Ibid., p. 121.
106. Ibid., p. 122.
107. See similar observations in Hatem, "Psychodynamics of Mothering and Gender in Egyptian Families," p. 302.
108. Mernissi, *Beyond the Veil*, p. 135.
109. Ibid., p. 119.
110. Ibid., pp. 64, 119–20, 148–49.
111. Bouhdiba, *Sexuality in Islam*, p. 225.
112. Bouhdiba, "Child and the Mother in Arab-Muslim Society," pp. 128–29.
113. Ibid., p. 131.
114. Ibid., p. 130.
115. In *The Thousand and One Nights*, trans. E. W. Lane (London: East-West Publications, 1981), vol. 3, pp. 168–214.
116. Bouhdiba, *Sexuality in Islam*, p. 227.
117. Ibid., p. 228.
118. Ibid.
119. Ibid., pp. 225–29; and Bouhdiba, "Child and the Mother in Arab-Muslim Society," pp. 135–36.
120. Bouhdiba, "Child and the Mother in Arab-Muslim Society," pp. 138, 140.
121. Ammar, *Growing Up in an Egyptian Village*, pp. 107–11.
122. Berger, *Arab World Today*, p. 170.
123. Rugh, *Family in Contemporary Egypt*, pp. 82, 152.
124. Joseph, *Intimate Selving in Arab Families*, p. 140; Donna Lee Bowen and Evelyn A. Early, eds., *Everyday Life in the Muslim Middle East* (2nd ed. Bloomington: Indiana University Press, 2002), p. 14.
125. Joseph, *Intimate Selving in Arab Families*, p. 117.
126. El Saadawi, *The Hidden Face of Eve*, p. 14. See Adhaf Soueif's short story "The Water-Heater," in her collection *Sandpiper* (London: Bloomsbury, 1996), pp. 63–86.
127. Hassan El-Shamy, "The Brother-Sister Syndrome in Arab Family Life, Socio-Cultural Factors in Arab Psychiatry: A Critical Review." *International Journal of Sociology of the Family* 2 (1981): 319.
128. Joseph, *Intimate Selving in Arab Families*, pp. 109–110, 123.
129. Joseph H. Pleck, *The Myth of Masculinity* (Cambridge, MA: The MIT Press, 1981), pp. 133–60, and "The Gender Role Strain Paradigm: An Update," in Levant and Pollack, *A New Psychology of Men*, pp. 11–32.

130. Patai, *Arab Mind*, p. 211.
131. Ibid., p. 100.
132. Pryce-Jones, *The Closed Circle*, p. 36.
133. Julie Peteet, "Male Gender and the Rituals of Resistance in the Palestinian Intifada: A Cultural Politics of Violence," in Ghoussoub and Sinclair-Webb, *Imagined Masculinities*, p. 107.
134. This discussion is informed by Gary R. Brooks and Louise B. Silverstein, "Understanding the Dark Side of Masculinity: An Interactive Systems Model," in Levant and Pollack, *A New Psychology of Men*, pp. 280–333.
135. Pryce-Jones, *The Closed Circle*, p. 37.
136. Ibid.
137. Pleck, *The Myth of Masculinity*, pp. 142–48; Brooks and Silverstein, "Understanding the Dark Side of Masculinity," pp. 309–11.
138. Pierre Bourdieu, "The Sentiment of Honour in Kabyle Society," in Peristiany, *Honour and Shame*, p. 212.
139. Patai, *Arab Mind*, pp. 97–107.
140. Pryce-Jones, *The Closed Circle*, p. 41; Sharabi, "Impact of Class and Culture on Social Behavior," pp. 247–50.
141. Pryce-Jones, *The Closed Circle*, p. 38.
142. Ibid., p. 395.
143. Patai, *Arab Mind*, pp. 80, 209. For more information on this custom, see Austin Kennett, *Bedouin Justice: Law and Customs among the Egyptian Bedouin* (London: Frank Cass, 1968), and Joseph Ginat, *Blood Revenge: Family Honor, Mediation and Outcasting* (Portland, OR: Sussex Academic, 1997).
144. See, for example, Habib Jamati's story "Blood Feud," in Dalya Cohen-Mor, *A Matter of Fate* (New York: Oxford University Press, 2001), pp. 118–25; and the title story in Yusuf al-Sharuni, *Blood Feud: Short Stories*, trans. Denys Johnson-Davies (London: Heinemann, 1983), pp. 120–37.
145. Sharabi, *Neopatriarchy*, pp. vii, 152–53; Pryce-Jones, *The Closed Circle*, p. 221; Patai, *Arab Mind*, pp. 209–210.
146. Rachid Boudjedra, *La Vie quotidienne en Algerie* (Paris: Librairie Hachette, 1971), p. 5. Quoted in Pryce-Jones, *The Closed Circle*, p. 131.
147. Dialmy, "Sexuality in Contemporary Arab Society," p. 3.
148. Mernissi, *Beyond the Veil*, pp. 113–20.
149. Patai, *Arab Mind*, pp. 28–29.
150. See Inhorn, *Infertility and Patriarchy*, pp. 176–79.
151. See, for example, Daisy al-Amir's story, "The Newcomer," in Dalya Cohen-Mor, trans. and ed., *Arab Women Writers: An Anthology of Short Stories* (Albany: State University of New York Press, 2005), pp. 189–91.
152. Muhammad Abdul-Rauf, *The Islamic View of Women and the Family* (New York: Robert Speller & Sons, 1977), p. 85.

153. Marcia C. Inhorn, "The Worms Are Weak: Male Infertility and Patriarchal Paradoxes in Egypt," in Ouzgane, *Islamic Masculinities*, pp. 217–37.
154. John Racy, "Psychiatry in the Arab East," in Brown and Itzkowitz, *Psychological Dimensions of Near Eastern Studies*, p. 321.
155. Dialmy, "Sexuality in Contemporary Arab Society," p. 10.
156. Ibid., p. 11.
157. Ibid.
158. Ibid., pp. 3, 4.
159. Abdellah Hammoudi, *Master and Disciple* (Chicago, IL: The University of Chicago Press, 1997), p. 145.
160. Deniz Kandiyoti, "The Paradoxes of Masculinity: Some Thoughts on Segregated Societies," in Andrea Cornwall and Nancy Lindisfarne, eds., *Dislocating Masculinity* (London: Routledge, 1994), p. 198.
161. Ibid.
162. See, for example, Durre S. Ahmed, "Gender and Islamic Spirituality: A Psychological View of 'Low' Fundamentalism," in Ouzgane, *Islamic Masculinities*, p. 28.

3 Fathers and Sons in Personal Histories

1. The Arabic version of the autobiography, titled *Mudhakkirat Jurji Zaydan*, was first published in 1966, some 50 years after Zaydan's death. It was edited and translated by Thomas Philipp as *The Autobiography of Jurji Zaidan* (Washington, DC: Three Continents Press, 1990). All quotations are from this translation.
2. Philipp, in the Introduction to *The Autobiography of Jurji Zaidan*, p. 15.
3. Ibid., p. 16.
4. Ibid., p. 6.
5. Ibid., p. 7.
6. Ibid., pp. 7, 16.
7. Ahmad Amin, *My Life* (*Hayati*, Cairo, 1950, 1952), trans. Issa J. Boullata (Leiden: Brill, 1978). All quotations are from this translation.
8. Mikhail Naimy, *Seventy: A Life Story* (*Sab'un: hikayat 'umr*. Beirut, 1960). This work is not available in English translation. Three chapters from the first volume, titled "A Lebanese Childhood," appear in Mikhail Naimy, *A New Year: Stories, Autobiography, Poems*, trans. J. R. Perry (Leiden: Brill, 1974), pp. 1–22.
9. Cited from Naimy, *A New Year*, p. 1.
10. Ibid., p. 5.
11. Ibid., p. 3.
12. Ibid., p. 4.
13. Ibid., p. 2.
14. Ibid., p. 4.
15. Ibid., p. 7.

16. Ibid., p. 6.
17. *Sab'un*, 1:38; Hussein Dabbagh, *Mikhail Naimy: Some Aspects of His Thought as Revealed in His Writings* (Durham, UK: University of Durham, 1983), pp. 2–3.
18. Naimy, *A New Year*, p. 6.
19. Ibid., p. 5.
20. Dabbagh, *Mikhail Naimy*, p. 19.
21. Ibid., p. 41.
22. Ibid.
23. This chapter appears in *Sab'un*, 3:129–34.
24. Cited from Dabbagh, *Mikhail Naimy*, p. 43.
25. Jabra Ibrahim Jabra, *The First Well: A Bethlehem Boyhood* (*Al-Bi'r al-ula*. London: Riad El-Rayyes, 1987), trans. Issa J. Boullata; Second volume, *Princesses' Street: Baghdad Memories* (*Shari' al-amirat*. Beirut, 1994), trans. Issa J. Boullata (Fayetteville: University of Arkansas Press, 1995, 2005 respectively). The second volume deals mainly with the year 1951, when Jabra met his wife in Baghdad. All quotations are from these translations.
26. Said's publications on the topic of Palestine include *The Question of Palestine* (1979), *Blaming the Victims* (1988), and *The Politics of Dispossession* (1994).
27. Edward E. Said, *Out of Place: A Memoir* (1999; New York: Vintage, 2000). All quotations are from this edition.
28. Both his parents were 76 years old at the time of their death. Said's mother died of breast cancer in 1990, and his father died of melanoma in 1971.
29. Malise Ruthven, "Obituary of Edward Said," *The Guardian* (September 26, 2003).
30. Ibid.
31. Bruce Bawer, "Edward W. Said, Intellectual," *The Hudson Review* (Winter 2002): 7.
32. Tawfiq al-Hakim, *The Prison of Life* (*Sijn al-'umr*. Cairo, 1964), trans. Pierre Cachia (Cairo: The American University in Cairo Press, 1992). All quotations are from this translation.
33. Anderson and Sabatelli, *Family Interaction*, pp. 208–9, 216–19.
34. Hanna Mina, *Fragments of Memory: A Story of a Syrian Family* (*Baqaya suwar*. Beirut, 1975), trans. Olive Kenny and Lorne Kenny (Austin: University of Texas Press, 1993). All quotations are from this translation.
35. Rooke, *In My Childhood*, pp. 47–48, 61, 64.
36. The third volume is not included in this discussion because of its highly fictionalized character.
37. It is interesting to note that although the mother belonged to the Greek Orthodox Church, she held fatalistic views. This shows that the core values of Arab culture are shared by all segments of Arab

society, regardless of sectarian affiliations. For a study of the belief in fate in the Arab world, see Dalya Cohen-Mor, *A Matter of Fate* (New York: Oxford University Press, 2001).

38. Mohamed Choukri, *For Bread Alone* (*Al-Khubz al-hafi*. Beirut, 1982), trans. Paul Bowles (1973; San Francisco, CA: City Lights, 1987); *Streetwise* (*Al-Shuttar*. Beirut, 1992), trans. Ed Emery (1996; London: Telegram, 2007). All quotations are from these translations.

39. "The Berbers of North Africa." Available: http://www.angelfire .com/az/rescon/mgcberbr.html (accessed October 24, 2012).

40. Mohamed Choukri, "Being and Place," in Ferial Ghazoul and Barbara Harlow, eds., *The View from Within* (Cairo: The American University in Cairo Press, 1994), p. 220.

41. David D. Gilmore, *Manhood in the Making: Cultural Concepts of Masculinity* (New Haven: Yale University Press, 1990), p. 223. Gilmore uses the word "impregnator" instead of "procreator."

42. "Mohamed Choukri: Voice of Morocco, Heard in Forty Languages," *Times Online* (November 24, 2003).

43. Halim Barakat, "Childhood Memories," trans. Bassam Frangieh, in Elizabeth Warnock Fernea, ed., *Remembering Childhood in the Middle East* (Austin: University of Texas Press, 2002), pp. 127–32. All quotations are from this source. His memoir, *The Crane* (*Ta'ir al-hawm*. Casablanca, 1988), trans. Bassam Frangieh and Roger Allen (Cairo: The American University in Cairo Press, 2008), deals mainly with his experiences in the United States.

44. Anderson and Sabatelli, *Family Interaction*, p. 272.

45. Guy Corneau, *Absent Fathers, Lost Sons* (Boston: Shambhala, 1991), p. 22. See similar conclusions in Josette G. Abdalla, "The Absent Father," in Hopkins, *The New Arab Family*, pp. 201–13.

46. Cited in Joseph, *Intimate Selving in Arab Families*, p. 176.

47. Cited in *UN Arab Human Development Report 2005*, p. 149.

48. Idris's childhood recollections, originally titled "Yusuf Idris on Yusuf Idris," appear in Roger Allen, ed., *Critical Perspectives on Yusuf Idris* (Colorado Springs, CO: Three Continents Press, 1994), pp. 5–13. All quotations are from this source. For clarity, I changed the title of Idris's recollections to "A Sketch of My Life as a Child," a phrase that he uses at the conclusion of his essay.

49. Frank McCourt, *Angela's Ashes* (New York: Touchstone, 1966), p. 9.

50. Harmut Fahndrich, "Fathers and Husbands: Tyrants and Victims in Some Autobiographical and Semi-Autobiographical Works from the Arab World," in Roger Allen et al., *Love and Sexuality in Modern Arabic Literature* (London: Saqi, 1995), pp. 106–15.

51. Kimmel and Messner, *Men's Lives*, p. 8.

52. Hammoudi, *Master and Disciple*, p. 145.

4 Fathers and Sons in Works of Fiction

1. The Trilogy consists of vol. 1, *Palace Walk* (*Bayn al-qasrayn*, 1956), trans. William Maynard Hutchins and Olive E. Kenney; vol. 2, *Palace of Desire* (*Qasr al-shawq*, 1957), trans. William Maynard Hutchins, Lorne M. Kenny, and Olive E. Kenney; vol.3, *Sugar Street* (*Al-Sukkariyya*, 1957), trans. William Maynard Hutchins and Angele Botros Samaan (New York: Doubleday, 1990, 1991, 1992). All quotations are from these translations.
2. Hafez, "Women's Narrative in Modern Arabic Literature: A Typology," in Roger Allen et al., eds., *Love and Sexuality in Modern Arabic Literature* (London: Saqi, 1995), p. 156
3. Gregg, *The Middle East*, p. 274.
4. Altorki, "Patriarchy and Imperialism," p. 225.
5. Yusuf Idris's "The Journey" ("Al-Rihla") was first published in *Al-Ahram* (June 5, 1970) and later included in his collection *Bayt min lahm* (Cairo, 1971). An earlier version of this analysis and interpretation appeared in Dalya Cohen-Mor, *Yusuf Idris: Changing Visions* (Potomac, MD: Sheba Press, 1992), pp. 111–17.
6. Yusuf Idris, "The Journey," trans. Roger Allen, *Journal of Arabic Literature* 3 (1972): 66.
7. Sigmund Freud, *Introductory Lectures on Psychoanalysis* (Harmondsworth, UK: Penguin, 1973), pp. 187–89.
8. Sigmund Freud, *On Psychopathology* (Harmondsworth, UK: Penguin, 1979), pp. 205–8.
9. Sigmund Freud, *Three Essays on the Theory of Sexuality* (New York: Basic Books, 1975), p. 48.
10. Freud, *Introductory Lectures on Psychoanalysis*, p. 478.
11. James Harrison, "Roles, Identities, and Sexual Orientation: Homosexuality, Heterosexuality, and Bisexuality," in Levant and Pollack, *A New Psychology of Men*, p. 371.
12. For a discussion of the theme of aberrant sex in the short stories of Yusuf Idris, see Cohen-Mor, *Yusuf Idris: Changing Visions*, chapter 5.
13. Charles Rycroft, *The Innocence of Dreams* (London: Hogarth, 1979), pp. 83–84.
14. Ibid.
15. Nasser died of a sudden heart attack in September 1970.
16. Muhammad Pickthall, *The Glorious Quran: Arabic Text and English Rendering* (Des Plaines, IL: Library of Islam, 1994), pp. 569, 570. My emphasis. The Koranic word that Pickthall translates as "journeying" is *al-masir*.
17. Yahya Haqqi, *The Saint's Lamp and Other Stories* (*Qindil Umm Hashim*. Cairo, 1944), trans. M. M. Badawi (Leiden: Brill, 1973). All quotations are from this translation.
18. Naguib Mahfouz, *Echoes of an Autobiography*, trans. Denys Johnson-Davies (Cairo: The American University in Cairo Press, 1996), p. 24.

19. Zakaria Tamer, "The Family," in his collection *Tigers on the Tenth Day and Other Stories*, trans. Denys Johnson-Davies (London: Quartet, 1985), pp. 35–36. All quotations are from this translation.

20. Ibrahim Muhawi, in the Introduction to Zakaria Tamer, *Breaking Knees*, trans. Ibrahim Muhawi (Reading, UK: Garnet, 2008), p. ix.

21. Rooke, *In My Childhood*, pp. 241–42.

22. Fathy Ghanem, *The Man Who Lost His Shadow* (*Al-Rajul alladhi faqad zillahu*. Cairo, 1962), trans. Desmond Stewart (London: Heinemann, 1980). All quotations are from this translation.

23. Fatma Moussa-Mahmoud, *The Arabic Novel in Egypt: 1914–1970* (Cairo: The General Egyptian Book Organization, 1973), p. 76.

24. Ibid., p. 73.

25. Mu'nis al Razzaz, "Abu Rashad," in his collection *Al-Namrud* (Beirut, 1980). Translated as "Abu Richard" by Yasir Suleiman in collaboration with Sandor Hervey, in *Journal of Arabic Literature* 22 (1991–92): 148–53. All quotations are from this translation.

26. Alaa al-Aswany, *The Yacoubian Building* (*'Imarat Ya'qubiyan*. Cairo, 2002), trans. Humphrey Davies (Cairo: The American University in Cairo Press, 2004). All quotations are from this translation.

27. Yusuf al-Qa'id, *War in the Land of Egypt* (*Al-Harb fi barr Misr*. Beirut, 1978), trans. Olive and Lorne Kenney and Christopher Tingley (New York: Interlink, 1998). All quotations are from this translation.

28. Fedwa Malti-Douglas, in the Afterword to *War in the land of Egypt*, p. 188.

29. Ibid., pp. 189–90.

30. *The Koran*, trans. N. J. Dawood (London: Penguin, 1993), p. 315.

31. Ibrahim al-Koni, *Anubis* (Beirut, 2002), trans. William M. Hutchins (Cairo: The American University in Cairo Press, 2005). All quotations are from this translation.

32. Ibid., Translator's Note, p. viii.

33. Margaret Obank, "Ibrahim al-Koni, *Anubis*: The Search for the Tuareg Desert Truth," *Banipal* 23 (Summer 2005).

34. Ibid.

35. al-Koni, *Anubis*, p. xvii.

36. See, for example, Barakat, *Arab World*, pp. 116–17, 175; Sharabi, *Neopatriarchy*, p. 64; Bouhdiba, *Sexuality in Islam*, p. 220.

37. Barakat, "The Arab Family and the Challenge of Social Transformation," in Fernea, *Women and the Family in the Middle East*, pp. 45–46.

38. Zakaria Tamer, "The Thunderbolt," in *Modern Syrian Short Stories*, trans. Michel Azrak, rev. M. J. L. Young (Washington, DC: Three Continents Press, 1988), pp. 106–7.

39. Fatima Mernissi introduces the notion of "the harem within" in her book *Dreams of Trespass* (New York: Addison-Wesley, 1994), pp. 61–62.

40. Abdellatif Laabi, *Rue de Retour*, trans. Jacqueline Kaye (London: Readers International, 1989), p. 27.
41. See Dalya Abudi, *Mothers and Daughters in Arab Women's Literature: The Family Frontier* (Leiden: Brill, 2011), pp. 277–78.
42. Rooke, *In My Childhood*, p. 237.
43. Ibid., p. 240.
44. Some examples are the Syrian poet Muhammad al-Maghut, the Egyptian playwright Alfred Farag, the Saudi novelist Abd al-Rahman Munif, and the Egyptian novelists Gamal al-Ghitani, Yusuf Idris, and Sonallah Ibrahim.
45. Mohamed Choukri, "Quotations." Available: http://en.wikipedia.org/wiki/Mohamed_Choukri (accessed April 1, 2008).
46. Harrison, "Roles, Identities, and Sexual Orientation," p. 371.
47. For more information on this topic, see Frederic Lagrange, "Male Homosexuality in Modern Arabic Literature," in Ghoussoub and Sinclair-Webb, *Imagined Masculinities*, pp. 169–98.

5 Fathers and Sons in Poetry and Politics

1. R. A. Nicholson, *A Literary History of the Arabs* (Cambridge: Cambridge University Press, 1976), p. 317.
2. Sa'd Darweesh, "I've Committed No Such Crime," in M. M. Enani, ed. and trans., *An Anthology of the New Arabic Poetry in Egypt* (Cairo: General Egyptian Book Organization, 1986), pp. 281–89.
3. Ibid., pp. 281 and 288–89 respectively.
4. For example, the Moroccan writer Mohamed Choukri rejected marriage and fatherhood for fear that he might repeat the cycle of abuse that he suffered in his childhood at the hands of his father.
5. This is the subtitle of Lewis Yablonsky's book *Fathers and Sons* (New York: Gardner, 1990).
6. For examples of how poems are informed by culture and culture is reflected in poetry, see Lila Abu-Lughod, *Veiled Sentiments: Honor and Poetry in a Bedouin Society* (Berkeley: University of California Press, 1986); and Paul Friedrich, "The Culture in Poetry and the Poetry in Culture," in E. Valentine Daniel and Jeffrey M. Peck, eds., *Culture/Contexture: Explorations in Anthropology and Literary Analysis* (Berkeley: University of California Press, 1996), pp. 37–57.
7. Jazia al-Hilalaite, "Worthy Men," in al-Amily, *The Book of Arabic Wisdom*, p. 103.
8. Cited in In Clinton Baily, *A Culture of Desert Survival* (New Haven, CT: Yale University Press, 2004), p. 184.
9. Jacques Berque, *The Arabs: Their History and Future* (New York: Praeger, 1964), p. 174.
10. Abd al-Aziz al-Maqalih, "Choice," trans. Lena Jayyusi and Christopher Middleton, in Salma Khadra Jayyusi, ed., *Modern*

Arabic Poetry: An Anthology (New York: Columbia University Press, 1987), p. 345.

11. Abdulilah Salhi, "Getting the Hell out of It," trans. from French James Kirkup, in Margaret Obank and Samuel Shimon, eds., *A Crack in the Wall: New Arab Poetry* (London: Saqi, 2001), p. 246.

12. Mohamed Metwalli, "Untitled," in *Angry Voices: An Anthology of the Off-Beat New Egyptian Poets*, trans. Mohamed Enani, compiled by Mohamed Metwalli (Fayetteville: The University of Arkansas Press, 2003), pp. 24–27.

13. Adonis, "Adam," in *Adonis: The Pages of Day and Night*, trans. Samuel Hazo (Marlboro, VT: Marlboro Press, 1994), p. 27.

14. Abu al-Atahiah (AD 748–826) was a major ascetic Arab poet who lived in Iraq.

15. Hashim Shafiq, "Mirage," trans. Saadi A. Simawe, Ralph Savarese, Ellen Dore Watson, and Melissa L. Brown, in Daniel Weissbort, ed., *Iraqi Poetry Today* (London: King's College, University of London, 2003), p. 232.

16. Adonis, "Celebrating Childhood," in *Adonis: Selected Poems*, trans. Khaled Mattawa (New Haven, CT: Yale University Press, 2010), pp. 260, 262, 263, respectively.

17. Adonis, "Beginning Speech," trans. Lena Jayyusi and John Heath-Stubbs, in Jayyusi, *Modern Arabic Poetry*, p. 139.

18. Anton Shammas, "I Have a Drawer," trans. from Hebrew Betsy Rosenberg, *Ariel*, no. 33–34 (1973): 174.

19. Sami Mahdi, "The Inheritance," trans. May Jayyusi, in Jayyusi, *Modern Arabic Poetry*, p. 313.

20. Khalid Saud al-Zayd, "My Son," trans. Sharif S. Elmusa and Naomi Shihab Nye, in Salma Khadra Jayyusi, ed., *The Literature of Modern Arabia: An Anthology* (London: Kegan Paul International in association with King Saud University, Riyadh, 1988), pp. 248–49.

21. Adonis, "Elegies (for my Father)," in *Adonis: Selected Poems*, trans. Khaled Mattawa, p. 5, part 1.

22. Abbas Beydhoun, "The Flower of Life and My Father's Black Heart," trans. Khaled Mattawa, in Obank and Shimon, eds., *A Crack in the Wall*, p. 61.

23. Fadhil Assultani, "My Mother, in Memoriam," trans. Saadi A. Simawe, Raghid Nahhas, Melissa L. Brown and the poet with thanks to Richard McKane, in Weissbort, *Iraqi Poetry Today*, p. 22.

24. Naguib Mahfouz, *Naguib Mahfouz at Sidi Gaber: Reflections of a Nobel Laureate, 1994–2001* (Cairo: The American University in Cairo Press, 2001), p. 36.

25. Lunde and Wintle, eds., *A Dictionary of Arabic and Islamic Proverbs*, p. 101.

26. Mohammad Bennis, "Belonging to a New Family," trans. Sharif Elmusa and Charles Doria, in Jayyusi, ed., *Modern Arabic Poetry*, pp. 181–82.

27. Sargon Boulus, "My Father's Dream," trans. Sargon Boulus and Alistair Elliot, in Jayyusi, *Modern Arabic Poetry*, pp. 185–86.
28. Ahmad Qandeel, "A Scream," trans. Bassam al-Hilu with Alan Brownjohn, in Mansour al-Hazimi, Salma Khadra Jayyusi, and Ezzat Khattab, eds., *Beyond the Dunes: An Anthology of Modern Saudi Literature* (London: I. B. Tauris, 2006), p. 59.
29. Abd al-Karim Kassid, "Tales about My Father," trans. Lena Jayyusi and Anthony Thwaite, in Jayyusi, *Modern Arabic Poetry*, pp. 291–92.
30. Anton Shammas, "No Man's Land," trans. from Hebrew Judith Levy, *Modern Hebrew Literature* 6, no. 1–2 (Summer 1980): 47.
31. Hammoudi, *Master and Disciple*, pp. 139–40.
32. Ibid., pp. 140, 141, 157.
33. Barakat, *Arab World*, pp. 116–17.
34. Ibid., p. 116.
35. Amal Dunqul, "The Murder of the Moon," in John Mikhail Asfour, trans. and ed., *When the Words Burn: An Anthology of Modern Arabic Poetry 1945–1987* (Dunvegan, ON: Cormorant Books, 1988), pp. 135–36.
36. Abd-Allah al-Baraduni, "From Exile to Exile," trans. Diana Der Hovanessian with Sharif Elmusa, in Jayyusi, *Modern Arabic Poetry*, pp. 157–58.
37. Abdallah Salih al-'Uthaymeen, "Legend," trans. Bassam al-Hilu with Alan Brownjohn, in al-Hazimi et al., *Beyond the Dunes*, pp. 160–62.
38. Kamal Nasir, "The Leaders of My Country," in Asfour, *When the Words Burn*, p. 215.
39. Nizar Qabbani, "Marginal Notes on the Book of Defeat," in Asfour, *When the Words Burn*, p. 98.
40. Nizar Qabbani, "The Ruler and the Sparrow," in Abdullah al-Udhari, trans. and ed., *Modern Poetry of the Arab World* (Harmondsworth, UK: Penguin, 1986), pp. 103–4.
41. Abd al-Aziz al-Maqalih, "Fear," trans. Lena Jayyusi and John Heath-Stubbs, in Jayyusi, *The Literature of Modern Arabia*, pp. 163–64.
42. Muhammad al-Maghut, "The Tattoo," in his collection *Fan of Swords: Poems*, trans. May Jayyusi and Naomi Shihab Nye, ed. Salma Khadra Jayyusi (Washington, DC: Three Continents Press, 1991), pp. 21–22.
43. El Saadawi, *The Nawal El Saadawi Reader*, p. 205. See also Michel G. Nehme, *Fear and Anxiety in the Arab World* (Gainesville: University Press of Florida, 2003).
44. Barakat, *Arab World*, p. 175.
45. Ibid., p. 277.
46. Ibid.
47. Said K. Aburish, *Saddam Hussein: The Politics of Revenge* (London: Bloomsbury, 2000), p. 13.
48. Ibid., p 23.

49. Hazim Saghieh, "'That's How I Am, World!': Saddam, Manhood and the Monolithic Image," in Ghoussoub and Sinclaire-Webb, *Imagined Masculinities*, p. 243.
50. Ibid.
51. Ibid., p. 244.
52. Ibid.
53. Ibid., p. 245.
54. Ibid, p. 248.
55. Patrick Seale, *Asad of Syria: The Struggle for the Middle East* (Berkeley: University of California Press, 1995), p. 7.
56. Ibid., pp. 7–8.
57. Ibid., p. 13.
58. Ibid., p. 56.
59. Ibid., p. 343.
60. Ibid., p. 344.
61. Cited in Moshe Ma'oz, *Asad, the Sphinx of Damascus: A Political Biography* (New York: Grove Weidenfeld, 1988), p. 43.
62. Ibid., p. 43.
63. "Middle Eastern Dynasties: Like Father, Like Son," *The Economist* (June 2, 2001), p. 45.
64. Richard Haass, "The Revolution Stops Here," *Time* (April 18, 2011), p. 22.
65. Robert Stephens, *Nasser: A Political Biography* (New York: Simon and Schuster, 1971), pp. 28–29.
66. Ibid., p. 28.
67. Jean Lacouture, *Nasser: A Biography* (New York: Alfred A. Knopf, 1973), p. 26.
68. Ibid., p. 355.
69. Ibid., pp. 355–56.
70. Ibid., p. 357.
71. Ibid.
72. Anwar el-Sadat, *In Search of Identity: An Autobiography* (New York: Harper and Row, 1978), p. 3.
73. Camelia Sadat, *My Father and I* (New York: Macmillan, 1985), p. 31.
74. Ibid., p. 129.
75. Ibid., p. 144.
76. Ibid., p. 5.
77. Ibid., p. 153.
78. Al-Aswany, *The Yacoubian Building*, p. 68.
79. Qabbani, "Marginal Notes on the Book of Defeat," in Asfour, *When the Words Burn*, p. 99.
80. Barakat, *Arab World*, p. 277.
81. For more information on youth in the Middle East and the complex change taking place on the ground, see Ali Akbar Mahdi, ed., *Teen Life in the Middle East* (Westport, CT: Greenwood Press, 2003), and Navtej Dhillon and Tarik Yousef, eds., *Generation in*

Waiting: The Unfulfilled Promise of Young People in the Middle East (Washington, DC: Brookings Institute, 2009).

82. "Middle Eastern Dynasties: Like Father, Like Son," *The Economist* (June 2, 2001), p. 46.

6 Conclusion: Embattled Selves and the Dream of Liberation

1. Herb Goldberg, *The Hazards of Being Male* (Gretna, LA: Wellness Institute, 2000), p. 179.
2. Progressive legislation varies from one Arab country to another. For a comparative view of Muslim family law, see *UN Arab Human Development Report 2005*, pp. 189–200.
3. Mohamed Choukri, "Men Have All the Luck," trans. Paul Starkey, in Peter Clark, ed., *Sardines and Oranges: Short Stories from North Africa* (London: Banipal, 2005), pp. 108–131.
4. Mernissi, *Beyond the Veil*, pp. 113–20; Hatem, "Psychodynamics of Mothering and Gender in Egyptian Families," p. 302.
5. Fatima Mernissi, *Women's Rebellion and Islamic Memory* (London: Zed, 1996), p. 37.
6. Abou-Zeid, "Honour and Shame among the Bedouins of Egypt," pp. 245–59; Patai, *Arab Mind*, pp. 120–23.
7. Pryce-Jones, *The Closed Circle*, p. 37. For statistics on honor crimes in the Arab world, see *UN Arab Human Development Report 2005*, pp. 116, 143–44, 198.
8. Nawal El Saadawi, "She Is Not a Virgin," trans. Dalya Cohen-Mor, in Cohen-Mor, *A Matter of Fate*, pp. 143–48.
9. Yusuf al-Qaʻid, *News from the Meneisi Farm* (*Akhbar ʻizbat al-Manisi.* Cairo, 1971), trans. Marie-Therese Abdel-Messih (Cairo: General Egyptian Book Publication, 1987).
10. Al-Sharuni, *Blood Feud*, pp. 120–37.
11. Patai, *Arab Mind*, p. 91.
12. Mona al-Aswaf and Ihsan al-Issa, "Sex and Sexual Dysfunction in an Arab-Muslim Society," in Ihsan al-Issa, ed., *Al-Junun: Mental Illness in the Islamic World* (Madison, CT: International Universities Press, 2000), p. 308.
13. Alifa Rifaat, "My Wedding Night," in Dalya Cohen-Mor, trans. and ed., *Arab Women Writers: An Anthology of Short Stories* (Albany: State University of New York Press, 2005), pp. 120–26.
14. Bouhdiba, "Child and the Mother in Arab-Muslim Society," p. 135.
15. Nizar Qabbani, "Schahriar's Tears," in Ben Bennani, ed., and trans., *Bread, Hashish and Moon: Four Modern Arab Poets* (Greensboro, NC: Unicorn, 1982), pp. 9–10.
16. Nizar Kabbani (Qabbani), "I Am Accused of Being like Shahrayar," in his collection *Arabian Love Poems*, trans. Bassam K. Frangieh

and Clementina R. Brown (Boulder, CO: Lynne Rienner, 1999), pp. 149–56.

17. Inhorn, "The Worms Are Weak," p. 229.

18. In Yusuf Idris, *The Cheapest Nights and Other Stories*, trans. Wadida Wassef (London: Heinemann, 1978), pp. 1–5.

19. Inhorn, "The Worms Are Weak," p. 226.

20. Joseph, *Intimate Selving in Arab Families*, p. 187.

21. For an analysis of this novel, see Dalya Abudi, *Mothers and Daughters in Arab Women's Literature: The Family Frontier* (Leiden: Brill, 2011), pp. 248–64.

22. Qasim Amin, *The Liberation of Women* (*Tahrir al-mar'a*, 1899), trans. Samiha Sidhom Peterson (Cairo: The American University in Cairo Press, 1992), p. 6.

23. Ibid., p. 12. Cited from an abridged version in Mernissi, *Beyond the Veil*, p. 14.

24. Germaine Tillion, *The Republic of Cousins*, trans. Quintin Hoare (London: Saqi, 1983), pp. 166–67.

25. Sulaiman al-Fulayyih, "Being," trans. Lena Jayyusi and Naomi Shihab Nye, in Jayyusi, *The Literature of Modern Arabia*, p. 84.

26. Dhabya Khamees, "Schizophrenia," trans. May Jayyusi and Naomi Shihab Nye, in Jayyusi, *The Literature of Modern Arabia*, p. 144.

27. Sami Mahdi, "Abel's Brothers," trans. Ferial J. Ghazoul, in Weissbort, *Iraqi Poetry Today*, pp. 117–18.

28. Muhammad Hasan Faqi, "Quartet # 7," trans. Laith al-Husain and Patricia Alanah Byrne, in al-Hazimi et al., *Beyond the Dunes*, p. 55.

29. Samira Aghacy, *Masculine Identity in the Fiction of the Arab East since 1967* (Syracuse, NY: Syracuse University Press, 2009), p. 5.

30. Reference to the Tunisian street vendor Mohammed Bouazizi whose self-immolation sparked the Jasmine Revolution.

31. Quoted from http://newanthems.blogspot.com. Posted by Adam Jones on January 9, 2011 (accessed May 15, 2011).

32. See Fuad I. Khuri, *Tents and Pyramids: Games and Ideology in Arab Culture from Backgammon to Autocratic Rule* (London: Saqi, 1990), pp. 27–50.

33. Michael Elliott, "Learn to Love the Revolution: Five Lessons from Change in the Arab World," *Time* (March 7, 2011), p. 34.

34. Fareed Zakaria, "A Region at War with Its History," *Time* (April 16, 2012), p. 24.

35. Hazim Saghieh, "The Other Arab Exception," *Open Democracy* (April 18, 2011). Available: http://www.opendemocracy.net (accessed June 3, 2012).

36. Elliott, "Learn to Love the Revolution," p. 35.

37. Wael Ghonim, *Revolution 2.0* (New York: Houghton Mifflin Harcourt, 2012), p. 292–93.

38. Mahfouz, *Naguib Mahfouz at Sidi Gaber*, p. 36.

39. See, for example, Lilia Labidi, "From Sexual Submission to Voluntary Commitment: The Transformation of Family Ties in Contemporary Tunisia," in Kathryn M. Yount and Hoda Rashad, eds., *Family in the Middle East: Ideational Change in Egypt, Iran, and Tunisia* (New York: Routledge, 2008), pp. 236–50.

40. Marcia C. Inhorn, *The New Arab Man: Emergent Masculinities, Technologies, and Islam in the Middle East* (Princeton, NJ: Princeton University Press, 2012), pp. 60–61.

41. John Borneman, *Syrian Episodes: Sons, Fathers, and an Anthropologist in Aleppo* (Princeton, NJ: Princeton University Press, 2007), p. xiv.

42. Gregg, *The Middle East*, p. 250.

43. Borneman, *Syrian Episodes*, p. 112.

44. Ibid., p. 148.

45. Ibid., p. 81.

46. Ibid., p. 222.

47. Barakat, *Arab World*, p. 182.

48. Inhorn, *The New Arab Man*, pp. 1, 60–61, 299–302.

49. Altorki, "Patriarchy and Imperialism," pp. 223–24.

50. Ibid.

Bibliography

Abd al-Ati, Hammudah. *The Family Structure in Islam.* [s.l.]: American Trust Publications, 1977.

Abdul-Rauf, Muhammad. *The Islamic View of Women and the Family.* New York: Robert Speller & Sons, 1977.

Abou-Zeid, Ahmed. "Honour and Shame among the Bedouins of Egypt." In *Honour and Shame: The Values of Mediterranean Society,* edited by Jean G. Peristiany, pp. 245–59. Chicago: University of Chicago Press, 1966.

Abu-Lughod, Lila. *Veiled Sentiments: Honor and Poetry in a Bedouin Society.* Berkeley: University of California Press, 1986.

Aburish, Said K. *Saddam Hussein: The Politics of Revenge.* London: Bloomsbury, 2000.

Adonis ('Ali Ahmad Sa'id). *The Pages of Day and Night.* Translated by Samuel Hazo. Marlboro, VT: Marlboro Press, 1994. Evanston, IL: Northwestern University Press, 2000.

———. *Selected Poems.* Translated by Khaled Mattawa. New Haven, CT: Yale University Press, 2010.

Aghacy, Samira. *Masculine Identity in the Fiction of the Arab East since 1967.* Syracuse, NY: Syracuse University Press, 2009.

Ahmed, Ramadan A., and Uwe P. Gielen, eds. *Psychology in the Arab Countries.* Menoufia, Egypt: Menoufia University Press, 1998.

Akhtar, Salman, and Henri Parens, eds. *Real and Imaginary Fathers: Development, Transference, and Healing.* Lanham, MD: Jason Aronson, 2003.

Ali, A. Yusuf. *The Holy Qur'an.* Washington, DC: Khalil al-Rawaf, 1946.

Allen, Roger, ed. *Critical Perspectives on Yusuf Idris.* Colorado Springs, CO: Three Continents Press, 1994.

———. *The Arabic Literary Heritage: The Development of Its Genres and Criticism.* Cambridge: Cambridge University Press, 1998.

———, Hilary Kilpatrick, and Ed de Moor, eds. *Love and Sexuality in Modern Arabic Literature.* London: Saqi, 1995.

Altorki, Soraya. *Women in Saudi Arabia: Ideology and Behavior among the Elite.* New York: Columbia University Press, 1986.

———. "Patriarchy and Imperialism: Father-Son and British-Egyptian Relations in Najib Mahfuz's Trilogy." In *Intimate Selving in Arab*

Families, edited by Suad Joseph, pp. 214–34. Syracuse, NY: Syracuse University Press, 1999.

al-Amily, Hussain Mohammed. *The Book of Arabic Wisdom*. Northampton, MA: Interlink, 2005.

Amin, Ahmad. *My Life* (*Hayati*. Cairo, 1950; 1952). Translated by Issa J. Boullata. Leiden: Brill, 1978.

Amin, Qasim. *The Liberation of Women* (*Tahrir al-mar'a*, 1899) and *The New Woman* (*Al-mar'a al-jadida*, 1900). Translated by Samiha Sidhom Peterson. Cairo: The American University in Cairo Press, 1992, 1995.

Ammar, Hamed. *Growing Up in an Egyptian Village: Silwa, Province of Aswan*. London: Routledge & Kegan Paul, 1954.

Anderson, Stephen A., and Ronald M. Sabatelli. *Family Interaction: A Multigenerational Developmental Perspective*. 3rd ed. Boston, MA: Allyn and Bacon, 2002.

Arberry, A. J. *The Koran Interpreted*. New York: Macmillan, 1955.

Asfour, John Mikhail, trans. and ed. *When the Words Burn: An Anthology of Modern Arabic Poetry, 1945–1987*. Dunvegan, ON: Cormorant Books, 1988.

al-Aswany, Alaa. *The Yacoubian Building* (*'Imarat Ya'qubiyan*. Cairo, 2002). Translated by Humphrey Davies. Cairo: The American University in Cairo Press, 2004.

Baily, Clinton. *A Culture of Desert Survival*. New Haven, CT: Yale University Press, 2004.

Barakat, Halim. "The Arab Family and the Challenge of Social Transformation." In *Women and the Family in the Middle East: New Voices of Change*, edited by Elizabeth Warnock Fernea, pp. 27–48. Austin: University of Texas Press, 1985.

——— *The Arab World: Society, Culture, and State*. Berkeley: University of California Press, 1993.

———. "Childhood Memories." Translated by Bassam Frangieh. In *Remembering Childhood in the Middle East*, edited by Elizabeth Warnock Fernea, pp. 127–32. Austin: University of Texas Press, 2002.

———. *The Crane* (*Ta'ir al-hawm*. Casablanca, 1988). Translated by Bassam Frangieh and Roger Allen. Cairo: The American University in Cairo Press, 2008.

Bates, Daniel G., and Amal Rassam. *Peoples and Cultures of the Middle East*. Englewood Cliffs, NJ: Prentice-Hall, 1983.

Bennani, Ben. ed. and trans. *Bread Hashish and Moon: Four Modern Arab Poets*. Greensboro, NC: Unicorn, 1982.

Benson, Paul, ed. *Anthropology and Literature*. Urbana: University of Illinois Press, 1993.

Berger, Morroe. *The Arab World Today*. New York: Doubleday, 1962.

———. *Real and Imagined Worlds: The Novel and Social Science*. Cambridge, MA: Harvard University Press, 1977.

Bergman, Stephen J. "Men's Psychological Development: A Relational Perspective." In *A New Psychology of Men*, edited by Ronald F. Levant and William S. Pollack, pp. 68–90. New York: Basic Books, 1995.

Berque, Jacques. *The Arabs: Their History and Future*. New York: Praeger, 1964.

Blos, Peter. *Son and Father: Before and Beyond the Oedipus Complex*. New York: The Free Press, 1985.

Boddy, Janice. *Wombs and Alien Spirits*. Madison: The University of Wisconsin Press, 1989.

Booth, Marilyn. "Arab Adolescents Facing the Future: Enduring Ideals and Pressures to Change." In *The World's Youth*, edited by B. Bradford Brown, Reed W. Larson, and T. S. Saraswathi, pp. 207–42. Cambridge: Cambridge University Press, 2002.

Bordieu, Pierre. "The Sentiment of Honour in Kabyle Society." In *Honour and Shame: The Values of Mediterranean Society*, edited by Jean G. Peristiany, pp. 191–242. Chicago: University of Chicago Press, 1966.

Borneman, John. *Syrian Episodes: Sons, Fathers, and an Anthropologist in Aleppo*. Princeton, NJ: Princeton University Press, 2007.

Bouhdiba, Abdelwahab. "The Child and the Mother in Arab-Muslim Society." In *Psychological Dimensions of Near Eastern Studies*, edited by L. Carl Brown and Norman Itzkowitz, pp. 126–41. Princeton, NJ: Darwin, 1977.

———. *Sexuality in Islam*. Translated by Alan Sheridan. London: Saqi, 2004.

———. "Festivities of Violence: Circumcision and the Making of Men." In *Imagined Masculinities*, edited by Mai Ghoussoub and Emma Sinclair-Webb, pp. 19–32. London: Saqi, 2006.

Bowen, Donna Lee, and Evelyn A. Early, eds. *Everyday Life in the Muslim Middle East*. 2nd. ed. Bloomington: Indiana University Press, 2002.

Brooks, Gary R., and Louise B. Silverstein. "Understanding the Dark Side of Masculinity: An Interactive Systems Model." In *A New Psychology of Men*, edited by Ronald F. Levant and William S. Pollack, pp. 280–336. New York: Basic Books, 1995.

Brown, L. Carl, and Norman Itzkowitz, eds. *Psychological Dimensions of Near Eastern Studies*. Princeton, NJ: Darwin, 1977.

Cath, Stanley H., Alan R. Gurwitt, and John Munder Ross, eds. *Father and Child: Developmental and Clinical Perspectives*. Boston, MA: Little, Brown and Company, 1982.

Chodorow, Nancy. *The Reproduction of Mothering: Psychoanalysis and the Sociology of Gender*. Berkeley: University of California Press, 1978.

Choukri, Mohamed. *For Bread Alone* (*Al-Khubz al-hafi*, Beirut, 1982). Translated by Paul Bowles (1973). 2nd ed. San Francisco, CA: City Lights, 1987.

———. "Being and Place." In *The View from Within*, edited by Ferial Ghazoul and Barbara Harlow, pp. 220–27. Cairo: The American University in Cairo Press, 1994.

———. "Men Have All the Luck." Translated by Paul Starkey. In *Sardines and Oranges: Short Stories from North Africa*, edited by Peter Clark, pp. 108–31. London: Banipal, 2005.

———. *Streetwise* (*Al-Shuttar*, Beirut, 1992). Translated by Ed Emery. 1996; London: Telegram, 2007.

Cohen-Mor, Dalya. *Yusuf Idris: Changing Visions*. Potomac, MD: Sheba Press, 1992.

———. *A Matter of Fate: The Concept of Fate in the Arab World as Reflected in Modern Arabic Literature*. New York: Oxford University Press, 2001.

———, ed. and trans. *Arab Women Writers: An Anthology of Short Stories*. Albany: State University of New York Press, 2005.

——— (Abudi). *Mothers and Daughters in Arab Women's Literature: The Family Frontier*. Leiden: Brill, 2011.

Connell, R. W. *Masculinities*. 2nd ed. Berkeley: University of California Press, 2005.

Corneau, Guy. *Absent Fathers, Lost Sons*. Boston, MA: Shambhala, 1991.

Dabbagh, Hussein. *Mikhail Naimy: Some Aspects of His Thought as Revealed in His Writings*. Durham, UK: University of Durham, 1983.

Daniel, E. Valentine, and Jeffrey M. Peck., eds. *Culture/Contexture: Explorations in Anthropology and Literary Studies*. Berkeley: University of California Press, 1996.

De Quincey, Thomas. *Autobiography*. In *The Collected Writings of Thomas De Quincey*, edited by David Masson. New York: Johnson Reprint Corporation, 1968.

Dhillon, Navtej, and Tarik Yousef, eds. *Generation in Waiting: The Unfulfilled Promise of Young People in the Middle East*. Washington, DC: Brookings Institute, 2009.

Dialmy, Abdessamad. "Sexuality in Contemporary Arab Society." Translated by Allon J. Uhlmann.*Social Practice* 49, no. 2 (Summer 2005). Available: http://www.berghahnbooksonline.com.

Elliott, Anthony. *Concepts of the Self*. Cambridge, UK: Polity, 2001.

Elliott, Michael. "Learn to Love the Revolution: Five Lessons from Change in the Arab World." *Time* (March 7, 2011): 30–35.

Enani, M. M. ed. and trans. *An Anthology of the New Arabic Poetry in Egypt*. Cairo: General Egyptian Book Organization, 1986.

———. trans. *Angry Voices: An Anthology of the Off-Beat New Egyptian Poets*. Fayetteville: University of Arkansas Press, 2003.

Fahndrich, Harmut. "Fathers and Husbands: Tyrants and Victims in Some Autobiographical and Semi-Autobiographical Works from the Arab World." In *Love and Sexuality in Modern Arabic Literature*, edited by Roger Allen et al., pp. 106–15. London: Saqi, 1995.

Fernea, Elizabeth Warnock. "And How's the Family?" *Arab Perspectives* 15 (1984): 13–17.

———, ed. *Women and the Family in the Middle East: New Voices of Change*. Austin: University of Texas Press, 1985.

———, ed. *Children in the Muslim Middle East*. Austin: University of Texas Press, 1995.

———, ed. *Remembering Childhood in the Middle East: Memoirs from a Century of Change*. Austin: University of Texas Press, 2002.

Freud, Sigmund. *Introductory Lectures on Psychoanalysis*. Harmondsworth, UK: Penguin, 1973.

———. *Three Essays on the Theory of Sexuality.* New York: Basic Books, 1975.

———. *On Psychopathology.* Harmondsworth, UK: Penguin, 1979.

Friedrich Paul. "The Culture in Poetry and the Poetry in Culture." In *Culture/Contexture: Explorations in Anthropology and Literary Studies,* edited by E. Valentine Daniel and Jeffrey M. Peck, pp. 37–57. Berkeley: University of California Press, 1996.

Ghanem, Fathy. *The Man Who Lost His Shadow (Al-Rajul alladhi faqad zillahu.* Cairo, 1962). Translated by Desmond Stewart. London: Heinemann, 1980.

Ghonim, Wael, *Revolution 2.0.* New York: Houghton Mifflin Harcourt, 2012.

Ghoussoub, Mai, and Emma Sinclair-Webb, eds. *Imagined Masculinities: Male Identity and Culture in the Modern Middle East.* London: Saqi, 2000.

Gilmore, David D. *Manhood in the Making: Cultural Concepts of Masculinity.* New Haven, CT: Yale University Press, 1990.

Ginat, Joseph. *Blood Revenge: Family Honor, Mediation and Outcasting.* 2nd ed. Portland, OR: Sussex Academic, 1997.

Goldberg, Herb. *The Hazards of Being Male.* Gretna, LA: Wellness Institute, 2000.

Gregg, Gary S. *The Middle East: A Cultural Psychology.* New York: Oxford University Press, 2005.

Guth, Stephen. "Why Novels—Not Autobiographies?" In Robin Ostle et al., *Writing the Self,* pp. 139–47. London: Saqi, 1998.

al-Hakim, Tawfiq. *The Prison of Life (Sijn al-'umr.* Cairo, 1964). Translated by Pierre Cachia. Cairo: The American University in Cairo Press, 1992.

Hall, Margaret C. *Individual and Society: Basic Concepts.* Boonsboro, MD: Antietam Press, 1981.

Hammoudi, Abdellah. *Master and Disciple: The Cultural Foundations of Moroccan Authoritarianism.* Chicago: The University of Chicago Press, 1997.

Haqqi, Yahya. *The Saint's Lamp and Other Stories (Qindil Umm Hashim.* Cairo, 1944). Translated by M. M. Badawi. Leiden: Brill, 1973.

Harrison, James. "Roles, Identities, and Sexual Orientation: Homosexuality, Heterosexuality, and Bisexuality." In *A New Psychology of Men,* edited by Ronald F. Levant and William S. Pollack, pp. 337–58. New York: Basic Books, 1995.

Hatem, Mervat. "Underdevelopment, Mothering and Gender within the Egyptian Family." *Arab Studies Quarterly* 8, no. 1 (Winter 1986): 45–61.

———. "Toward the Study of the Psychodynamics of Mothering and Gender in Egyptian Families." *International Journal of Middle East Studies* 19 (1987): 287–306.

al-Hazimi, Mansour, Salma Khadra Jayyusi, and Ezzat Khattab, eds. *Beyond the Dunes: An Anthology of Modern Saudi Literature.* New York: I. B. Tauris, 2006.

Hearn, Jeff, and David Morgan, eds. *Men, Masculinities and Social Theory*. London: Unwin Hyman, 1990.

Hopkins, Nicholas S., ed. *The New Arab Family*. Cairo: The American University in Cairo Press, 2003.

Hourani, Albert. *Arabic Thought in the Liberal Age: 1798–1939*. Cambridge: Cambridge University Press, 1971.

Idris, Yusuf. "The Journey" ("Al-Rihla." *Al-Ahram*, June 5, 1970). Translated by Roger Allen. *Journal of Arabic Literature* 3 (1972): 7–11.

———. *The Cheapest Nights and Other Stories*. Translated by Wadida Wassef. London: Heinemann, 1978.

———. "Yusuf Idris on Yusuf Idris" (A Sketch of My Life as a Child). In *Critical Perspectives on Yusuf Idris*, edited by Roger Allen, pp. 5–13. Colorado Springs, CO: Three Continents Press, 1994.

Inhorn, Marcia C. *Infertility and Patriarchy: The Cultural Politics of Gender and Family Life in Egypt*. Philadelphia: University of Pennsylvania Press, 1996.

———. "'The Worms Are Weak': Male Infertility and Patriarchal Paradoxes in Egypt." In *Islamic Masculinities*, edited by Lahoucine Ouzgane, pp. 217–37. London: Zed, 2006.

———. *The New Arab Man: Emergent Masculinities, Technologies, and Islam in the Middle East*. Princeton: Princeton University Press, 2012.

al-Issa, Ihsan, ed. *Al-Junun: Mental Illness in the Islamic World*. Madison, CT: International Universities Press, 2000.

Jabra, Jabra Ibrahim. *The First Well: A Bethlehem Boyhood* (*Al-Bi'r al-ula*. London: Riad El-Rayyes, 1987). Translated by Issa J. Boullata. Fayetteville: The University of Arkansas Press, 1995.

———. *Princesses' Street: Baghdad Memories* (*Shari' al-amirat*. Beirut, 1994). Translated by Issa J. Boullata. Fayetteville: University of Arkansas Press, 2005.

Jayyusi, Salma Khadra, ed. *Modern Arabic Poetry: An Anthology*. New York: Columbia University Press, 1987.

———, ed. *The Literature of Modern Arabia: An Anthology*. London: Kegan Paul International in association with King Saud University, Riyadh, 1988.

Joseph, Suad, ed. *Intimate Selving in Arab Families: Gender, Self, and Identity*. Syracuse, NY: Syracuse University Press, 1999.

Kabbani (Qabbani) Nizar. *Arabian Love Poems*. Translated by Bassam K. Frangieh and Clementina R. Brown. Boulder, CO: Lynne Rienner, 1999.

Kandiyoti, Deniz. "Islam and Patriarchy: A Comparative Perspective." In *Women in Middle Eastern History*, edited by Nikki Keddie and Beth Baron, pp. 23–42. New Haven, CT: Yale University Press, 1991.

———. "The Paradoxes of Masculinity: Some Thoughts on Segregated Societies." In *Dislocating Masculinity*, edited by Andrea Cornwall and Nancy Lindisfarne, pp. 197–213. London: Routledge, 1994.

Kennett, Austin. *Bedouin Justice: Law and Customs among the Egyptian Bedouin*. London: Frank Cass, 1968.

Khuri, Fouad I. *Tents and Pyramids: Games and Ideology in Arab Culture from Backgammon to Autocratic Rule*. London: Saqi, 1990.

Kimmel, Michael S., and Michael A. Messner, eds. *Men's Lives*. 2nd ed. New York: Macmillan, 1992.

al-Koni, Ibrahim. *Anubis* (Beirut, 2002). Translated by William M. Hutchins. Cairo: The American University in Cairo Press, 2005.

Korany, Bahgat, ed. *The Changing Middle East: A New Look at Regional Dynamics*. Cairo: The American University in Cairo Press, 2010.

Laabi, Abdellatif. *Rue de Retour*. Translated by Jacqueline Kaye. London: Readers International, 1989.

Lacouture, Jean. *The Demigods: Charismatic Leadership in the Third World*. New York: Alfred A. Knopf, 1970.

———. *Nasser: A Biography*. New York: Alfred A. Knopf, 1973.

Lagrange, Frederic. "Male Homosexuality in Modern Arabic Literature." In *Imagined Masculinities*, edited by Mai Ghoussoub and Emma Sinclaire-Webb, pp. 169–98. London: Saqi, 2000.

Lane, Edward William, trans. *The Thousand and One Nights*. 3 vols. London: East-West, 1979–81.

Le Gassick, Trevor. "The Faith of Islam in Modern Arabic Fiction." *Religion and Literature* 20, no. 1 (Spring 1988): 97–110.

Levant, Ronald F., and William S. Pollack, eds., *A New Psychology of Men*. New York: Basic Books, 1995.

Lunde, Paul, and Justin Wintle, eds. *A Dictionary of Arabic and Islamic Proverbs*. London: Routledge, 1984.

al-Maghut, Muhammad. *Fan of Swords: Poems*. Translated by May Jayyusi and Naomi Shihab Nye. Edited by Salma Khadra Jayyusi. Washington, DC: Three Continents Press, 1991.

Mahdi, Ali Akbar, ed. *Teen Life in the Middle East*. Westport, CT: Greenwood Press, 2003.

Mahfouz, Naguib. Cairo Trilogy (Cairo, 1956–57). Vol. 1, *Palace Walk* (*Bayn al-qasrayn*, 1956). Translated by William Maynard Hutchins and Olive E. Kenny. Vol. 2, *Palace of Desire* (*Qasr al-shawq*, 1957). Translated by William Maynard Hutchins, Lorne M. Kenny, and Olive E. Kenny. Vol. 3, *Sugar Street* (*Al-Sukkariyya*, 1957). Translated by William Maynard Hutchins and Angele Botros Samaan. New York: Doubleday, 1990, 1991, 1992.

———. *Echoes of an Autobiography* (*Asda' al-sira al-dhatiyya*, 1994). Translated by Denys Johnson-Davies. Cairo: The American University in Cairo Press, 1996.

———. *Naguib Mahfouz at Sidi Gaber: Reflections of a Nobel Laureate, 1994–2001*, from conversations with Mohamed Salmawy. Cairo: The American University in Cairo Press, 2001.

Ma'oz, Moshe. *Asad, the Sphinx of Damascus: A Political Biography*. New York: Grove Weidenfeld, 1988.

Meijer, Roel, ed. *Alienation or Integration of Arab Youth: Between Family, State and Street*. Richmond, UK: Curzon Press, 2000.

Mernissi, Fatima. *Beyond the Veil: Male-Female Dynamics in Modern Muslim Society*. Rev. ed. Bloomington: Indiana University Press, 1987.

————. *Women's Rebellion and Islamic Memory*. London: Zed, 1996.

Mina, Hanna. *Fragments of Memory: A Story of a Syrian Family (Baqaya suwar.* Beirut, 1975). Translated by Olive Kenny and Lorne Kenny. Austin: University of Texas Press, 1993.

————. *Al-Mustanqa'* (The Swamp). Beirut, 1977.

————. *Al-Qitaf* (The Picking). Beirut, 1986.

Moghadam, Valentine M. *Modernizing Women: Gender and Social Change in the Middle East*. 2nd ed. Boulder, CO: Lynne Reinner, 2003.

Naimy, Mikhail. *Sab'un: Hikayat 'umr* (Seventy: A Life Story). Beirut, 1959–60.

————. *A New Year: Stories, Autobiography, Poems*. Translated by J. R. Perry. Leiden: Brill, 1974.

Nehme, Michel G. *Fear and Anxiety in the Arab World*. Gainesville: University Press of Florida, 2003.

Nicholson, R. A. *A Literary History of the Arabs*. Cambridge: Cambridge University Press, 1976.

Nijland, C. *Mikhail Nu'aymah: Promoter of the Arabic Literary Revival*. Istanbul: Nederlands Instituut voor het Nabije Oosten, 1975.

Obank, Margaret. "Ibrahim al-Koni, *Anubis*: The Search for the Tuareg Desert Truth." *Banipal* 23 (Summer 2005).

————, and Samuel Shimon. eds. *A Crack in the Wall: New Arab Poetry*. London: Saqi, 2001.

Osherson, Samuel. *Finding Our Fathers*. New York: Contemporary Books, 2001.

Ostle, Robin, Ed de Moor, and Stefan Wild, eds. *Writing the Self: Autobiographical Writing in Modern Arabic Literature*. London: Saqi, 1998.

Ouzgane, Lahoucine, ed. *Islamic Masculinities*. London: Zed, 2006.

Patai, Raphael. *The Arab Mind*. Rev. ed. New York: Charles Scribner's Sons, 1983.

Pellegrini, Robert J., and Theodore R. Sarbin, eds. *Between Fathers and Sons: Critical Incident Narratives in the Development of Men's Lives*. New York: The Haworth Clinical Practice Press, 2002.

Peristiany, Jean G., ed. *Honour and Shame: The Values of Mediterranean Society*. Chicago: University of Chicago Press, 1966.

Phillips, Shelley. *Beyond the Myths: Mother-Daughter Relationships in Psychology, History, Literature, and Everyday Life*. London: Penguin, 1991.

Pickthall, Muhammad. *The Glorious Quran: Arabic Text and English Rendering*. Des Plaines, IL: Library of Islam, 1994.

Pittman, Frank. *Man Enough: Fathers, Sons, and the Search for Masculinity*. New York: Perigee, 1993.

Pleck, Joseph H. *The Myth of Masculinity*. Cambridge, MA: The MIT Press, 1981.

————. "The Gender Role Strain Paradigm: An Update." In *A New Psychology of Men*, edited by Ronald F. Levant and William S. Pollack, pp. 11–32. New York: Basic Books, 1995.

Pryce-Jones, Davies. *The Closed Circle: An Interpretation of the Arabs.* Chicago: Ivan R. Dee, 2002.

al-Qaʻid, Yusuf. *War in the Land of Egypt* (*Al-Harb fi barr Misr.* Beirut, 1978). Translated by Olive and Lorne Kenney and Christopher Tingley. New York: Interlink, 1998.

Racy, John. "Psychiatry in the Arab East." In *Psychological Dimensions of Near Eastern Studies,* edited by L. Carl Brown and Norman Itzkowitz, pp. 279–329. Princeton, NJ: Darwin, 1977.

al-Razzaz, Muʼnis. "Abu Richard" ("Abu Rashad." In *Al-Namrud.* Beirut, 1980). Translated by Yasir Suleiman in collaboration with Sandor Hervey. In *Journal of Arabic Literature* 22 (1991–92): 148–53.

Reich, Bernard, ed. *Political Leaders of the Contemporary Middle East and North Africa: A Biographical Dictionary.* Westport, CT: Greenwood Press, 1990.

Rooke, Tetz. *In My Childhood: A Study of Arabic Autobiography.* Stockholm: Almqvist & Wiksell, 1997.

Rugh, Andrea. *Family in Contemporary Egypt.* Cairo: The American University in Cairo Press, 1985.

Rutherford, Jonathan. *Men's Silences.* London: Routledge, 1992.

Rycroft, Charles. *The Innocence of Dreams.* London: Hogarth, 1979.

El Saadawi, Nawal. *The Hidden Face of Eve.* London: Zed, 1980.

———. *The Nawal El Saadawi Reader.* London: Zed, 1997.

———. "She Is Not a Virgin." In Dalya Cohen-Mor, *A Matter of Fate,* pp. 143–48. New York: Oxford University Press, 2001.

el-Sadat, Anwar. *In Search of Identity: An Autobiography.* New York: Harper and Row, 1978.

Sadat, Camelia. *My Father and I.* New York: Macmillan, 1985.

al-Safti, Madiha. *Impact of Social and Economic Changes on the Arab Family: An Exploratory Study.* New York: United Nations, 1992.

Saghieh, Hazim. "'That's How I Am, World!': Saddam, Manhood and the Monolithic Image." In *Imagined Masculinities,* edited by Mai Ghoussoub and Emma Sinclaire-Webb, pp. 236–48. London: Saqi, 2000.

———. "The Other Arab Exception." *Open Democracy* (April 18, 2011). Available: http://www.opendemocracy.net

Said, Edward W. *Orientalism.* New York: Vintage, 1979.

———. *The World, the Text, and the Critic.* Cambridge, MA: Harvard University Press, 1983.

———. *Out of Place: A Memoir.* New York: Vintage, 2000.

Seale, Patrick. *Asad of Syria: The Struggle for the Middle East.* Berkeley: University of California Press, 1995.

El-Shamy, Hassan. "The Brother-Sister Syndrome in Arab Family Life, Socio-Cultural Factors in Arab Psychiatry: A Critical Review." *International Journal of Sociology of the Family* 2 (1981): 313–23.

Sharabi, Hisham. *Neopatriarchy: A Theory of Distorted Change in Arab Society.* New York: Oxford University Press, 1988.

————, in collaboration with Mukhtar Ani. "Impact of Class and Culture on Social Behavior: The Feudal-Bourgeois Family in Arab Society." In *Psychological Dimensions of Near Eastern Studies,* edited by L. Carl Brown and Norman Itzkowitz, pp. 240–56. Princeton, NJ: Darwin, 1977.

al-Sharuni, Yusuf. *Blood Feud: Short Stories.* Translated by Denys Johnson-Davies. London: Heinemann, 1983.

Singerman, Diane, and Homa Hoodfar, eds. *Development, Change, and Gender in Cairo: A View from the Household.* Bloomington: Indiana University Press, 1996.

Snodgrass, Joan Gay, and Robert L. Thompson, eds. *The Self Across Psychology.* New York: The New York Academy of Sciences, 1997.

Stephens, Robert. *Nasser: A Political Biography.* New York: Simon and Schuster, 1971.

al-Suhrawardy, Allama Sir Abdullah al-Mamun. *The Sayings of Muhammad.* New York: Citadel Press, 1990.

Tamer, Zakaria, "The Family." In *Tigers on the Tenth Day and Other Stories.* Translated by Denys Johnson-Davies, pp. 35–36. London: Quartet, 1985.

————. "The Thunderbolt." In *Modern Syrian Short Stories.* Translated by Michel Azrak, revised by M. J. L. Young, pp. 106–7. Washington, DC: Three Continents Press, 1988.

————. *Breaking Knees.* Translated by Ibrahim Muhawi. Reading, UK: Garnet, 2008.

Tillion, Germaine. *The Republic of Cousins.* Translated by Quintin Hoare. London: Saqi, 1983.

al-Udhari, Abdullah, trans. and ed. *Modern Poetry of the Arab World.* Harmonsdworth, UK: Penguin, 1986.

United Nations Development Program. *Arab Human Development Report 2005: Towards the Rise of Women in the Arab World.* New York: United Nations Publications, 2006.

Weissbort, Daniel, ed. *Iraqi Poetry Today.* London: King's College, University of London, 2003.

Yablonsky, Lewis. *Fathers and Sons: The Most Challenging of All Family Relationships.* New York: Gardner, 1990.

Young, William C., and Seteney Shami. "Anthropological Approaches to the Arab Family: An Introduction." *Journal of Comparative Family Studies* 28, no. 2 (Summer 1997): 1–13.

Yount, Kathryn, M., and Hoda Rashad, eds. *Family in the Middle East: Ideational Change in Egypt, Iran, and Tunisia.* New York: Routledge, 2008.

Zaydan, Jurji. *The Autobiography of Jurji Zaidan* (*Mudhakkirat Jurji Zaydan.* Cairo, 1966). Translated, edited and introduced by Thomas Philipp. Washington, DC: Three Continents Press, 1990.

Permissions

The scope of quotations from poetry in this volume made it at times difficult, despite sincere and sustained efforts, to locate some of the poets, their translators, or publishers. The author regrets any omissions or errors, which will be corrected in subsequent printings. Permission to reprint copyrighted material is gratefully acknowledged as follows:

Abd-Allah al-Baraduni, "From Exile to Exile." Translated by Diana Der Hovanessian with Sharif Elmusa; Abd al-Aziz al-Maqalih, "Choice." Translated by Lena Jayyusi and Christopher Middleton; Abd al-Karim Kassid, "Tales about My Father." Translated by Lena Jayyusi and Anthony Thwaite; Adonis ('Ali Ahmad Sa'id), "Beginning Speech." Translated by Lena Jayyusi and John Heath-Stubbs; Mohammad Bennis, "Belonging to a New Family." Translated by Sharif Elmusa and Charles Doria; Sami Mahdi, "The Inheritance." Translated by May Jayyusi; Sargon Boulus, "My Father's Dream." Translated by Sargon Boulus and Alistair Elliot. From *Modern Arabic Poetry: An Anthology*, edited by Salma Khadra Jayyusi. Copyright © 1987 by Columbia University Press. Reprinted by permission of the publisher.

Adonis, "Adam." From *Adonis: The Pages of Day and Night*. Translated by Samuel Hazo. English translation copyright © 1994 by Samuel Hazo. First published by Marlboro Press, Marlboro, Vermont. Northwestern University Press paperback published in 2000. All rights reserved. Reprinted by permission of the translator and the publisher.

Ahmad Qandeel, "A Scream." Translated by Bassam al-Hilu with Alan Brownjohn; Abdallah Salih al-'Uthaymeen, "Legend." Translated by Bassam al-Hilu with Alan Brownjohn; Muhammad Hasan Faqi, "Quartet." Translated by Laith al-Husain and Patricia Alanah Byrne. From *Beyond the Dunes: An Anthology of Modern Saudi Literature*, edited by Mansour al-Hazimi, Salma Khadra Jayyusi, and Ezzat

Index

Printed in the United States of America